URBAN PASTORAL

CONTEMPORARY NORTH AMERICAN POETRY SERIES

Series Editors Alan Golding, Lynn Keller, and Adalaide Morris

TIMOTHY GRAY

URBAN PASTORAL

Natural Currents in the New York School

UNIVERSITY OF IOWA PRESS

Iowa City

UNIVERSITY OF IOWA PRESS, IOWA CITY 52242
Copyright © 2010 by the University of Iowa Press
www.uiowapress.org
Printed in the United States of America

Design by Teresa W. Wingfield

The University of Iowa Press is a member of Green Press Initiative and is
committed to preserving natural resources.

Printed on acid-free paper

Library of Congress Cataloging-in-Publication Data

Gray, Timothy, 1964–
    Urban pastoral: natural currents in the New York School / Timothy Gray.
        p.   cm.—(Contemporary North American poetry series)
    Includes bibliographical references and index.
    ISBN-13: 978-1-58729-909-4
    ISBN-10: 1-58729-909-7
        1. American poetry—New York (State)—New York—History and criticism.
2. Nature in literature.   3. American poetry—20th century—History and
criticism.   I. Title.
    PS255.N5G73   2010
    811'.540997471—dc22   2010005243

FOR ALEXANDER, CHARLOTTE, AND MARIA

CONTENTS

ACKNOWLEDGMENTS

I AM EXCITED to be publishing again with the Contemporary North American Poetry Series at the University of Iowa Press. Alan Golding, Lynn Keller, and Dee Morris deserve kudos for establishing the nation's best forum on contemporary poetics. Additional thanks go to friends at the Press, including Holly Carver and Allison Thomas Means, who first heard of my project over lunch at the Grand Central Oyster Bar. Editor Joe Parsons merits a special note of thanks, for he has supported me during every step of the submission process, offering sage advice or a healthy dose of humor whenever I need it. Thanks also to Charlotte Wright, Karen Copp, and my favorite copyeditor, Leslee Anderson, for turning the manuscript into a book.

Several far-flung friends, including Andrew Epstein, Marit MacArthur, Ann Mikkelson, Mark Silverberg, and Terry Diggory, graciously shared their knowledge of the New York School of Poets over the years. I am thankful to them and urge readers of *Urban Pastoral* to consult their fine scholarly writings. At my home institution, the College of Staten Island, City University of New York, I wish to thank my colleagues in the English Department and acknowledge Francisco Soto for financial support of my project. And I want to thank my students, whose perspectives on New York City informed my research and influenced my analyses.

Many thanks to Andy Arnot at Tibor de Nagy Gallery for his generous support of my research on New York School poetry and art. Thanks also to the poets and artists who shared their recollections in conversation and allowed me to use portions of their discourse.

Chris Betts, Jason Bott, Greg Campbell, Alan Sun, and Kathleen Winter are friends and artists I cannot fathom living without. Their wisdom is behind every essay in *Urban Pastoral*.

On the domestic front, I thank the Barnett, Cummings, and Gray clans for sticking with me through a decade's worth of hard work. A big thank-you goes to Don and Grace Barnett, Carolyn Gray, Harold Gray, and Irene Gammon for their long-standing interest in this project. I humbly dedicate *Urban Pastoral* to my wife, Maria, and my young children, Alexander and Charlotte. May the blessings of the natural world be yours, always.

In memoriam: Milt Cummings, Hani Hasweh, Tony Hilfer.

I gratefully acknowledge the following, who gave me permission to cite specific material:

Excerpt from *Sammy and Rosie Get Laid* by Hanif Kureishi, copyright © 1988 by Hanif Kureishi. Used by permission of Penguin, a division of Penguin Group (USA) Inc.

"Fragment: Little N.Y. Ode," "Poem (My footsteps in the shallow)," and "Love Rockets," from *Fear of Dreaming: The Selected Poems of Jim Carroll* by Jim Carroll, copyright © 1993 by Jim Carroll. Used by permission of Viking Penguin, a division of Penguin Group (USA) Inc.

Excerpts from the poems "Excerpts from the Angel Handbook" and "At a Window, New York City," from *Journey: New and Selected Poems, 1969–1999* by Kathleen Norris, copyright © 2001. Reprinted by permission of the University of Pittsburgh Press.

"A True Account of Talking to the Sun at Fire Island," "Nocturne," and "Four Little Elegies," from *The Collected Poems of Frank O'Hara* edited by Donald Allen, copyright © 1971 by Maureen Granville-Smith, administratrix of the estate of Frank O'Hara. Used by permission of Alfred A. Knopf, a division of Random House, Inc.

"A Big Clown-Face-Shaped Cloud," "West Wind," "Where Am I Kenneth?", and "On Beauty," from *The Collected Poems of Kenneth Koch* by Kenneth Koch, copyright © 2005 by the Kenneth Koch Literary Estate. Used by permission of Alfred A. Knopf, a division of Random House, Inc.

"Love," from *Rose, Where Did You Get That Red?* by Kenneth Koch, copyright © 1973 by Kenneth Koch. Used by permission of Random House, Inc.

"Parachutes, My Love, Could Carry Us Higher," section 32 of "The Countess of Minneapolis," and six short excerpts from *The Collected Poems of Barbara Guest*, copyright © 2008 by Barbara Guest. Reprinted by permission of Wesleyan University Press.

"The Chateau Hardware" and "Soonest Mended" from *The Double Dream of Spring*, copyright © 1966, 1967, 1968, 1969, 1970, 1997 by John Ashbery. Both originally appeared in *Paris Review*. "At North Farm" from

A Wave, copyright © 1981, 1982, 1983, 1984 by John Ashbery. Originally appeared in *The New Yorker*. "The Picture of Little J. A. in a Prospect of Flowers" from *Some Trees*, copyright © 1956, 1997 by John Ashbery. "Crazy Weather" from *Houseboat Days*, copyright © 1975, 1976, 1977 by John Ashbery. Originally appeared in *Antaeus*. Reprinted by permission of Georges Borchardt, Inc., on behalf of John Ashbery.

Portions of *Urban Pastoral* first appeared, in slightly different form, in the following journals:

"Semiotic Shepherds: Gary Snyder, Frank O'Hara, and the Embodiment of an Urban Pastoral," by Timothy Gray. Originally published in *Contemporary Literature* 39.4 (Winter 1998): 523–59. Copyright © 1998 by the Board of Regents of the University of Wisconsin System. Reproduced courtesy of the University of Wisconsin Press.

"Process and Plurality in New York's Urban Pastoral," by Timothy Gray. Originally published in *Contemporary Literature* 44.2 (Summer 2003): 362–78. Copyright © 2003 by the Board of Regents of the University of Wisconsin System. Reproduced courtesy of the University of Wisconsin Press.

"New Windows on New York: The Urban Pastoral Vision of James Schuyler and Jane Freilicher," by Timothy Gray. Originally published in *Genre* 33.2 (Summer 2000): 171–98. Reprinted by permission of the University of Oklahoma Regents.

"'Fictions Dressed Like Water': Aqueous Imagery in the Poetry of Barbara Guest," by Timothy Gray. Originally published in *Jacket* 28 (October 2005). http://jacketmagazine.com.

"'A World without Gravity': The Urban Pastoral Spirituality of Jim Carroll and Kathleen Norris," by Timothy Gray, in *Texas Studies in Literature and Language* 47.3 (Fall 2005): 213–52. Copyright © 2005 by the University of Texas Press. All rights reserved.

"Fun City: Kenneth Koch among Schoolchildren," by Timothy Gray, in *Texas Studies in Literature and Language* 51.2 (Summer 2009): 223–62. Copyright © 2009 by the University of Texas Press. All rights reserved.

"'The Place Where Your Nature Meets Mine': Diane di Prima in the West," by Timothy Gray. Originally published in *Journal X: A Journal in Culture and Criticism* 8.1 (Autumn 2003): 1–31. Copyright © 2003 by the University of Mississippi.

ABBREVIATIONS

PARENTHETICAL REFERENCES to editions of *Collected Poems* by Frank O'Hara, John Ashbery, Barbara Guest, James Schuyler, Kenneth Koch, and Allen Ginsberg are marked by the abbreviation *CP*. Complete reference information on these editions is contained in the Works Cited section. All citations included in the book follow guidelines adopted by the Modern Language Association.

URBAN PASTORAL

INTRODUCTION
Pastures New

IN THE EARLY 1950S, a group of young poets converged on New York City. Blessed with sophistication and wit, they forged close relationships with each other and with the avant-garde artists whom painter Robert Motherwell half-seriously dubbed the "School of New York." Over time, thanks to their first publisher, gallery director John Bernard Myers, five of these poets (Frank O'Hara, John Ashbery, Barbara Guest, James Schuyler, and Kenneth Koch) came to share the appellation with the artists, even though they resisted being pigeonholed in this way. The New York School is a curious designation. After all, its charter members were fiercely independent in their aesthetic allegiances, and their writings decidedly antiacademic in style and sentiment. "One of the definable characteristics of the New York School," Ashbery noted in 1968, is "its avoidance of anything like a program" (*Selected Prose* 113). As in many literary milieus, however, these poets seemed to be heading in the same general direction. Koch compared his writer friends to "members of a team, like the Yankees or the Minnesota Vikings. We inspired each other, we envied each other, we emulated each other, we were almost entirely dependent on each other for support. Each had to be better than the others but if one flopped we all did" (*Art* 213). Viewed another way, the New York School's confluence of poets and artists resembled a school of fish: creatures coming together to explore currents outside the mainstream.

Regardless of the labels used to describe them, members of the New York School found in their city a charged atmosphere conducive to their ambitions, a realm where the discussion, exhibition, and performance of literature, art, and music quickened their creative energies. In the 1950s and early 1960s, poets went to the Cedar Tavern, on the corner of Eighth Street and University Place, to overhear what the painters were saying about modern art, and the painters returned the favor, visiting the nearby San Remo Bar, the poets' favorite hangout, to eavesdrop on their literary discussions. Before long, poets and painters were collaborating on mixed-media works. Ashbery, O'Hara, Guest, and Schuyler wrote art criticism for leading journals, and some of the painters tried their hand at poetry. Such interchange had a palpable effect on the work produced there. "New York poets, except I suppose for the color blind, are affected most by the floods of paint in whose crashing surf we all scramble," Schuyler explained, adding that, "if you try to derive a strictly literary ancestry for New York poetry, the main connection gets missed" ("Poet and Painter" 418, 419). An interarts emphasis continued to influence the New York School's second generation, a group of downtown writers who came to the fore after O'Hara's death in 1966, even if they preferred pop art over abstract expressionism, American Beats over European modernists, rock and roll over classical music.

Like their fellow New Yorkers, members of the School were renowned for their boundless energy and joie de vivre, yet they also seemed to enjoy a sense of calm in the midst of all their rushing around. In so doing they nurtured the idea of an *urban pastoral*. I first heard this provocative term mentioned twenty years ago by David Perkins in a Harvard lecture on Frank O'Hara and James Merrill. Perkins in turn may have picked it up from O'Hara's earliest academic critics, like Herbert Leibowitz. The term has stuck in my mind, even as it has taken on different meanings. Urban pastoral often refers to a cosmopolitan retreat conducive to the development of aesthetic experimentation and countercultural community, though as evident throughout this book, it refers as well to the natural sensibilities city writers secretly harbor.

The former definition is closer to what Perkins spelled out in his lecture, and it accommodates a widely accepted view of the New York School milieu. Unlike suburban or small-town America, from which most of the New York School poets hailed, the big city offered writers greater artistic freedom as well as an unusual variety of repose. Losing themselves amid millions of others, these experimentalists could not only be who they wanted to be but also join forces with a select group of like-minded souls in urban sites of refuge. Within those havens, avant-garde poets and painters could relax, let their guard down, and be more "natural." Taking advantage of New York's opportunities, and its (sexual) tolerance, they proved that the green pastures celebrated by Robert Frost and Winslow Homer were not the only places conducive to pastoral meditation.[1] Like rural dreamers chewing on shoots of hay, members of the School calmly waited for their surroundings to work inspirational magic on their consciousness, at the same time avoiding the facile "rural felicity" (Marx 6) dominating popular portrayals of pastoral settings (television Westerns, Norman Rockwell paintings).

The bulk of my book is devoted to the second aspect of urban pastoral. Taking an unconventional approach, I argue that poets of the New York School, however devoted they may have been to avant-garde techniques like abstraction, should be placed alongside Annie Dillard, Wendell Berry, and Mary Oliver in the ranks of contemporary American nature writers. The legacy of the postwar avant-garde is also in need of revision. Among the favored sites of the New American Poetry movement (delineated in Donald Allen's 1960 anthology by that name), San Francisco and Black Mountain College (in North Carolina) usually take pride of place in ecocritical discussions. The mythic rituals and indigenous nature worship incorporated into verse by Charles Olson, Robert Duncan, and Gary Snyder indicate earnest attempts on the part of these poets to make the wisdom of primitivism jibe with postmodern realities. Poets of the New York School did not take this route, and in the opinion of most, their writings about gallery openings, ballet performances, and other city events are about as distant from natural discourse as is possible. My aim in *Urban Pastoral* is to rethink such assessments, looking beyond the School's celebration of cosmopolitan energy to shake up common conceptions of what constitutes nature writing. Dodging sentimentality at every turn, poets of the New York School grafted onto their surprisingly abundant natural imagery a devil-may-care attitude, a seriocomic urbanity, a sophisticated artifice offering resonant commentary on urban nature. Flowers are more beautiful in their garden of verses because no one expects them to bloom there.

These confounded expectations carry over to the critical realm. Since urban pastoral tends to be based on a feeling or an atmosphere rather than a fixed set of conventions, its conceptual synthesis is not easy to define, let alone follow. When literary scholars Alastair Fowler (106–29) and Paul Alpers (*What* 44–78) speak of pastoral as a mode rather than a genre, they are highlighting its combinatory indeterminacy, which tends to be even stronger in its urban version. In typical pastoral plots handed down by ancient Greeks and Romans, stressed-out city dwellers leave the city for the country, taking on new identities while hoping to recover a sense of *otium* (leisure) and brotherhood destroyed by encroaching civilization. Such logic is highly oppositional. Raymond Williams reminds us that "country" derives from the Latin *contra* (meaning "against" or "opposite"), which originally referred to "land spread out against the observer" but has come to signal whatever stands in contrast to the city (307). Over time, Williams explains, "the country has gathered the idea of a natural way of life: of peace, innocence, and simple virtue. On the city has gathered the idea of an achieved centre: of learning, communication, light. Powerful hostile associations have also developed: on the city as a place of noise, worldliness and ambition; on the country as a place of backwardness, ignorance, limitation" (1).

In actuality, though, the geographical polarities Williams delineates are highly mutable; in creative hands they break down and filter into one another. Critics enjoy the same leeway as artists. As Alpers notes, "it sometimes seems as if there are as many versions of pastoral as there are critics and scholars who write about it"; indeed, because pastoral is so situational, "representative anecdotes" prove more useful than blanket definitions (*What* 8, 11). My essays on urban poets certainly hew to this trend, for as Richard Sennett points out, in language eerily akin to that of Alpers, "there are probably as many ways of conceiving what a city is as there are cities" (39).

Urban pastoral shares with traditional versions the "creation of imaginative space," a sovereign "domain" where one can do as one pleases (Alpers, "Pastoral"). Whether it is coded rural or urban, pastoral's *locus amoenus*, or "happy place," allows those who enter it the chance to forge beneficial friendships considered off-limits in everyday life. Disguise is important here. Aristocrats masquerading as shepherds in classical and early modern pastoral adopt new identities not only to entertain themselves but also to recover communitarian models that have been blindly eschewed by appetitive civilization. Adopting a "useful disguise" (Ettin 28) and lighting out for pastoral spaces cause whatever problems the sojourners have left behind—national affiliations, regional prejudices, literary or social expectations—to seem less binding, somehow less real. Many centuries ago, Virgil (as Tityrus) and Edmund Spenser (as Colin Clout) took on rustic aliases in order to finesse their literary ambitions and offer pointed cultural commentary. Just the same, in his two versions of *Arcadia*, Sir Philip Sidney has the lovelorn aristocrats Pyrocles and Musidorus parade as an Amazon and a shepherd as they embark on picaresque adventures. A preference for alter egos colors contemporary urban pastoral as well. Literary émigrés from the hinterlands may reverse ordinary lines of flight, traveling toward the metropolis instead of away from it, but otherwise they mimic the shepherds populating classical and early modern texts, playing roles denied them back home in an attempt to realize their dreams or ambitions. It is just that the street has replaced the meadow as the happy place where the harried pace of life slows down and new aesthetic possibilities open up.

Traditional pastoral tends to see the city as degraded and sinful, its seductions best avoided by those who reside in the countryside. Polybius, in *The Histories*, claimed that the Arcadian emphasis on music and poetry had kept that bucolic region at peace, and that only after its rural populace exchanged leisurely pastimes for sophisticated civic concerns did Arcadia, like the large cities it unwisely emulated, fall into strife (Sidney 369n). Though it is a highly stylized literary form, pastoral champions the simplicity and innocence of a rural Golden Age, before civilization knocked at the door. Typically, the city plays the role of rapacious villain. For centuries now, Lawrence Buell notes, pastoral has been "given over to representation of country ways that are being displaced by enclosure and/or urbanization" (144). Accordingly, when literary writers of pastoral elegy (John Milton on Edward King, Walt Whitman on Abraham Lincoln) include catalogs of flora and fauna, they are lending solace to mourners and suggesting the cyclical rebirth nature promises, but they are also implicitly commenting on the ills of urban civilization, which may have had a hand in the early death of their subjects.

Members of the New York School loved turning this argument on its head. Recalling his temporary residence in a picturesque upstate hamlet, poet-critic David Lehman described the restlessness he felt amid the rustic splendor: "One day I walked into the woods with my friend Tom's coonhound Bruno, and we sat at our favorite rocks where three streams meet. A bird chirped, but in my brain it was a phone ringing, and I knew then that I would have to return to the city, to its civilization and billboards. I have something of the city within me wherever I go" (Ashton 8). In 1958, painter Franz Kline expressed the same uneasiness: "Hell, half the world wants to be like Thoreau at Walden worrying about the noise of traffic on the way to Boston; the other half use up their lives being part of that noise. I like the second half. Right?" (O'Hara, *Art* 52). Even sculptor David Smith, who moved his studio from the Terminal Iron Works on Brooklyn's waterfront to the idyllic hills of Bolton Landing, near Lake George, found it difficult to abandon his urban sensibilities, creating massive industrial totems and placing them precariously, almost confrontationally, in his new property's lush, expansive meadows (viewing these in situ, O'Hara remarked, "nature looks intimate and vulnerable, the sculptures powerful, indomitable" [*Standing* 121]). By most accounts, Smith spent his time at Bolton Landing productively and happily, yet he seemed to long for the rancor of New York

City, locating WQXR on his radio's AM band and measuring the distance he had traveled:

> [Brooklyn] was awake 24 hours a day, harbor activity in front, truck transports on Furman Street behind. In contrast the mountains are quiet except for occasional animal noises. Sometimes Streever's hounds run foxes all night and I can hear them baying as I close up shop. Rarely does a car pass at night, there is no habitation between our road and the Schroon River four miles cross country. I enjoy the phenomenon of nature, the sounds, the Northern lights, stars, animal calls, as I did the harbor lights, tugboat whistles, buoy clanks, the yelling of men on barges around the TIW in Brooklyn. I sit up here and dream of the city as I used to dream of the mountains when I sat on the dock in Brooklyn. (Lauterbach, *Night* 202)

Like Lehman and Kline, Smith feared that immersion in rural areas would mean not only saying goodbye to the home space of the metropolis but also abandoning the basic geographical tension giving the pastoral mode its melancholy aspect, its bittersweet longing for landscapes glimpsed fleetingly in the rearview mirror of temporal consciousness. Ultimately, his fears failed to materialize. Like some second-generation New York School poets (Diane di Prima and Bill Berkson in rural California, Kathleen Norris in South Dakota), Smith learned that he could settle in the countryside without obliterating his urban identity. Instead, his city-bred art made rural settings a little edgier, a little more hip.

Another variety of urban pastoral emerged when members of the New York School reversed course and brought countrified sensibilities to bear on city life. As William Empson notes (185–240), this practice has been evident in Anglo-American literature since *The Beggar's Opera*, John Gay's "Newgate pastoral," which with its street urchin rustics and rollicking mixture of city images satirized a literary convention gone stale.[2] A more tranquil synthesis affected urban pastoral literature from nineteenth- and twentieth-century London, which softened the edges of an industrialized cityscape, luxuriating in its circumscribed parks, foggy waterfront docks, and sooty rail yards. William Wordsworth's "Composed upon Westminster Bridge," Oscar Wilde's "Impression du Matin," Ezra Pound's "The Garden," and the opening scene of E. M. Forster's *Howards End* are illustrative of this trend, as are a more recent crop of popular English songs, including the Kinks' "Waterloo Sunset," Robyn Hitchcock's "Trams of Old London," and Jamie Cullum's "London Skies." Across the Channel, Paris provided

nineteenth-century poet Charles Baudelaire, the strolling intellectual or
flaneur, an uncanny web of crowded, interconnected images, alternately
strange and beautiful. Walter Benjamin, Baudelaire's most sympathetic explicator, took a similar approach in the twentieth century with his Arcades
Project, its name echoing the hallowed ground of pastoral Arcadia even as
it designated the Parisian shops where Benjamin sought discarded curios
filled with aura.

Meanwhile, New Yorkers were busy fashioning their own pastoral art.
Poets Walt Whitman, Hart Crane, and William Carlos Williams suffused
gritty cityscapes with bucolic flourishes, as did, on more isolated occasions
in ensuing decades, Elizabeth Bishop and James Merrill. New York urban
pastoral was chronicled just as effectively in collage art and avant-garde
cinema. Joseph Cornell's boxed assemblages, filled with discarded material scavenged from Fourth Avenue's used bookstores and print shops,
framed (in the words of Jed Perl) "meltingly romantic expressions of the
past," the artist's sepia-toned nostalgia softening the "jangling, hard-edged
city" (*New Art* 288). Powered by risk and awash in beauty, films by Rudy
Burckhardt, Jonas Mekas, and Peter Hutton aimed for similar effects, juxtaposing disparate fragments of contemporary urban experience, creating a
bittersweet symphony, a new take on the pastoral impulses millions of city
dwellers secretly share.[3]

Poets of the New York School belong in this company. Unbeknownst to
many devotees of avant-garde poetry, and unbeknownst as well to readers
of environmental literature—who might scan *The Norton Book of Nature
Writing, Urban Nature: Poems about Wildlife in the City,* and other such
anthologies in vain—members of the School were, at heart, nature writers. For all their experimental derring-do, they dug deep into the mysteries of environmental phenomena, allowing the wonders of nature to shape
their appreciation of city life. More subtly than their literary peers in San
Francisco and Black Mountain, they learned how to fashion an "open field"
poetics within city limits instead of constantly heading out to the countryside to enjoy nature (though they sometimes did this, too). When Schuyler
equated a yellow taxi with a sunburst, or when di Prima tracked fugitive
cockroaches in her cold-water flat as though she were stalking big game,
these writers were being highly imaginative, but not altogether delusional.
Rather, they were acceding to a way of seeing that is as practicable in the
metropolis as it is in the hinterlands, offering readers a fresh viewpoint on
New York's bucolic surprises and revealing its hidden lyrical charms.

While aficionados of country living may be reluctant to associate the
hustle of Manhattan with the leisurely atmosphere depicted in poems by

Wordsworth or paintings by Constable, New Yorkers are attuned to those moments when time and space seem miraculously suspended, lending an air of beauty and comfort to all the steel and concrete. In such moments, New York City becomes America's biggest small town. During her early years in New York, Barbara Guest wrote a letter to relatives, enthusing over the "intimate" atmosphere she had found in the big city (Lundquist, "Fifth Point" 20). When quoted in an anonymously penned *New York Times* article, artist Alfred Leslie, a native New Yorker, recalled that the prospect of running into creative types at "intellectual destinations" like the Museum of Modern Art caused the city to become "sort of rural in its character" ("Modern Gone By"). The effect on recent arrivals could be dizzying. Introducing O'Hara's *Collected Poems*, Ashbery recalled finding "a kaleidoscopic lumber-room where laws of time and space are altered—where one can live a few yards from a friend whom one never sees and whom one would travel miles to visit in the country" (*Selected Prose* 133).

For some of the New York School poets, personal and professional crises ensued once the city's aleatory freedoms became an insidious trap. William Watkin maintains that New York's intoxicating mix of flash and finery bridged the gap the highly popular Frank O'Hara felt between himself and those he loved, assuaging the anxiety that attended his otherwise urbane persona (251). Yet at key moments O'Hara's initial connection with New York became as elusive as a taxi during a downpour. Just when he thought he had settled in, the city kept moving, forcing him to run faster. In the opinion of his peers, this energetic urban shepherd embodied New York City, making his attempts to escape it essentially futile. O'Hara clearly embraced the semiotic freedom of Manhattan, but in the end he was weighed down by the exemplary role he was forced to play. As Larry Rivers noted at O'Hara's funeral, scores of New Yorkers considered this magnetic poet to be their best friend. By the early 1960s, O'Hara was being wined and dined by a new breed of art collector, and sought out by younger poets who arrived on the scene. He had become the center of a vibrant art world network. As his poems suggest, the attention was too much and the pressure increasingly unbearable, prompting him to seek refuge outside the metropolis, even if that meant the nearby beaches of Fire Island, where he was struck and killed by a dune buggy in July 1966.

Like Guillaume Apollinaire, to whom he has been compared, O'Hara died young, leaving behind a cult of personality at whose altar many a second-generation New York School poet has worshipped.[4] While it remains debatable whether O'Hara deliberately stepped in front of the oncoming beach vehicle, his wish for pastoral escape was haunted by images of death.

In chapter 1, which serves alternately as case study and cautionary tale, I analyze O'Hara's escapist impulses, viewed best in his achingly beautiful poems about James Dean, the ill-starred actor, whom he memorialized repeatedly in lonely seaside retreats. In a sense, the natural detail issuing from O'Hara's pen shows him writing his own pastoral elegy in advance of his fatal accident. Death may have finally delivered this urban shepherd to his place of rest, but he was searching for a *locus amoenus* long before then, in bucolic spots closed off from his constant stream of admirers. By his own admission, his quest was futile. "I can't even find a pond small enough / to drown in without being ostentatious," he complained in 1961 (*CP* 434).

Other poets in the New York School found greater happiness because of lower profiles and better escape routes. In the remaining six chapters—which I have arranged according to the chronology of each poet's career and to the amount of critical attention each has received—I attempt to show how various aspects of country life shaped a body of literature renowned for its portrayal of the city. Combing the work of these poets for urban pastoral trends, I am amazed at their creative conceptualizations of space, viewed best in their startling geographical juxtapositions. I have witnessed, for instance, a dialectical pull between agrarian and urban landscapes in Ashbery's poetry, much of which draws upon his boyhood in upstate New York. Similarly, I have noted how Guest's girlhood memories of coastal Florida and California influenced the surrealistic imagery of her brilliant, art-based poems. I have considered how Schuyler's extended residence in Fairfield Porter's country homes in the Hamptons and Maine shaped his poetry after Porter's death, when Schuyler's view of flora was limited to the wrought-iron chrysanthemum design on the Chelsea Hotel's balustrade. I have marveled as Koch taught imaginative writing techniques to Lower East Side schoolchildren, encouraging them to let fly their escapist fantasies while bedecking cheerless city blocks with garlands of flowers. I have tracked the route of Brooklyn-born di Prima as she took her nontraditional family unit on extended sojourns (and eventual residence) in the American West. And I have come to appreciate the resolve of Norris and her friend Jim Carroll, second-generation writers who fled Andy Warhol's decadent orbit in the early 1970s to seek spiritual salvation in various *loci amoeni*, sometimes beyond city limits and occasionally within them.

Further details about these poets are reserved for the chapters themselves, which remain more or less self-contained, to be taken individually or out of order, as readers wish. For the moment, suffice it to say that each New York writer includes beneath the opacity of avant-garde language natural currents I find highly invigorating. Their willingness to suspend familiar definitions of city and country, artificiality and organicism, has inspired my own investigations.

As hinted earlier, I am not alone in spotting pastoral trends in New York City art and literature. In the 1960s and 1970s, urban pastoral caught the attention of several New York intellectuals, including Susan Sontag, who invoked the term to showcase the faux-naïf mannerisms prevalent in gay literature and film ("Notes"); Peter Schjeldahl, who employed it in a rave review of Jane Freilicher's paintings ("Urban"); and Walter Clemons ("New York") and Herbert Leibowitz ("Pan"), who used it to herald the publication of O'Hara's *Collected Poems*. Interestingly, none of these writers really explained what urban pastoral is; instead, they let the term represent a type of mood.[5] Since that time, a few scholars writing about the New York School have alluded to urban pastoral motifs, sorting through different definitions and managing varying degrees of consistency.

Helen Vendler, for instance, has spoken about the "full assent to city life" she espies in O'Hara's work ("Frank O'Hara"), only to turn around and highlight the "retreat from the active life" she finds in Schuyler's writings (*Soul* 62–70). Similarly, Terence Diggory spends one essay lauding architects Ludwig Mies van der Rohe and Siah Armanji for making New York a more livable environment ("'Picturesque'"). Yet in another, he shifts attention beyond city limits to Allen Ginsberg's farm in Cherry Valley, which in the late 1960s and early 1970s served as an upstate retreat for Lower East Side bohemians ("Allen Ginsberg's"). Then again, Diggory notes that Ginsberg, with his "whitmanesque mania & nostalgia for cities," grew impatient with agrarian life and thereafter disarmed all idyllic fantasies with the protective sheath of satire, viewing his city apartment as a bucolic setting and his Cherry Valley farm as a deluding fiction (or "lie," as Ginsberg says in his ironically titled "Ecologue" [*CP* 547]). In their books on the New York School, Geoff Ward and William Watkin concentrate on the "new nature" that abounds in New York, citing poems from O'Hara and Schuyler as they equate streets with meadows and skyscrapers with trees.

The subject also attracted those outside academia. Charles Siebert's 1998 memoir, *Wickerby: An Urban Pastoral*, bears a strong resemblance to Annie Dillard's *Pilgrim at Tinker Creek*, except that half of Siebert's narrative is set in Brooklyn. And why not? In *New Art City: Manhattan at Mid-Century*, art critic Jed Perl refers several times to urban pastoral, maintaining that "even a major metropolis could take on a pastoral character, if a painter or photographer chose to emphasize the city dweller's easy, rhythmic, almost primitive relationship with the place" (254). Perl casts his net wide, citing as practitioners of the urban pastoral mode a variety of artists and writers, from expressionist and figurative painters (Jackson Pollock and Nell Blaine), to assemblage artists (Cornell), to filmmakers (Burckhardt), to poets (O'Hara), each working at a different rhythm to capture the city's alluring atmosphere. In 2005, around the time Perl's book appeared, journalist Laura Sinagra extended the discussion to music, referring to Animal Collective, an experimental city-based ensemble, as "moody junkyard folk-poppers [who] find a kind of romance in walls and clatter," explaining that their "urban pastoral chant-alongs map a landscape where fantastical beasts gather for ritual rocking around trashcan campfires" (E26). More recently, Cold Spring Jazz Quartet, a Baltimore-based group, released a CD entitled *Urban Pastoral*, complete with "city" and "country" sides.

Remaining consistent across these various invocations of urban pastoral is an adventurous, combinatory spirit. Startlingly new approaches to the mode emerge when natural and artificial elements collide kaleidoscopically, as when O'Hara likens blinking stars to a hairnet, or claims he cannot enjoy a blade of grass unless he knows there is a subway handy; when Freilicher places a jar of irises in her studio window to mirror plumes of smoke rising from Consolidated Edison smokestacks; or when Norris equates rooftop water towers with grain silos as she plans her journey to the Great Plains. Appreciations of the mode are influenced just as much by the background of the critic analyzing such texts. *Urban Pastoral* certainly reflects the arc of my own experiences, from the distant longings of a country boy who aspired to live in the big city, to my eventual realization of that dream, to my increasingly apparent (and somewhat unsettling) desire to say goodbye to all that and get back to the land. Assembling this book for publication, I have recognized with newfound clarity how conflicting geographical allegiances led me to conceive this series of essays, composed intermittently during my first decade in New York. Attempting to capture on paper whatever pastoral aesthetic happened to influence a particular poet at a particular time, I realize that I have actually been tracking my own imaginative journeys in and out of the city.

Readers should note that I have taken a scholarly approach to my research, but a rather creative approach to my writing, which aims to be broadly accessible, unabashedly subjective, even entertaining. Paging through *Urban Pastoral*, you will find endnotes veering off into the realm of popular culture (film, television, and music), literary terminology tempered with everyday speech, and critical objectivity cut through with personal impressions of the city I have gathered over the years. Whether I am susceptible to strange frequencies, or just plain eclectic, I cannot say for sure. But lately I have been able to hear the Velvet Underground's swirling 1969 performance of "The Ocean" as a psychedelic update of Claude Debussy's Impressionistic 1905 composition *La Mer*, and to regard Jared Leto's and Jennifer Connelly's exhibitions of strung-out ecstasy in the 2000 film *Requiem for a Dream* as a powerful visual analogue to Lou Reed's 1976 anthem, "Coney Island Baby." Tapping such multifarious but interlinked sources has enriched my understanding of natural currents in urban environments. I take an equally diverse approach in my analyses of poetry, not as a substitute for traditional academic discourse, but rather as evidence of what postmodern urban culture prompts me to see and hear. After all, as Reed sings, "the city is a funny place."

More than anything, I want my writings on urban pastoral to be shareable. Aside from a handful of background interviews I have conducted with New York poets and painters, I have based my scholarship on published materials. For the sake of convenience, I have keyed citations to the most comprehensive and widely available volumes, including the spate of Collected Poems editions released recently. My hope is that readers accessing these sources will make their own judgments and contributions. Although it pains me not to include a chapter on Victor Hernandez Cruz, a talented Nuyorican writer, the truth is that I am now able to locate urban pastoral motifs in any number of contemporary New York City writers, from Eileen Myles to Colson Whitehead. In that spirit, I invite you to move beyond the eight poets whose work I consider in *Urban Pastoral*, to seek out new pastures while tending to your own.

During my time in New York, various green ideas (Chelsea's High Line railway garden; the Greenstreets initiative; vertical farming on skyscrapers; the mention of Central Park's red-tailed hawk, "Pale Male," in word and song) have taken root, making urban planning more bucolic and environmentally friendly. I like to think the poets of the New York School were there first, even if their experimental language hardly resembles the terminology we find in policy statements, Greenpeace leaflets, or Earth Day dedications. Over the years, they have assumed prominence in contemporary avant-garde literature and won major awards, but they still elude the notice of nature-writing anthologists and academic eco-critics, and that, I believe, is unfortunate.[6] For me, their writings have had a personal impact, serving as a kind of crazy compass, helping me recognize the different landscapes I have encountered while pointing out new directions for me to travel. Whatever your relationship to New York and its great literary tradition, I offer this work with the enthusiasm of a city dweller handing you a site map and with the pride of a country cousin handing you a bouquet of his choicest cuttings.

1

SEMIOTIC SHEPHERD
Frank O'Hara and the Embodiment of Urban Pastoral Community

FROM PAUL ALPERS to Annabelle Patterson, most literary scholars concur about the freedoms pastoral havens offer, but the specific place or placement of these realms remains a point of contention, and for good reason. Celebrated as sites of disguise, play, and rearrangement, pastoral spaces remain mysterious, teasingly ambiguous, and indeterminate. Edmund Spenser's *Shepheardes Calendar* (1579) may have been written for the pleasure of the Elizabethan court, but its English dialect was mixed with archaisms gleaned from Greek and Roman sources (Theocritus and Virgil), placing its singing shepherds in a fictional landscape that is neither here nor there. It is the semiotic vibrancy of pastoral and its resultant placelessness that contemporary avant-garde practitioners of the mode have sought to nurture rather than (re)place. I find this aspect relevant to my study of the New York School and urban pastoral. On one hand, I am interested in learning how writers and artists who traveled to New York City at midcentury in search of avant-garde community cognitively mapped the domain drawing them into its orbit. On the other, I want to explore the circumstances leading them to seek traditional pastoral spaces in the countryside when the placeless city wore out its welcome. Poets of the New York School are renowned for celebrating urban life, but their work is filled with fluid pathways linking the gray space of the metropolis with the green space of outlying areas. In their most affecting poems, claustrophobia gives way to mobility, abstract ideas to palpable experiences, a hard view of the streets to a softer focus on organic beauty.

Throughout his career, Frank O'Hara nurtured this heterogeneous blend of imagined geographies, though somewhat secretly. O'Hara moved frenetically through various urban venues, shepherding the eclectic aesthetic desires of his avant-garde cohorts while fashioning sophisticated verse that kept up with the city's frantic pace. During midcentury, O'Hara's vapor trails redrew the cultural landscape of New York, announcing the city as a safety zone, a haven for free-thinking individuals at odds with cold war America's mainstream ideals. Adopting the "useful disguise" prevalent in pastoral literature (Ettin 28), poets arriving in New York could take on any identity they wanted, accessing a more easygoing relationship to the world than they could in the country. "One need never leave the confines of New York to get all the greenery one wishes," O'Hara crowed at the height of his powers. "I can't even enjoy a blade of grass unless I know there's a subway handy, or a record store or some other sign that people do not totally *regret* life" (*CP* 197). Notice, though, that in this quote from "Meditations in an Emergency" the blade of grass lingers, a talisman of rural allegiances the city poet never totally abandoned.

To get a better idea of the metropolitan magic that drew O'Hara and his peers to New York, I want to move briefly across the Atlantic to consider the urban pastoral sensibility on display in Hanif Kureishi's 1987 screenplay, *Sammy and Rosie Get Laid*. In the following scene, a young English citizen of Pakistani heritage (Sammy) tries to explain to his father (Rafi) his refusal to leave London and return "home" to South Asia, where according to Rafi, "you will be valued . . . you will be rich and powerful." Sammy is thus prompted to defend the bohemian life he leads with his lover, a white radical named Rosie, in a nation increasingly hostile to "Pakis" and others perceived as different.

> RAFI: London has become a cesspit. You'd better come home, Samir.
> SAMMY: I am home, Pop. This is the bosom.
> RAFI: . . . What can you possibly like about this city now?
> SAMMY: Well . . .
> (*Now we see a number of London scenes that* SAMMY *and* ROSIE *like:* SAMMY *and* ROSIE *are walking along the towpath towards Hammersmith Bridge.*)
> (*Voice-over*) On Saturdays we like to walk along the towpath at Hammersmith and kiss and argue.
> (*Next we see* SAMMY *and* ROSIE *in "Any Amount of Books."*)
> (*Voice-over*) Then we go to the bookshop and buy novels written by women.

(*Next,* SAMMY *and* ROSIE *outside the Albert Hall*)

(*Voice-over*) Or we trot past the Albert Hall and up through Hyde Park. On Saturday nights things really hot up.

(*Cut to: outside the Royal Court Theatre in Sloane Square*)

(*Voice-over*) If we can get cheap seats we go to a play at the Royal Court. But if there's nothing on that hasn't been well reviewed by the *Guardian*—

(*Now we are in the small amused audience of a cabaret above a pub. This is the Finborough in Earl's Court. A man wearing a huge fat man's outfit, head disappeared into the neck, is dancing to an old French tune. . . .* SAMMY *and* ROSIE *sit in the audience laughing and drinking.*)

(*Voice-over*) We go to an Alternative Cabaret in Earl's Court in the hope of seeing our government abused. Or if we're really desperate for entertainment—

(*We are now in the seminar room at the ICA.* COLIN MCCABE *is talking to an enthralled audience about Derrida. A member of the audience has her hand up.*)

(*Voice-over*) We go to a seminar on semiotics at the ICA which Rosie especially enjoys.

(*Rosie also has her hand up. But* MCCABE *points to someone else.* ROSIE *looks at* SAMMY, *disgusted with* MCCABE's *indifference to her.*)

AUDIENCE MEMBER: What, would you say, is the relation between a bag of crisps and the self-enclosed unity of the linguistic sign?

(COLIN MCCABE *starts to laugh.*)

SAMMY: (*Voice-over*) We love our city and we belong to it. Neither of us are English, we're Londoners you see. (233–34)

This is a marvelous description of urban pastoral. The riches of the city are on display as we see the couple sampling myriad cultural events, many of which run counter to England's prevailing conservatism. Disguise and difference are constantly in play, liberating participants of the metropolitan carnival from ordinary troubles and identities. Notice that Colin McCabe's lecture is on semiotics, a shifting signification system open to various readings. Such indeterminacy liberates Sammy and Rosie as they traipse through London. In their favorite haunts, harmful aspects of mainstream society (imperialism, racism, sexism, homophobia) are deconstructed and recoded. That their walking tour ends in a specific gathering place, in this case a seminar room, should not surprise us if we recall the etymological root of "semiotics." In *Postmodern Geographies*, Edward Soja explains that the word derives from the Greek *semeion*, "which means sign, mark, spot or *point in space*. You arrange to meet someone at a *semeion*, a particular place. The significance of this connection between semiotics and spatiality is too often forgotten" (246n). The ICA lecture hall, like the other spots on Sammy and Rosie's itinerary, is such a point in space. Traveling among the city's *semeions*, the interracial couple celebrates zones where binary separations and cultural prescriptions are subject to reconfiguration. "Londoners" move beyond "English" citizenship.

New York City functioned in the same way for progressive Americans during the cold war. Writers and artists arriving from the hinterlands flocked to gathering spots (bars, coffeehouses, galleries, studios, jazz clubs) where diverse cultures intermingled. Abstract expressionist artwork evolving from a confluence of European émigrés and America's own internal exiles was forged in *semeions* conducive to social exchange. The lively discussions that took place in intellectual contact zones like the New School for Social Research, Hans Hofmann's painting workshops, the Eighth Street Artists Club, and the Cedar Tavern allowed New York School painters to rethink cultural values and assay new directions in American art. Wandering onto this scene were several young poets who adhered to similar aesthetic principles. Foremost among them was O'Hara, who not only reveled in New York's polyvalent, abstract atmosphere but also managed physically to embody it.

Crucial to my understanding of O'Hara's role within the New York School is a style of movement that makes semiotic spaces attractive and shareable. According to Michel de Certeau, an astute observer of postmodern cities, "space is composed of intersections of mobile elements. It is in a sense actuated by the ensemble of movements deployed within it. . . . In short, *space is practiced place*" (117). The allure of the city derives from people whose "spacings" announce new realms of being, even as they playfully undermine the stability typically ascribed to place. When rigorously "practiced" by mobile figures, these spatial realms become pastoral havens of relentlessly directional play. In Kureishi's screenplay, Sammy realizes he need only retrace Rosie's trajectory through London to articulate the freedom he has found. Similarly, John Ashbery remembers how he and his friends relied upon the peripatetic genius of O'Hara, whose tireless wanderings connected the dots in New York: "The one thing lacking in our privileged little world (privileged because it was a kind of balcony overlooking the interestingly chaotic events happening in the bigger worlds outside) was the arrival of Frank O'Hara to kind of cobble everything together and tell us what we and they were doing" (*Reported* 241). Apparently, urban pastoral realms benefit from freewheeling individuals blessed with charisma and intellect, not to mention a sturdy pair of feet.

In his short and eventful life, O'Hara achieved success as a poet, a museum curator, and an art critic. Others remember him as the ultimate social butterfly, the popular figure making the scene at galleries, studios, and the Hamptons party circuit. Because O'Hara hit so many spots on his daily rounds, theories of cultural geography prove useful. And because geography is at base a literary construction—an inscription (-*graph*) on the earth (*geo-*)—it makes sense to investigate the way the city gets written as an experimental language. The task is daunting. In "Semiology and Urbanism," Roland Barthes explains that urban geography has a semantic content that outstrips its functionality. A site that appears unitary upon first glance is actually heterogeneous, or in linguistic terms, *polysemic*. No metaphor can fix the meaning of the city. Like a fading neon sign on a Baltimore morning (Jacques Lacan's analogy for the human unconscious), the imagined city exists just beyond our cognitive grasp, somewhere out there on the receding horizon of consciousness, teasing those drawn to its flash and flicker. Instead of getting hung up on fixed meanings, Barthes says, urban theorists would do better to analyze "the world of signifiers, of correlations, and above all of correlations which can never be imprisoned in a full signification, in a final signification" (198). Like the unconventional literature and art proliferating within its permeable borders, the postmodern city, a site of "combination and transformation," eludes formalist closure. "The city is a poem," Barthes explains, "but not a classical poem, not a poem centered on a subject. It is a poem which deploys the signifier, and it is this deployment which the semiology of the city must ultimately grasp and make sing" (201).

Yet even in an open system, some places get marked as central, inasmuch as they make aleatory energies recognizable and shareable. McCabe's seminar room in *Sammy and Rosie* is one such place. The Cedar Tavern, the downtown watering hole where New York's avant-garde pioneers robustly defended their art, is another. The centrality of such spots is accordant with their ability to give free rein to signification and to be, as Barthes says, "the privileged site where the other is and where we ourselves are the other, as the site where one plays" (200). Because these gathering places rely upon pragmatic movement, or "spacing," I want to turn to one who moves effortlessly among them. Frank O'Hara stood out in the New York School not simply because of his writing, but because he was able to embody, in a distinctly mobile form, the semiotic energy fueling his milieu's avant-garde desires. Moving with verve through the city's *semeions*, O'Hara announced New York as a realm of difference. Before long, it was he who got figured as semiotic, his physical presence captured not so much by symbolic fixation as by a metonymic tracing of the routes he traveled. As semiotic shepherd of the New York School, he was a fluidly affective site where the desires of an arts community conveniently converged.[1]

O'Hara participated actively in city life, sampling a diverse array of cultural offerings, tendering his opinions nightly at dinner parties and gallery openings, and recording his original observations in witty poetry and insightful art criticism. His pronouncements were a barometer of adventurous good taste. So long as O'Hara was on the scene, New Yorkers felt secure in their own aesthetic risk-taking. Following the poet through Manhattan, from the revolving door of the Museum of Modern Art (MoMA) to the bathroom door of the Five Spot, his admirers calibrated their own potential for hip eclecticism and urbane sophistication. "He taught me to really see New York for the first time," Allen Ginsberg said (Gooch 238). "Frank seemed to be a priest who got into a different business," Alex Katz recalled. "Even on his sixth martini-second pack of cigarettes and while calling a friend 'a bag of shit' and roaring off into the night. Frank's business was being an active intellectual. He was out to improve our world whether we liked it or not. . . . The frightening amount of energy he invested in our art and our lives often made me feel like a miser" (99). O'Hara liked to say that "style at its highest ebb is personality" (*Art* 149). By this measure, he was highly successful.

Yet O'Hara's embodiment of artistic freedom proved burdensome, not so much in an existentialist sense as in the claustrophobic arena of social expectation. Once he got tapped as semiotic shepherd, the guiding force for flocks gathering in New York's urban pastoral, it was difficult for him to enjoy rest or solitude. His "useful disguise," coveted by shepherds in literary pastoral, became utterly transparent, necessitating new forms of concealment. But where could he hope to go without having the adoring eyes of his community follow his every action? What kind of haven awaited a writer whose movements cut the borders of urban pastoral community? How could he retreat beyond the metropolis he had come to signify? To understand how O'Hara facilitated the abstract dreams of his avant-garde community, only to become trapped within its semiotic crucible, we must temper our appreciation of his "urban world of fantasy" (Ashbery, *Selected*

Prose 128) with a fresh consideration of the pressures he faced and a look at the natural escape route he secretly dreamed of following.

LIKE THE SCHOOL'S other charter members, O'Hara was not a native New Yorker. Born in Baltimore in 1926, he moved soon thereafter to the small town of Grafton, Massachusetts, settling near a farm depot, where he and his family sometimes worked. As Brad Gooch explains in *City Poet*, O'Hara chafed at farm chores and other aspects of rural life, although he seems to have enjoyed riding horses. At the same time, he appears to have soaked up the natural imagery of rural Massachusetts, since several Grafton anecdotes—many of them pertinent to his sexual awakening—appear in "Commercial Variations," "For Bob Rauschenberg," "Ode to Michael Goldberg ('s Birth and Other Births)," and other poems. As Gooch says, "in his erotic life, [O'Hara] seemed to have been drawn back to the very hay bins and farm animals he was so bored by in the workaday world" (52). In this manner he resembled Ashbery, who repeatedly recalls his adolescent antipathy toward work on his family's upstate farm but routinely employs the imagery of agrarian America in his avant-garde verse, often when sexuality is involved.

Grafton's hold was tenuous, however. O'Hara proclaimed in his high school yearbook his plans "to live in a big city" (Gooch 39), and at Harvard there exists further evidence of this ambition, as though Cambridge was but a way station on the golden road to Gotham. Enamored of music, O'Hara began college with the intention of becoming a classical composer, though he eventually switched to the English department, where Ashbery and Koch were upperclassmen. When these two moved to New York to pursue the writer's life, O'Hara took note of their trajectory. "One must not be stifled in a closed social or artistic railway station waiting for the train," he emoted in his journal. "I've a long long way to go, and I'm late already." Restlessness is O'Hara's predominant motif here, as it is in his most famous New York poems. As he put it in another journal entry, "My own writing is so far in the future that it may well be a mirage." Happily, literature allowed O'Hara the chance to leave childhood alienation behind, and soon he started to believe that "something wonderful may happen" (*Early Writing* 101, 103, 109). In "Autobiographia Literaria," written during his final year at Harvard, he exults, "here I am, the / center of all beauty! / writing these poems! / Imagine!" (*CP* 11).

In 1950, O'Hara's writing prowess earned him a graduate scholarship to the University of Michigan. Success proceeded apace, as he won Michigan's prestigious Hopwood award. Meanwhile, he kept his eyes peeled for what was happening in New York City, where he was already establishing a network of friends. Anticipating the community he was about to join, he wrote to painter Jane Freilicher from Ann Arbor in the summer of 1951, recommending Paul Goodman's "Advance Guard Writing," an essay celebrating the "physical establishment" of personal ties in urban settings (Diggory, "Community" 18–19).[2] O'Hara's decision to share Goodman's message proved eerily prescient, since his own physicality would become the adhesive holding the New York School together. Sensing this, Freilicher traveled to Michigan, where she captured O'Hara's physical allure in a portrait, the first of many done by his artist friends.

O'Hara admired the resilience of New York's visual artists, a hearty bunch whose challenging works reflected the environment in which they were created. "New York is one of the most violent cities in the world and its pace is hectic," O'Hara explained. "What can survive must have had some quality, what can be done under all the different pressures of circumstance must have meant something to the artist who managed to get it done" (*Standing* 97). Over time, O'Hara would experience firsthand the "pressures of circumstance" that circulated in the New York art world, responding to its hothouse atmosphere with joie de vivre, assuaging whatever doubts lesser figures might have had about the avant-garde life. "By the early sixties he had become a kind of culture hero," Marjorie Perloff says in her pioneering critical study (*Frank* xi). O'Hara's peers had weighed in years earlier. His "*cult du moi* is overpowering," Ashbery noted in 1966 (*Selected Prose* 82). In a memorial piece, Bill Berkson referred to O'Hara as a "one-man movement," echoing Willem de Kooning's effusive praise of Marcel Duchamp ("Frank" 161). Larry Rivers, meanwhile, thought of him as the New York School's "central switchboard," musing in his eulogy that there were at least sixty people who considered Frank O'Hara to be their best friend ("Speech" 138). Barbara Guest recalled that O'Hara "had this wonderful gift of love which so many of us withheld" (Lehman 176). Kenneth Koch praised his "way of feeling and acting as though being an artist were the most natural thing in the world" (*Art* 22).

Many of the accolades took aim at O'Hara's body, an energetic vessel whose all-over trajectory, like Jackson Pollock's skeins of dripped paint, signified the heroic act of moving spontaneously and speedily through postmodern space. As Koch recalls, "Frank was trying to run faster than ordinary consciousness" (Ferguson 27). Zeroing in on the poet's mobile figure, avant-garde types discerned a "heterotopian" mind-set, defined by Michel Foucault as "what type of storage, circulation, marking, and classification of human elements should be adopted in a given situation to achieve a given end" (23). O'Hara's lunchtime walks, his gift purchases, his movie- and theatergoing, his "big artistic tipsy kisses" (Ginsberg 458), his worship of painters and musicians, his spats with lovers: these actions were read by a community defining its spatial aesthetic, the boundaries of which O'Hara seemed constantly to expand. Here was someone comfortable above and below Fourteenth Street, at gala openings at MoMA or benefit readings for struggling Lower East Side magazines, at the Metropolitan Opera or a bebop session at the Five Spot. As the person mutually agreeable to up-town wealth and downtown bohemianism, which depended upon each other but were hesitant to meet, O'Hara was responsible for an amazing social confluence. He brought to New York an added injection of energy. Peter Schjeldahl remembers that O'Hara's "physical presence in a room was like that of an exclamation point on a page," citing Mike Goldberg's judg-ment that, "if you were close to him, Frank forced you to live at a terribly high intensity" ("Frank" 141–42). Those able to keep pace regarded him the same way Jasper Johns regarded Duchamp, as an avant-garde pioneer who "changed the condition of being here" (22). In sum, O'Hara had the same quality he admired in Whitman: "gatheringness" (*Standing* 162).

O'Hara's gatheringness was especially apparent on his urban perambu-lations. For him, a walk through Manhattan was not the relaxed sampling of a Baudelairean flaneur, but rather the emboldened ambition of a world-city impresario racing against time to orchestrate components of a cultural crescendo.[3] His hectic lunchtime walks resulted in terrific poems, several of which ("The Day Lady Died," "A Step Away from Them," and "Personal Poem") are now regularly anthologized. Years after they were written, these poems remain representative of New York. Sidewalks are bustling with crowds, kiosk attendants and street vendors are hawking products, sweaty construction workers are taking their lunch break, cabs are flashing by in a blur down busy avenues. O'Hara shows us that in New York hardly any-thing remains motionless, including personal relationships, which are as fluid as the traffic. The effect on his writing is palpable. Whether he was oc-cupying adjacent bar stools with a friend or wooing a distant lover, O'Hara realized that in order to represent the New York arts community, he had to develop a breathless style. On this level he succeeded brilliantly. Nearly a half century after his death, many readers feel like they have an intimate knowledge of his social scene.[4]

"Personal Poem" showcases O'Hara's kinetic communitarianism. Walking to meet LeRoi Jones at Moriarty's, a bar, O'Hara takes in the streetscape, letting his sensations guide him: "I walk through the luminous humidity / passing the House of Seagram with its wet / and its loungers and the construction to / the left that closed the sidewalk if / I ever get to be a construction worker / I'd like to have a silver hat please" (*CP* 335). The intellectual admits that commercialism dominates in Manhattan, hence the appeal of silver-helmeted construction workers going about their business. Responding to a friend who was complaining about the demolishing of Manhattan's grand old buildings, O'Hara once said, "Oh no, that's the way New York is. You have to just keep tearing it down and building it up" (Gooch 218).[5] No surprise, then, that in "Personal Poem" he dismisses the mothballed status of a "poets' walk" in San Francisco, opting instead for a careening tour of New York's demolition sites. Beneficial as it is for his fluid style of writing, O'Hara notes that the city's ceaseless commercial flow facilitates friendships, marked here by his repartee with Jones and his subsequent thoughts of his lover, Vincent Warren:

> we don't want to be in the poets' walk in
> San Francisco even we just want to be rich
> and walk on girders in our silver hats
> I wonder if one person out of the 8,000,000 is
> thinking of me as I shake hands with LeRoi
> and buy a strap for my wristwatch and go
> back to work happy at the thought possibly so (*CP* 336)

According to an old cab driver's joke, even if you are one in a million, in New York there are eight people just like you. The joke provides one way to dismiss the intimidating size of the city. O'Hara takes a slightly different tack, but his logic is not so different. His comment on hardhat workers, his valedictory handshake with a friend, and his purchase of a watchband awaken thoughts of an absent lover, who may be thinking of him at the same time. Somehow, the fact that there are eight million people moving between O'Hara and Warren during this New York minute draws the lovers closer together. The two men stand apart, but they join the same urban weave, the same quirky social contract whereby strangers and friends accede to a surprising level of intimacy, inseparable from the bustling transactions going on around them. O'Hara not only shows his willingness to "enter the city's flows, but also [his desire] to 'stand still' by recording love and desire that oppose the rush of the city," Susan Rosenbaum notes (162). Still, I have the feeling that the "love" and the "rush" are one and the same.

O'Hara conveys a similar message in "Having a Coke with You," which is addressed directly to Warren. "It is hard to believe when I'm with you that there can be anything as still / as solemn as unpleasantly definitive as statuary," he emotes, "when right in front of it / in the warm New York 4 o'clock light we are drifting back and forth / between each other like a tree breathing through its spectacles" (*CP* 360). Let old-fashioned son-neteers talk about building stately monuments in verse to their beloveds. O'Hara prefers the fizzy kick of a Coke and the effervescent notion of love-as-kinesis. He avoids the solemn fixity of statuary the same way he backed away from the poets' walk in "Personal Poem," submitting to the drift that is part of any relationship, surrealistically likening that drift to a whoosh of wind through the trees, or to New York streets at rush hour (take your pick). "Whether engagé or exhausted," Maggie Nelson says, O'Hara "consistently replaces the drama of 'caring' about Poetry and/or literary accomplishment with the drama of 'caring' or 'not caring' for the moment at hand—a shift that grants the poetry much of its remarkable euphoria, melancholy, and freedom" (92). Proving invaluable in such instances, O'Hara implies in his mock-manifesto "Personism," is a willingness to "just go on your nerve." Writers should not get hung up on how the establishment receives their art any more than they should plan in advance the way personal relationships play out. "Suppose you're in love and someone's mistreating (*mal aimé*) you, you don't say, 'Hey, you can't hurt me this way, I care!' you just let all the different bodies fall where they may, and they always do may after a few months. But that's not why you fell in love in the first place, just to hang onto life, so you have to take your chances and try to avoid being logical. Pain always produces logic, which is very bad for you" (*CP* 498).

O'Hara's love affair with Warren ended shortly after "Having a Coke," and his friendship with Jones was altered when the latter changed his name to Amiri Baraka and joined the Black Arts movement. The cool tone of "Personism" suggests that O'Hara may have taken these upheavals in stride. After all, a number of his muses (Freilicher, Bunny Lang, Grace Hartigan) had exited his life, only to be replaced by others (Berkson, Patsy Southgate). In "To the Harbormaster" (*CP* 217) and "Joe's Jacket" (329–30), O'Hara reg-isters his regret over failed relationships but returns rather quickly to his main goal, which is "to be true to a city," confident that this commonly held third term will prevent his social world from crumbling. In the former poem, he treads water in a crowded harbor, a stand-in for New York, try-ing to skirt danger and "reach" his ex-lover Larry Rivers, the titular master of that realm. In "Joe's Jacket," O'Hara remains in the apartment he shared with Joe LeSueur long after their relationship has cooled, feeling depressed over present circumstances but continuing to find security in LeSueur's seersucker blazer, which he wears proudly on the street to signal their lasting bond. In both poems, the city helps O'Hara save a relationship that has been torn asunder. In *Casablanca*, Bogart tells an old flame they will always have Paris. O'Hara may have believed he and his friends would always have New York.

But as Barthes reminds us, semiotic situations are characterized by ambiguities and rapid reversals, such that when it comes to chronicling O'Hara's fate as city poet, it might make more sense to say "New York always had him." Once this semiotic shepherd was called upon by his admirers to embody the city, the objective third term he professed to share with members of his milieu suddenly disappeared. His relationship with New York collapsed back into a dialectical formula, closing off most escape routes. For better or worse, O'Hara equaled New York, meaning that those seeking connection with the city's avant-garde necessarily sought personal contact with him. Judging by his poems, O'Hara's recognition of his figural entrapment hit him only intermittently, though we can see his recognition growing stronger as years go by.

INITIALLY, O'Hara seems to have thrived in New York's heady environment. In "1951," he speaks enthusiastically about immersing himself in a cityscape "Far from burgeoning // verdure," where "the literal drifts / colorfully" (*CP* 73–74). By the time of "Steps," composed in 1960, he was adept at capturing the swirl of cultural energies making Manhattan a propitious contact zone. Ginger Rogers, Lana Turner, and Greta Garbo appear in this poem's magically skewed cityscape, a cartoonlike realm where ballet dancers in the park are mistaken for "worker-outers at the West Side Y," old men drinking beer on discarded delicatessen boxes are knocked on their backsides by their wives, and even Saint Bridget's steeple is caught "leaning a little to the left." The sheer craziness of the place allows for an unprecedented amount of personal freedom. In what appears to be a direct address to the city, O'Hara praises a realm that "accepts me foolish and free" and promises to pay the city back in kind: "oh god it's wonderful / to get out of bed / and drink too much coffee / and smoke too many cigarettes / and love you so much" (370–71). Like many a swain in Renaissance pastoral, he finds in the metropolis a happy place to wile away his time among like-minded souls. The difference, of course, is that O'Hara prefers New York's filth and traffic to a life sitting on rural hillocks. In such moments, Russell Ferguson asserts, "the city can be seen as the *new* nature, superseding the old rather than obliterating it" (35).

Grafton, in any case, seems like a distant memory. "I'm not the pastoral type anymore," O'Hara proclaims in "Corresponding Foreignly" (*Poems*

Retrieved 161). "I'm dropping my pastoral pretensions," he enthuses in "To the Mountains of New York" (*CP* 198). Other early poems, such as "A Pastoral Dialogue" and "Two Shepherds, a Novel," relegate traditional pastoral landscapes to the realm of parody. For Ferguson, such poems indicate "a hostility to the country" (35), and for other readers they might signal the metropolitan triumphalism O'Hara exhibited in "Meditations in an Emergency." From this perspective, the sidewalk "ballet" Jane Jacobs famously celebrated (*Death*) affords O'Hara all the solace (and greenery) he requires. It matters little that "Meditations" was written as a riposte to Larry Rivers, whose breakup with O'Hara removed the poet from the Hamptons beach scene that summer, leaving him lonely and sweltering in the city (Gooch 253–54). That is not why its lines about not being able to enjoy a blade of grass are etched today in Battery Park. Rather, as Ashbery says, it is because O'Hara provides "a vernacular corresponding to the creatively messy New York environment . . . shaping his already considerable gifts toward a remarkable new poetry—both modest and monumental, with something basically usable about it—not only for poets in search of a voice of their own but for the reader who turns to poetry as a last resort in trying to juggle the contradictory components of modern life into something like a livable space" (*Selected Prose* 132).

O'Hara's life grew more complicated once he got marked out as a "livable space," a popular point of convergence, a mobile signifier of New York's avant-garde thrusts. O'Hara's genius was announced publicly whenever he walked. Several younger poets camped out just to catch a glimpse of him. Jim Carroll trailed O'Hara down Fifty-third Street as he left work at MoMA. Ted Berrigan, Joe Brainard, and Ron Padgett, who traveled from Tulsa to New York to immerse themselves in the poetry scene, recognized their hero walking on Second Avenue and showered him with praise (Gooch 399). The Tulsa poets particularly liked the way their idol moved through space. "I remember Frank O'Hara's walk," Brainard writes. "Light and sassy. With a slight bounce and a slight twist. It was a beautiful walk. Confident. 'I don't care' and sometimes 'I know you are looking'" (14). Larry Rivers shares a similar appraisal: "He was a charming madman, a whoosh of air sometimes warm and pleasant, sometimes so gusty you closed your eyes and brushed back the hair it disarranged. He was thin and about five seven. He walked on his toes, stretched his neck, and angled his head, all to add an inch or two to his height. I never walked the same after I met him" (*What* 228). Members of the New York School realized what critics discovered only belatedly, namely that the "Emergency" upon which O'Hara based his "Meditations" was tied to the physical emergence of his being. As Berkson recalls, he was "a centripetal force that held everybody against the drum" (Gruen 152). Berrigan spoke for many of O'Hara's fans when he latched onto the phrase "perfectly frank" (11) and said of his hero's body of verse, "It's all there, I don't need anything else" (Shaw 38).

O'Hara's stylish movement through urban *semeions* was rendered expertly in paintings composed by his friends. In the portrait Freilicher painted in Ann Arbor, O'Hara stands at an angle in a nondescript doorway, a semiabstract figure gesturing with an upraised hand. His face is devoid of detail save for the curvaceous swell of nose linking the small dots of eye and mouth. Freilicher has said that her depiction "was just an attempt to capture a fleeting sense of his physical presence as he seemed, often, to be standing in the doorway of a room, one arm bent up at the elbow, his weight poised on the balls of his feet, maybe saying something funny or charming, proffering a drink or listening attentively, alert & delightful" ("It really" 23). In her 1954 painting *The Masker*, Grace Hartigan finds her own representational balance. She lends O'Hara's oval head a bit of detail, but once more his features tend to be geometric, almost exaggeratedly so. His hairline and eyebrows rise into high arcs, while his broken nose is flattened into a messy triangle, the base of which takes the measure of his perfectly straight lips. His head and his motley-attired torso are bisected, nearly perpendicularly, by the thin black lines severing his nose and tracing his neck.

In Elaine de Kooning's 1962 portrait, O'Hara again emerges from an abstract background, embodying the energetic gesture of the painter's geometric brushstrokes. Like Freilicher and Hartigan, de Kooning captures O'Hara's aura by subtracting detail from his body, particularly his face, relying upon her memory of his agile, abstract bearing. "The thing about people one knows intimately is, you don't even have to look," de Kooning explains. "First I painted the whole structure of his face; then I wiped out the face, and when the face was gone, it was more Frank than when the face was there." Advance planning is not necessary, she implies, since O'Hara simply "*occurs* within the painting" (Ferguson 89). Tapping Barthesian theory, I regard O'Hara's "occurrence" here as a semiotic event, fleeting but at the same time shareable, the metonymical aspects of his being retaining the centrality and purposefulness of metaphor. Indeed, Ferguson finds in these paintings "an ambiguous figure ready to take on any character" (90).[6]

O'Hara's can't-sit-still personality was evident even when he embarked on rural jaunts. John Button's 1956 canvas *Swimmer* shows O'Hara plunging headlong into the heavy surf off Long Island. It is hard to determine whether this figure is simply perpetuating the energetic mobility for which he has become renowned or actively fleeing the social attention he has attracted. A strong swimmer, O'Hara was known to take extraordinary chances in the water, as he did in his writing, venturing into currents others deemed too dangerous. To his credit, Button underscores O'Hara's risk-taking, rendering in a swirling wash of blue paint the kinetic force with which the poet approached all experiences.[7] Equally revealing is Fairfield Porter's 1957 portrait of O'Hara. Here we see the barefoot poet, clad in Bermuda shorts and a polo shirt, jackknifed uneasily into the corner of a couch in Porter's Southampton house. The sofa's floral design may whisper country casual, and the window in the background may let in a refreshing draft of Atlantic air, but O'Hara seems rather tightly wound. Even in this most leisurely of settings, the city poet's legs are in motion, as though he has just spilled himself into the sofa or is just now preparing to leave, swinging his lower limbs like a pendulum to gain momentum. Either way, he cannot have held this awkward position for very long. His relaxed pastoral self is dominated by his restless urban self.

O'Hara's agility is captured expertly in Alex Katz's 1959 cutout portrait, which depicts the poet on the balls of his feet, ready to spring into movement. Katz used oil paint on plywood, which he proceeded to cut along the boundaries of the represented figure. Easily transportable, the cutout is ready for any number of deployments. Katz's mobile representations jibed well with the New York School's emphasis on placelessness, a trend O'Hara notes in a 1966 essay. Speaking as someone with firsthand knowledge of the subject, O'Hara explains that "one of the most often discussed problems of New York painting in the mid-fifties was that of the figure." He then delineates the strategies Katz and other artists have undertaken to solve this problem:

> [Willem] De Kooning's alarming solution was an environment of paint as miraculously deft and beautiful as the figure itself. Katz's less-known but much-discussed (among painters) solution was a "void" of smoothly painted color, as smoothly painted as the figure itself, where the fairly realistic figure existed (but did not rest) in a space which had no floor, no walls, no source of light, no viewpoint. Unlike De Kooning's Women, they were not looking at you; unlike Larry Rivers's figures and nudes, they had no attitude and no atmosphere; Katz's people simply existed, somewhere. They stayed in the picture as solutions of a formal problem, neither existential nor lost, neither deprived nor dismayed. They were completely mysterious, pictorially, because there seemed to be no apparent intent of effect. They knew they were there.
> (*Art* 145–46)

But it was Katz's cutout portraits, such as the one that takes O'Hara as its locus, which came even closer to pure signification and which truly "did not rest," removed as they were from any background environment: "Katz then proceeded to remove even the 'void.' He began to paint figures which he then cut out of the plywood, thus removing any possibility of a pictorial space or environment. Wherever they stood was their environment" (146). Accordingly, O'Hara is not the subject of Katz's cutout. Rather, he is what Barthes would call a "deployed signifier." Removed from any conceptualization of fixed spatiality or "emplacement," the poet's mobile figure becomes a placeless site of pure signification, a barely traceable point on an otherwise elusive trajectory. Wherever O'Hara stands, viewers will locate the shifting borders of his aesthetic milieu.

O'Hara's perceptive analysis of Katz's cutouts matched what other New York artists and writers were saying about their placeless city and, by extension, about O'Hara himself. Willem de Kooning termed the New York School milieu a "no-environment" (Sandler 327). Robert Motherwell likewise insisted that the New York School was "not geographical but denoting a direction," that it was meant to describe a "placeless community" in which one could "invent oneself" (68, 83). As poet Alice Notley says, "somehow people don't connect the New York in the New York School with the city itself" (Nelson 210). Still, the New York School had its limits, the contours of which were attributable to the mobile bodies cutting its borders. Qualifying Motherwell's assessment, I maintain that the invention of oneself in urban pastoral settings is often enabled by the presence of an alluring figure, a third term whose trajectory through city space reveals to interested observers new aesthetic horizons.

However placeless it may have appeared, the New York art world required someone like O'Hara to position himself tactically, to shoulder the environmental expectations Ashbery claimed were not there, to be in the right place at the right time, and thus to "make the scene." O'Hara was the figure toward whom writers and artists repeatedly turned, even as the notion of figuration was being rigorously questioned. In a 1962 review, Berkson lampooned MoMA's latest exhibit, *Recent Painting U.S.A.: The Figure*, for being misnamed and "silly to start with," supplying a humorous scenario by way of explanation: "Two critics, walking through the exhibition rooms, invented the game, 'Spot the figger' and were occasionally, sometimes happily stumped. 'Where's the figger? Where's the figger?'" ("Art" 38–39). Perhaps, if they wanted to see the real, ceaselessly directional New York "figger," they should have left MoMA's exhibition room and entered its curatorial offices, where O'Hara had his desk, or else camped outside its revolving doors to follow him down Sixth Avenue on his lunch break.

Over time, a bitter irony emerged. Although he embodied the freedom avant-garde artists found attractive, O'Hara's own ability to place himself in pleasurable situations was effectively co-opted. Deemed agreeable to diverse groups of people, he had become a signifier of his city's big canvas fantasies, which followed him out of town. "I will get off the 4:19 in Easthampton / at 7:15 and then go straight to dinner / and I don't know the people who will feed me," O'Hara reports bemusedly in "The Day Lady Died" (*CP* 325). Just as his walks attracted onlookers, the bon mots O'Hara uttered at cocktail parties were passed on to other ears in other social circles. Like Katz's figures, he had become a "solution to a formal problem," or to use Barthes's language, a "deployed signifier" his city had "grasped and made sing." To invoke an image from "Personism," we might say that not even a "track star for Mineola Prep" can outrun signification's reach if his mobility has become the raison d'être of the New York School.

O'Hara tried to deflect attention onto peers and protégés, to little avail. He acknowledged Koch as the "backbone" and Southgate as the "Grace Kelly" of the New York School (*CP* 331, 389). He named one of his best poems from the 1960s ("Bill's School of New York") after Berkson and posed with him in nautical regalia for another Katz portrait, *Marine and Sailor*, as if to announce a new leader coming up through the ranks. Yet it was O'Hara, more than any other artist or writer, who remained in demand by socialites and collectors. Meanwhile, his old friends grew increasingly frustrated by their lack of access. We are left to speculate what O'Hara's life might have been like had he, like Ashbery (who spent a decade in Paris), left the milieu he signified for any length of time. But by the 1960s this semiotic shepherd had become tamed by his own adoring flocks.[8]

ALL ALONG, O'Hara had been firing warning volleys in his poems, reckoning the costs of avant-garde fame, at first indirectly and from afar, though increasingly on a more personal level. In "Interior (with Jane)," a poem composed in Ann Arbor, O'Hara honors Freilicher's decorative artistry, her ability to transform a cramped city apartment—bedecked with Persian carpets, patterned shawls, and bouquets of flowers—into the exotic lair she subsequently captured on canvas. "The eagerness of objects to / be what we are afraid to do // cannot help but move us," he enthuses (*CP* 55). Ostensibly, O'Hara is praising Freilicher's figurative style, but he might also be championing those whose eagerness to penetrate dangerous territory moves a legion of experimental artists forward. Acceding to this role in "Second Avenue," O'Hara takes up arms for the sake of his artistic confreres, who lie back in passive-aggressive fashion, latching on to whatever they see him doing. "I suffer accelerations that are vicarious and serene," O'Hara says of his closely monitored avant-garde thrusts, "just as the lances of an army advance the heat of the soldiery, / so does my *I* tremble before the getting-out-of-bedness / of that all-encompassing snake" (140). Although it would be a mistake to read the surrealistic "Second Avenue" too literally, we see here the insidious tendency of art world denizens to live out their adventures vicariously. The effect on O'Hara is real. He trembles at the duty of semiotic representation, his ongoing need to adopt for the sake of his community a consistently open self, depicted here as an "all-encompassing snake," herpetological kin to the serpent side-winding its way through "In Memory of My Feelings."

In "Memory," New York's shepherd speaks approvingly of the "Grace / to be born and live as variously as possible," yet he also exposes the "sordid identifications" constituting New York's avant-garde "masque." Specifically, he laments his figural entrapment in a milieu that wants him always to be available, to be everything to everybody. Steady ground is hard to find in such a weightless atmosphere, especially if you are the "various" figure called upon to create it. "I have lost what is always and everywhere / present, the scene of my selves, the occasion of these ruses," O'Hara admits (*CP* 252, 256–57). Losing a scene of selfhood that nevertheless remains "always and everywhere present" awakens in him a fresh consideration of his fate. Five years after arriving in New York City, he fears that he has lost control over his own scene-making potential, and hence any semblance of singularity and interiority. He surmises that he "must now kill" the false "occasion" and "scene" he embodies if he hopes to "save the serpent in their midst" or recover the true self (or "I") missing in the swirl of attention. The multiplicity that is the hallmark of New York School poetics has become in O'Hara's case a dangerous symptom.[9]

"I am what people make of me," O'Hara quips in "On Rachmaninoff's Birthday (I am so glad)" (*CP* 190). Similarly, in "Meditations in an Emergency," he declares, "I am needed by things as the sky must be above the earth. I can spare myself but little sleep" (197). "Grand Central" and "Nocturne," two other poems from the mid-1950s, ratchet up the codependency quotient, for they show the city poet taking on the physical features of Manhattan. The first poem is on its surface a parable about homosexual cruising in public, its letter carrier receiving sexual favors under Grand Central Terminal's expansive dome. On another level, we see the extent to which O'Hara, like the massive rail station, got depicted as the meeting ground where urbanites felt free to pursue their desires. "The wheels are inside me thundering," O'Hara admits, as though the foundations of his own being have been shaken by the city's social traffic. "Nocturne" covers similar territory, although it moves in the opposite direction, beginning with the poet's personal lament and moving toward his identification with a midtown building. Pressed by unhappy circumstances (failed love affairs, loneliness) into naming what shapes his life as city poet, O'Hara declares, "It's space." By way of example, he alludes to another architectural marvel:

A tiny airliner drops its
specks over the UN Building.
My eyes, like millions of
glassy squares, merely reflect.
Everything sees through me,
in the daytime I'm too hot
and at night I freeze; I'm
built the wrong way for the
river and a mild gale would
break every fiber in me.
Why don't I go east and west
instead of north and south?
It's the architect's fault.
And in a few years I'll be
useless, not even an office
building . . . (225)

To describe his lovelorn plight of "feeling bad and not / being able to tell you," O'Hara scans Manhattan for appropriate spatial coordinates. He does so at first through simile, suggesting that his eyes, like the "millions of glassy squares" comprising the UN Building and other modern sky-scrapers, "merely reflect" the teeming city he walks through. He quickly shifts to outright identification with the building, describing its footprints as though they were his own. Speaking as the sleek landmark, with lines running north and south along Manhattan's shoreline, O'Hara finds that he is susceptible to mild gales (social windstorms in his case) and violable to anyone passing through his architectural "fault," or fissure. His iden-tification with the UN Building reveals the stark reality of his situation. "Everything sees through me," he says. O'Hara's aptitude for reflecting the panorama of New York proves irresistibly attractive, but as years go by his genius has led celebrants of city life to think they can look right through him, as though he were a pane of glass, finding what they want to find in the depths of his being. In his own eyes, O'Hara enjoyed none of the protection a purely reflective exterior would have provided.[10]

As pressure built, O'Hara began to dream about leaving New York's avant-garde hothouse. A poignant expression of his wish arrives in "Sleeping on the Wing," a poem he wrote hastily in his apartment, acting on a dare proffered by Schuyler and LeSueur. "Soaring above the shoreless city," the persona of this poem takes flight, feeling New York's hardness dissipate. "Fear drops away too, like the cement," the suddenly aloft figure explains, as he finds himself "over the Atlantic," far from Manhattan's maddening crowd. "A sudden down-draught reminds you of gravity and your position in respect to human love," he admits. "But / here is where the gods are, speculating, bemused." Following his dream vision beyond city limits, O'Hara renounces his iconic status for the liberty of anonymous wandering. "Once you are helpless, you are free, can you believe / that? Never to waken to the sad struggle of a face? / to travel always over some impersonal vastness, / to be out of, forever, neither in nor for!" (*CP* 235). Disturbed by his circumscribed role in the New York School, the adventurer in "Sleeping on the Wing" leaps into the thin air of forgetfulness and detachment, pursuing indeterminacy on his own terms.

> . . . swooping,
> you relinquish all that you have made your own,
> the kingdom of your self sailing, for you must awake
> and breathe your warmth in this beloved image
> whether it's dead or merely disappearing,
> as space is disappearing and your singularity. (236)

The last line highlights the peculiarity of O'Hara's situation. We know that his singular personality made him a lightning rod in his milieu, and that attention followed him to pastoral settings outside Manhattan, complicating his search for solitude. At the same time we see that his "singularity," regarded here as the control of his own image, was slipping from his grasp. New American Poets enamored of multivalent identities might regard this scenario as favorable. The downside for O'Hara is that the concept of personal "space," identified as crucial in "Nocturne," seems sadly evanescent. Whatever safety zone he desires for himself shrinks as soon as it opens up, so virulent is the social buzz his presence creates. The crisis returns in "Southampton Variations," as O'Hara stands near the shore and notes

that his "boots / are bloody at the heel," expressing in violent terms †
adulation that trails him mercilessly to land's end. Thus trapped, he thi
it better to commune with turbulent ocean storms than to head inland.
"There's a warmth alive / to danger," he postulates, knowing full well that
the tempest brewing off Long Island's southern shore pales in comparison
to Manhattan's roiling atmosphere.

A few months prior to writing "Sleeping on the Wing," O'Hara began
a series of poems illustrative of his predicament and his desperate wish
to escape it. On September 30, 1955, the poet learned of James Dean's fatal
car crash in California. Within a week, he was recording his emotional responses to this tragedy, taking Dean's troubled life in Hollywood and transposing it to his own situation in the New York School. "For James Dean,"
the first of these poems to be written, sparked controversy when it appeared
in *Poetry* in March 1956. *The New Republic* lambasted O'Hara for suggesting that Hollywood was responsible for the actor's death. But O'Hara knew
whereof he spoke. Whether he was talking about Los Angeles or New York,
Dean's situation or his own, he realized that a star's proclivity "to be true to
a city" means little if that city is secretly prepared to ruin him.[11] Dean possessed "unnatural vigor," O'Hara realized, but he could only stand so much
"inane mothlike adoration" from "unctuous starers" and "navel-suckers."
O'Hara's empathy with Dean grows strongest in the following lines:

> Men cry from the grave while they still live
> and now I am this dead man's voice,
> stammering, a little in the earth.
> I take up
> the nourishment of his pale green eyes,
> out of which I shall prevent
> flowers from growing, your flowers. (*CP* 230)

Choppy phrasing leaves us unsure of whether O'Hara is emphasizing life-
in-death or death-in-life. Regardless, we notice that Dean, aided by O'Hara,
manages to "cry from the grave" in Marion, Indiana, and that the poet, in
giving voice to "this dead man," dies a little in the process, finding himself
already "a little in the earth." O'Hara bucks a major convention of pastoral
elegy here, cutting off at the root the traditional catalog of shrouded hills
and mourning flowers. In so doing, he refuses to nourish celebrity culture's false sentimentality, its perpetuation of a beauty myth that requires
the endless sacrifice of young, beautiful bodies. In the revisionist scenario
O'Hara lays out, Hollywood's crocodile tears will no longer reach the young

man lying six feet below the earth, pushing up daisies so others can marvel at their pastoral beauty.

In ensuing years, O'Hara wrote about other doomed heroes (Jackson Pollock and Billie Holiday) as though they were close friends, and about deceased friends (Bunny Lang, John Latouche) as though they were heroes, ruminating on their fate in order to ask a convoluted but crucial question: "is the /earth as full as life was full, of them?" (*CP* 258). In "A Step Away from Them" (composed after Pollock died) and "The Day Lady Died" (composed after Holiday died), O'Hara again considers his own mortality. Readers will note a shift from the Dean poems, for as he walks hurriedly through the streets of Manhattan, O'Hara responds enthusiastically to the vital rush of city living, its stimulation pushing him forward in the wake of personal loss. It is not the affecting lines about death that loom largest, but rather the details of O'Hara's daily routine, as he eats cheeseburgers and reads the *Post*. We recognize the harried pace of a swaggering New Yorker going about his business, refusing to "regret life" while he is still living it. At the time, O'Hara was entering his "I do this, I do that" phase, recording his daily rounds as though they possessed cultural value. As he walks toward Times Square—encountering in succession the "hum-colored / cabs," the construction workers who "feed their dirty / torsos sandwiches / and Coca-Cola, with yellow helmets /on," the "blonde chorus girl [who] clicks," the "Negro [who] stands in a doorway with / a toothpick," grinning and rubbing his chin, and the "lady in / foxes on such a day [who] puts her poodle / in a cab"—O'Hara offers readers a cross section of democracy in action. Tellingly, these faces in the crowd never crystallize into a Poundian epiphany. Instead, they remain indistinguishable from the cacophonous carnival of the street. Rambling through midtown Manhattan at "12:40 of / a Thursday," just one moment of convergence among many, O'Hara delights in the immediacy of urban life: "Everything suddenly honks" (257).

Yet O'Hara's message of egalitarianism, his notion that no single person or thing stands apart in the metropolis, exists only on the surface of his writing. He knows from personal experience that New Yorkers hewing to Whitman's democratic legacy still gravitate toward charismatic types who cobble together their city's multifarious strains. He realizes that his prominent social position in the New York School keeps him "a step away" from the people and places he mentions in his poems. He remains equally cognizant of his mortality, implying that he is but a step away from Pollock, Lang, and Latouche, fated to die within two weeks of each other in 1956. With one foot, the city poet ends his lunch break and walks jauntily back to work, pocketing his Reverdy and savoring his papaya juice, so full of life, it would seem, and so in love with his environment. But with the other, he takes a step toward the grave, summoning the starkest possible form of egalitarianism so as to escape the madness surrounding him. "If life were merely a habit I should commit suicide," the fledgling writer admitted in his Harvard journal (*Early Writing* 108). Notwithstanding persuasive arguments to the contrary penned by critics I admire, I am led to wonder whether, years later, O'Hara recalled his own advice.[12]

Even in death, O'Hara's presence was inescapable, haunting, and representative of his community's aesthetic momentum, now apparently lost. In his graveside speech, Rivers detailed in excruciating language the trauma his friend suffered after being struck by a dune buggy on Fire Island. The façade of this shepherd's indefatigable energy was shattered as mourners reflected upon the physical toll that had been exacted: "On paper he was improving," Rivers said. "In the crib he looked like a shaped wound, an innocent victim of someone else's war" ("Speech" 138). Ironically, as the story of O'Hara's death got replayed, and as painters like Alfred Leslie re-created the crash scene, the figure of a fatally injured poet came to carry as much kinetic force as did his adventures around Manhattan.[13]

Two artworks by Jasper Johns offer unusually sensitive commentary on O'Hara's predicament. Begun in 1961, five years before the dune buggy accident, these "memorial pieces" underscore the sadness in O'Hara's poetry and spookily foreshadow his untimely death. The first was an abstract painting called *In Memory of My Feelings—Frank O'Hara*. In the poem by that name, O'Hara bemoans the loss of his private life, his inability to feel anything without his community on hand to make sense of it. Aptly enough, Marjorie Perloff notices, Johns places in the margins of his abstract field the outline of a skull "buried in paint" ("Watchman" 208) along with two faintly visible words: "DEAD MAN." These ghostly images are a visual equivalent of the cryptic impulse that led O'Hara, shortly after Dean's crash, to view himself as "this dead man's voice" (*CP* 230). The difference, of course, is that in 1961 Johns's subject is not yet dead. Closer inspection reveals that the two canvases composing *In Memory of My Feelings* are connected by a hinge. Significantly, this hinge does not move, indicating that a writer perceived as a pivot point—one upon whom the collective desires of the New York art world so often hinged—was immobilized by overwhelming expectations. Taking its cue from its literary prototype, Johns's painting not only anticipates O'Hara's actual death but also mournfully reflects upon the poet's dead feelings, his shaky emotional state and his compromised tactile capacity, which together limited his ability to place himself in scenes of his own choosing.

Another notable artwork by Johns is a sculpture entitled *Memory Piece (Frank O'Hara)*, which was not completed until 1970, four years after O'Hara's death. As described by Roberta Bernstein, "a rubber cast of O'Hara's foot (made in 1961 when the study was done) is centered on the inside flap of a lid hinged to the top of a wooden box construction with drawers. When the lid is closed, the foot presses against a layer of sand, so that when it is opened we see both the cast and the footprint it has made in the sand. The foot brings the image of a figure into the work" (83). Arguably, this footprint signifies the trajectory O'Hara charted in the New York School. With the completed sculpture, which is actually a working contraption, viewers can continue to have O'Hara's peripatetic foot, or at least a mold of it, make its mark. Long after the poet's death, we can continue to see the paths he walks.

One of these paths is decidedly pastoral. In a letter sent to Johns in 1963, after the mold of his foot was cast, O'Hara enclosed a poem entitled "Dear Jap." In it he links his relationship with the painter to a physical sensation: "when I think of you in South Carolina I think of my foot in the sand." Although O'Hara could be alluding directly to *Memory Piece*, he might also be referring to their shared love of the seashore, which served as a retreat from the New York art scene. Whereas Johns walked the beaches of Edisto, South Carolina, O'Hara continued to visit friends in the Hamptons. More and more, though, he preferred prowling the beaches of Fire Island. It was in Water Island, hard by Fire Island's shore, that O'Hara composed his most moving elegies for James Dean. The first, dated October 9, 1955, was collected in "Four Little Elegies":

> *Written in the Sand at Water Island and Remembered*
> James Dean
> actor
> made in USA
> stopped short . . .
>
> Do we know what
> excellence is? it's
> all in this world
> not to be executed (*CP* 248)

The second stanza contains an inversion not often considered by critics. In "In Memory of My Feelings," composed in Manhattan nine months later,

O'Hara celebrates the "Grace to be born and live as variously as possible." In this little elegy, by contrast, he waxes darkly existential by the seaside, suggesting that, for our brightest stars, such grace might exist only beyond this life. He intimates that the excellent performances expected of talented performers are "not to be executed" in an increasingly restrictive world, and that the vitality of creative people is often endangered by admirers who threaten to kill it off (to invoke a different meaning of "executed"). Artists like Dean and O'Hara (or Pollock and Holiday) are unlikely to realize their potential if their personal lives remain so closely monitored and their social roles so rigidly pigeonholed.

Elsewhere in "Four Little Elegies," O'Hara speaks admiringly of an actor who "opposed the film colony's / hostility with sullenness, refused / to pose for movie-mag photographers or / talk about his dates, fought with directors, / insulted columnists, rode his sickle, / played his drum and raced his car" (*CP* 249). O'Hara had praised Pollock in much the same fashion, mentioning the painter's desire for unbridled freedom and his ability to break down aesthetic barriers. O'Hara implies that in Dean's case, as in Pollock's and perhaps his own, the "Made in USA" label loomed as an obstacle to personal fulfillment. What does artistic liberty mean if art world sycophants and cold war politicians are always on hand to co-opt it? More frequently than ordinary citizens, the best artists (those who "make it," but end up being "made") are "stopped short," entangled in America's star-maker machinery. O'Hara thus not only mourns the death of celebrities but also identifies with them, recognizing in their sad stories his own entrapment. Perhaps for this reason, he prefers to think of himself as "already dead" (250), or at least "out / of this world" (251). Here as elsewhere, the seaside setting is poignant. A week before he was killed, O'Hara reportedly asked Norman Bluhm's children to bury him in the sand "like I was dead" (Ferguson 137). Not for nothing did Rivers, in his funeral speech, make reference to the "soft, safe white sand of Long Island" that accepted O'Hara's body ("Speech" 138). Diane di Prima responded similarly in an elegiac poem for O'Hara: "I consign you to sand," she wrote. "I see you disperse on the North American coast" ("For Frank" 157).

In "Thinking of James Dean," the second elegy he composed in Water Island, O'Hara describes in greater detail the way the seashore affected his meditations on death. Gooch refers to "Thinking of James Dean" as "method poetry," alluding to the style of acting Dean practiced. Indeed, we might view "Thinking of James Dean" as we view Button's painting of O'Hara diving into a wave. Taking a "first plunge in dolorous surf / and the brilliant sunlight declaring all the qualities of the world" (*CP* 230), O'Hara's immersion in the turbulent Atlantic aligns with his reputation for making courageous leaps into the unknown. Then again, when we take into account his emotional response to Dean's death and the pressure the New York art world was exerting on him, O'Hara's dive into the waves contains a decidedly melancholy undertow. The ocean he encounters off Long Island is "dolorous," its sadness offering him a delicious invitation to death, much as it had Whitman a century before in "Out of the Cradle Endlessly Rocking." Likening himself to "an ant, dragging its sorrows up and down the sand to find / a hiding place never," O'Hara knows that he must take an extra few steps into ocean waters if he is to find the anonymity and resurrection he privately desires. He aims "To reach the depths and rise, only in the sea; / the abysses of life, incessantly plunging not to rise to a face / of heat and joy again; habits of total immersion and the stance // victorious in death" (230).

Significantly, O'Hara's most vivid identification with Dean comes "after hours of lying in nature, to nature, / and simulated death in the crushing waves" (*CP* 230), imagining what it would have been like to have died at twenty-four. Obviously, fate held different cards. As his hosts rise from last night's party, O'Hara has a few moments to enjoy "the cold last swim / before the city flatters meanings of my life I cannot find, // squeezing me like an orange for some nebulous vitality" (231). Ending his mournful meditation on Dean, O'Hara offers a valediction, "A leaving word in the sand, odor of tides: his name" (231). In a few hours the tides will reclaim the site of writing and wash away Dean's name. Given his high-stakes role as urban signifier, I wonder whether O'Hara wished the same for himself, asking the powerful ocean water to pull him away from the city's firm clutches.

O'Hara's beachside meditations reach their apotheosis in "A True Account of Talking to the Sun at Fire Island," a poem Koch retrieved from his friend's apartment immediately after his death and read at his memorial service. Written in 1958, "True Account" begins as a humorous take on literary inspiration. "When I woke up Mayakovsky he was / a lot more prompt" (*CP* 306), the chastising sun tells O'Hara, an incorrigible writer it has nonetheless decided to bless with godlike imaginative powers. Despite its frivolity, the poem is a wrenching complaint about finding one's way in the New York hothouse. From its panoptic position in the sky, the sun recognizes the troubled path O'Hara is traveling. "Wherever you were / I knew it and saw you moving," the simpatico sun tells the poet. "And now that you / are making your own days, so to speak, / even if no one reads you but me / you won't be depressed" (307). Accepting its role as the ultimate source of natural knowledge, the sun tells the poet that they are able to communicate so well because of where they find themselves:

> It's
> easier for me to speak to you out
> here. I don't have to slide down
> between buildings to get your ear.
> I know you love Manhattan, but
> you ought to look up more often.
> And
> always embrace things, people earth
> sky stars, as I do, freely and with
> the appropriate sense of space. That
> is your inclination, known in the heavens
> and you should follow it to hell, if
> necessary, which I doubt. (307)

As happens in Romantic crisis poems, O'Hara sees his dream-vision fade as the morning sun rises. The sun explains that "they're calling me" and tells O'Hara that "They're calling you too," hinting at the poet's impending death, his ascension as literary legend, or maybe both. Before departing, the sun says it will leave a poem as a farewell gift. If "True Account" is that gift, it is one any urban beachcomber would be delighted to have.

In "Dear Jap," the epistolary poem he sent to Johns, O'Hara refers more obliquely to his favorite seaside location, the one that offered him, in the language of "True Account," an "appropriate sense of space." He tells Johns, "I want someday / to have a fire-escape // in 1951 I became crazy for fire-escapes / as you remember" (*CP* 471). Although the term appears elsewhere in O'Hara's oeuvre, contextual circumstances I have been describing imply that the "fire-escape" mentioned here is Fire Island, a pastoral site where the city poet felt he might elude the attention he had attracted in New York since his arrival in 1951.[14] If a "fire-escape" had been at the ready, O'Hara could have made his own marks in the sand, free from social significance, free from the public's appropriation of his tactile and emotional "feelings." Sadly, I suspect his escapist fantasy was never fulfilled. We know that he returned to his hectic life in Manhattan after each brief retreat to the beach, and that his final marks in the sand were at the scene of a fatal accident, which became in turn another signification in the O'Hara myth.

In a telling line appearing in "Dear Jap," O'Hara laments that "accidental simplicity has become a horrible law" (*CP* 471), an ironic indication that the vertiginous energies he was thought to embody had become over time a rigid set of expectations over which he had no control. Perhaps he had finally decided to let his guard down. Previously, O'Hara had warned sculptor David Smith, another victim of a car accident, that "the slightest loss of attention leads to death" (Gooch 468). This may be true, but O'Hara might have also felt that remaining so attentive to the proceedings of the New York art world was killing him little by little, day by day. At least one friend appeared to notice. Upon returning to New York from Paris in 1965, Ashbery recalls seeing a changed man. "There was a kind of melancholy I didn't remember from before, a kind of tiredness. . . . I remember being surprised to see him feeling so down, physically and mentally" (Gooch 440). Little wonder. As everybody's semiotic genius, O'Hara occupied an increasingly impossible position. Almost inevitably, this shepherd of the New York School, this "Pan piping on city streets" (Leibowitz), became his community's sacrificial lamb.

AS WITH THE bag of crisps question put to Colin McCabe in *Sammy and Rosie*, we may laugh at the relation of a poet's body to a linguistic register. I hope to have suggested, however, a few instances in which a popular poet's physical presence codes a type of semiotic movement, and by so doing embodies the desires of avant-garde artists gathering in the urban *semeion*. Even though the desires of the New York School are polyvalent, we should recognize that they convene at, and settle upon, some limit, and that this convergence has a profound effect on the poet whose bodily movement is believed to trace that limit's contours. As an experimental writer enamored of linguistic play, O'Hara might have been "concerned with humorously debunking the idea of a centered and authentic self," as Hazel Smith argues (131). It might also be true, as Michael Clune suggests, that "the self-centered world of O'Hara's "I-do-this," "I-do-that" poems requires a self without a center" (184). But we should also realize that O'Hara was the center of attention in the New York School. He tried valiantly, but in vain, to outrace signification's reach, trapped as he was by "wanting to be everything to everybody everywhere" (*CP* 331).

Marjorie Perloff likes to think O'Hara "transcended" the New York School (*Frank* 196; *Poetic* 253), but I am not so sure. "Bad artists throughout history have always tried to make their art like life," a sorrowful Morton Feldman mused shortly after O'Hara's passing. "Only the artist who is close to his own life gives us an art that is like death" (14). O'Hara made that kind of art, identifying with doomed heroes like Dean and Pollock and admitting outright that "I historically belong to the enormous bliss of American death" (*CP* 326). Those in a position to save him were either late in getting the message or ineffectual in getting through to him. Only after he was dead would friends like Edwin Denby and John Button recognize the social pressures O'Hara faced, both of them sadly admitting that "a center" had gone out of their lives (Waldman, "Paraphrase" 32; Button 43).

Amiri Baraka, who says that "the New York School was chiefly, to me, O'Hara," believes he knows how his friend would have reacted to the assigned title of literary leader: "Listen, my dear, you can take that leadership business and shove it" (Epstein 198). But in a postmodern arts milieu celebrating abstraction, placelessness, and instability, O'Hara's refusal of leadership is precisely what made him its de facto leader. As Barthes liked to point out, semiotic systems, so prone to reversals, always have the last laugh, parceling out joy and sadness, freedom and entrapment, vitality and mortality, in strange and ever-changing combinations. Knowing this, I find it bitterly ironic, but altogether telling, that "Grace / to be born and live as variously as possible," the lines that in 1956 heralded Frank O'Hara's vital literary experiment, his unparalleled openness and freedom, ended up serving as his epitaph.

2 | LOCUS SODUS
Tracking Time and Place
in John Ashbery's Landscapes

THE COMPLEX INTERCHANGE between the country and the city looms large in the work of John Ashbery, a charter member of the New York School who has become one of America's most revered poets, albeit one of its most controversial. For decades, critics have commented on Ashbery's "difficulty," assigning the "most important living poet" label with a knowing wink, much as middlebrow art critics in the 1950s simultaneously extolled and called into question the prominence of Jackson Pollock.[1] Perhaps the most backhanded compliment Ashbery ever received was the one paid him by the *Saturday Review*, which labeled him the "Doris Day of Modernism" (Lehman 117). Ashbery is not only famous, it turns out, but famously hard to classify. Renowned for his eclecticism, he seems equally comfortable discussing painters from Europe (Parmigianino, De Chirico) and cartoon characters from America (Popeye, Daffy Duck). His poem titles range from the philosophical ("The New Realism") to the mundane ("The Wrong Kind of Insurance") to the parodic ("Farm Implements and Rutabagas in a Landscape"). Challenging customary divisions—self/other, past/present, modern/romantic, surreal/real, urban/pastoral—is his stock and trade.

The power of human memory serves Ashbery well in this regard, though not in any traditional way. Using his rural childhood as a benchmark, this city-based poet has waxed rhapsodic on temporality's unpredictable effect on conceptualizations of place and identity, his emphasis on spontaneity complicating all journeys into the past. The convoluted phrases and teasingly ironic images filling his poems help him evade the facile escapism prompting pastoral writers since Virgil to dream of a sentimental return to a Golden Age.[2] "Much of my poetry comes out of memories of childhood, the feeling of some lost world that can't be recovered," Ashbery admits. "At the same time, I think the present daily world which I happen to be in is what's writing the poem, what's dealing with these experiences of loss" (Poulin 253). Like Joseph Cornell, James McCorkle asserts, Ashbery strives to "compel both nostalgia and immediacy" in his work while heralding the "possibilities of a recalled geography" (102, 112). When Ashbery is successful, memory trumps reality, town and country merge, and a new pastoral setting floats into view. Or as he reports in "A Wave," "What is restored / Becomes stronger than the loss as it is remembered; / Is a new, separate life of its own" (*CP* 796).

Ashbery was raised on a fruit farm in Sodus, New York, near Lake Ontario. In the region he dubbed the "Holy Land / of western New York State" (*CP* 430), the precocious child harvested orchard crops and performed other chores, albeit very grudgingly. "I wasn't cut out to be a farm boy and Huck Finn type," Ashbery recalls (Lehman 122). Snowbound winters brought boredom. "I felt isolated and lonely," he told Marit MacArthur (28). The abuse he suffered at the hand of Chester Ashbery, his short-tempered father, added to his misery (Ford 21). Seemingly cut off from the world, the farm was in many ways a *locus solus*, a term that Ashbery, analyzing a Raymond Roussel novel by that name, translates alternately as "lonely place" and "only place" (*Other Traditions* 62). In 1959, when Ashbery joined a literary magazine named *Locus Solus*, his New York School coeditors, acting on a tip from Janice Koch, nicknamed the magazine "Locus Sodus" (Lehman 120; Schuyler, *Just* 124). The original assignation was jocular, but it has assumed a measure of poignancy over the years. As an adolescent, Ashbery planned his escape from lonely Sodus, but not before taking measure of upstate New York's stark beauty, storing its rural images away for future use. As he embarked on his writing career, initially at Deerfield Academy and Harvard, subsequently in New York and Paris, he would return quite frequently to the family farm, in mind if not in body.

Like O'Hara, Ashbery remembers that as a boy he "always wanted to live in a metropolis" (Ford 30). He even claims to have felt "nostalgia for the city" after his maternal grandfather, with whom he spent his preschool years, moved from metropolitan Rochester to Pultneyville, on the outskirts of Sodus (Herd, "John Ashbery" 32). Yet his attitude toward city life as an adult has been more ambivalent. When he moved to New York City in 1949, Ashbery remembers feeling intimidated by its size (MacArthur 162). Since then, he has found most urban centers to be blandly interchangeable, telling

David Herd that he does not regard New York as an "occasion" for his poetry "in the Frank O'Hara sense," but simply as a "benignly neutral space to write in" ("John Ashbery" 37). At other times, he has referred to "the crazy geometry of New York" (*Selected Prose* 290), calling it "an anti-place, an abstract climate," adding that he "would much rather be living in San Francisco" (114). Questioning the New York School label, he claims that the city is "merely a convenient place to live and meet people, rather than a specific place whose local color influences the literature produced there" (133).

According to Ashbery, "Living in New York doesn't seem to be taking a stand or making a statement as it would if one worked in San Francisco or Black Mountain, North Carolina, and other places where one is always conscious of living in the right place, which is something very few people have the luxury to do" (Murphy 22). Instead, New York exists primarily as "a logarithm / Of other cities" (*CP* 480). The advantage of migrating to New York, he recalls, was that "once one was there one didn't have to think about where one was" (Lehman 27). Paris, his home from 1955 to 1965, receives similar treatment. "After you've lived in Paris for awhile, you don't want to live anywhere, including Paris," Ashbery quips (*Selected Prose* 249). The effect the intellectually restless poet conveys in such statements is of "going around cities / To get to other places" (*CP* 126). The family farm, by contrast, appears to have cast an indelible impression. During the heyday of the New York School, Ashbery referred repeatedly, if vaguely, to an agrarian sensibility he managed to harvest during a less-than-idyllic childhood.

MY AIM in this chapter is to hail the country boy who calls out from Ashbery's lyric landscapes, from *Some Trees* (1956) to *Flow Chart* (1991). Tracking this figure is not easy, for Ashbery has always been a reticent man. "My own autobiography has never interested me very much," he confessed in 1977. "Whenever I try to think about it, I seem to draw a complete blank" (Gangel 10). "I have such an imprecise impression of what kind of person I am," he noted elsewhere, adding, "I suppose [my poems] come from a part of me that I am not in touch with very much except when I am actually writing" (Stitt, "Art" 49). Although he disdains "most poetry that's called Confessional," Ashbery admits that "I've probably written some confessional poetry myself only nobody recognizes it as such" (Murphy 23). Some of the confusion is attributable to the demotic language he uses. "What I am trying to get at is a general, all-purpose experience—like those stretch socks that fit all sizes," he says. "Something which a reader could dip into without knowing anything about me, my history, or sex life, or whatever" (Poulin 251). Lacking direct commentary from Ashbery, critics are left to sort through the poet's influences—including, it turns out, his sex life—in an attempt to trace the contours of his identity, which do not always line up so neatly in his convoluted syntax. Moreover, Ashbery's homoerotic explorations of pastoral manage to avoid both the sincere longings of Whitman and the campy irony of O'Hara. As Lynn Keller remarks, even if his "love affairs and friendships can frequently be glimpsed in his poetry . . . the glimpses are brief, the situations immediately generalized into larger abstractions" (*Re-Making* 40).[3]

Ashbery is "a poet of perceptions rather than of events and actual objects," Peter Stitt observes, "and just as our attention passes quickly from impression to impression, often without any sort of completion, coherence, or connection, so do his poems" (*Uncertainty* 32).[4] In this manner he resembles Ralph Waldo Emerson, who preferred the thinking process over intellectual end products, the abstract over the concrete. "I know that the world I converse with in the city and in the farms is not the world I *think*," Emerson admitted in "Experience," staying neutral in the battle between town and country while accessing a shareable imaginative realm (347). Emerson "demonstrates that deliberately shifting points of view can open new vistas [not only for] himself [but also for] his audience," editor Donald McQuade writes, so that while "readers are finally not given enough time to locate either Emerson or themselves in any of the viewpoints offered," they are at least able to sense the opportunity bestowed upon them to create an American identity (xxxi, xxxii). Reading an elliptically representative writer like Emerson or Ashbery can be instructive, provided we enter the magical zone where perception trumps reality. As Helen Vendler remarks, in a review Ashbery acknowledges as one of his favorites, "By entering into some bizarrely tuned pitch inside myself I can find myself on Ashbery's wavelength, where everything at the symbolic level makes sense. The irritating (and seductive) thing about this tuning in is that it can't be willed; I can't make it happen when I am tired or impatient. But when the frequencies meet, the effect on me is Ashbery's alone, and it is a form of trance" (*Soul* 130).[5]

Mary Kinzie explains that Ashbery's predilection for splitting the difference between two aesthetic modes, the surreal and the meditative, results in a frame of "suspended reference" (271, 281), which in turn gives rise to an ambiguous topography. Wandering the entrancing mindscapes mapped out by the poet, readers experience for themselves new conceptualizations of time. These "decentered landscapes" offer "new possibilities for reverie in temporal extension instead of spatial depth," Bonnie Costello argues. They are "uncharted 'spaces' in which temporality is dramatized rather than suppressed." Operating on a register that is serial rather than sequential, Ashbery participates in a process of cognitive mapping that is radically unstable "since there is no extra-textual system," but also strangely calming since he charts "pellucid moments" when all temporal and spatial variation collapses into an "open jar of space" (174, 175, 184–86, 190). Accordingly, an episode that took place in Sodus in the 1940s may recur decades later in Manhattan. But what was it that motivated Ashbery, haunted by certain aspects of his childhood and immersed in a literary milieu enamored of immediacy, to seek communion with his rural past?

The Unbearable Lightness of Being, a novel by Milan Kundera, seems an unlikely source, but it offers one clue. Following Nietzsche, Kundera distinguishes between a world shaped by eternal return and a world where access to the past is virtually nonexistent. To dwell in the first of these scenarios, he explains, is "to think that everything recurs as we once experienced it, and that the recurrence itself recurs ad infinitum." This is not to say that we respond to recurring events the same way every time. Indeed, for Kundera, "the idea of eternal return implies a perspective from which things appear other than as we know them: they appear without the mitigating circumstance of their transitory nature." "Nailed to eternity," a person who constantly travels back in time suffers "the heaviest of burdens," even as he experiences "life's most intense fulfillment." In the second scenario, by contrast, one's identity and personal attachments are ephemeral in nature. In the ever-fleeting present, "everything is pardoned in advance and therefore everything cynically permitted."[6] By steering clear of the past and its attendant burdens, a person enmeshed in the second scenario enjoys the spontaneous liberties of immediacy but struggles to attain a basic grasp of reality, referred to organically in our lexicon as "grounding." As Kundera puts it, "The absolute absence of a burden causes man to be lighter than air, to soar into the heights, take leave of the earth and his earthly being, and become only half real, his movements as free as they are insignificant" (3–5).

Ashbery's verse maneuvers freely between the opposing scenarios Kundera describes. On the surface, his poetry is rather weightless and au courant, attuned to the transitory nature of "logarithmic" New York City. Yet closer inspection indicates that it remains anchored in rural landscapes where childhood episodes are serially repeated. In Ashbery's most affecting work, time circles back upon itself, providing a pastoral cure for the restlessness he feels in urban environments. In the preface to *Some Trees* (1956), Ashbery's first volume, W. H. Auden praised the inner world the poet invoked in childhood and in daydreams, where time tends to be cyclical and ritualistic (Mendelson 408). Auden was only half right. If it were possible to encounter lost experiences "without the mitigating circumstances of their transitory nature," as Kundera postulates, Ashbery could linger endlessly in the past, there to work through the troublesome aspects of his upbringing. Yet Ashbery knows he cannot turn back the clock at will, subject as he is to the pressing demands of city living. Fortunately, he is that unique pastoral writer who would rather foreground this tension than succumb to facile nostalgia.

A devotee of Romanticism who disavows the solipsism holding sway in that tradition, Ashbery crafts experimental verse that is personal and retrospective, but for the most part egoless and evanescent.[7] "I have a feeling that everything is slipping away from me as I'm trying to talk about it," he told one interviewer (Poulin 245). In his best poems, he told another, "time thinks about me" (Koethe 183). Addressing autobiographical moments in his work, Ashbery has said: "I'm not aware of these things until after I've written them. I don't sit down and think, now I'm going to write about 'I' and really mean me. It's only, well, sometimes a long time afterwards that I sense that I was talking of myself rather than through a persona" (Herd, "John Ashbery" 35). He does not deny that formative experiences in Sodus loom large in his memory. He merely wants to suggest that the past, though it is always with us, makes house calls at odd hours, and that for writers attuned to strange frequencies, the recurrence of childhood events can seem just as weightless, just as melancholy and foreign, as the fugitive moments Kundera describes. To appreciate Ashbery's pastoral return to Sodus, we need to move beyond his poetry's abstraction, sorting through the "aesthetic remoteness blossoming profusely / but vaguely around what *does* stand out here and there" (*Can* 15).

"THE PICTURE of Little J. A. in a Prospect of Flowers," a typically abstruse poem from *Some Trees,* announces Ashbery's return to native landscape. In this update of Andrew Marvell's "The Picture of Little T. C. in a Prospect of Flowers," Little J. A. appears in a family snapshot, signaling a moment of innocence, befuddlement, and premonition. As the boy's head peeps out, it merges with other organic shapes in his environment, only to grow more conspicuous as time goes by:

> . . . I cannot escape the picture
> Of my small self in that bank of flowers:
> My head among the blazing phlox
> Seemed a pale and gigantic fungus.
> I had a hard stare, accepting

Everything, taking nothing,
As though the rolled-up future might stink
As loud as stood the sick moment
The shutter clicked. . . .

Like Francesco Parmigianino, the sixteenth-century artist who became the subject of Ashbery's most famous poem, "Self-Portrait in a Convex Mirror," Little J. A. "cannot escape the picture" that seals his identity, nor can the man he has grown into successfully escape the awkward image he stores in his brain.[8] But as the poem proceeds, Ashbery realizes the slipperiness of language gives him an out he did not have as a boy:

 . . . as the loveliest feelings

Must soon find words, and these, yes,
Displace them, so I am not wrong
In calling this comic version of myself
The true one. For change is horror,
Virtue is really stubbornness

And only in the light of lost words
Can we imagine our rewards. (*CP* 14)

At an early juncture, Ashbery discovers that his misrepresentative poetics—so paradoxically full of "lost words," or what he referred to in "The Skaters" as "this leaving-out business" (*CP* 152)—must "displace" his "loveliest feelings" about adolescence (homophonically understood as a *lost world*) if he hopes to resolve his complicated relationship with his past. Even when he is not leaving things out, Ashbery rewords episodes from his personal history to reap poetic "rewards." At first glance, the land around Sodus serves for him the way a California meadow did for Robert Duncan: as "a place of first permission, / everlasting omen of what is" (37). But whereas Duncan described a formative sexual encounter in this meadow, and Frank O'Hara alluded to boyhood liaisons he enjoyed in rural Massachusetts, Ashbery has refrained from commenting explicitly on his sexual experiences, preferring to register episodes from his rural past in broadly representative language. In "The Picture of Little J. A.," he shifts from a "comic version" of himself to a more general "we," making his snapshot ours. As the title of a later volume implies, Ashbery offers readers an invitation to put "your name here."[9]

Although Ashbery declines to identify him by name, Little J. A. lurks in the margins of other early works, and over time he comes to serve as the poet's alter ego.[10] His youthful escapades and insecurities get reevaluated years later, sentimentally at times, more cynically at others. "The Young Son," for instance, features a boy whose "absolute smile," transformed by "supreme good fortune" into a Munch-like "celestial scream," awakens in Ashbery "denials, thoughts of putrid reversals as he traced the green paths to and fro" (CP 20). Presumably, these green paths connect town and country, as the Bowery once did in New York City or as Cottage Grove Avenue, featured in "Pyrography" (495), does in metropolitan Chicago. Yet the predominant message of "The Young Son" is that retrospective flights of fancy back to the countryside, rendered here as "putrid reversals," are best avoided by avant-garde writers seeking immediacy. "Much that is beautiful must be discarded / So that we may resemble a taller / Impression of ourselves," Ashbery reminds himself in "Illustration" (25). "Our youth is dead," he declares in "Our Youth," a poem from *The Tennis Court Oath* (1962). "You will never have that young boy" (71). New York City trumps Sodus in these instances. Elsewhere, the erstwhile country boy validates his decision to repair to the "vast gloom of cities," since "only there you learn / How the ideas were only good because they had to die" (190).

Ashbery struggled mightily to keep up his urbane façade, but Sodus memories kept rushing forward to confront him. *The Tennis Court Oath*, written in Paris, abounds with agrarian images (hay, dandelions, flowers, honey, pastures), many of which contain an erotic charge. Items from Whitman's pastoral catalog (pillars of grass, roots fit for swallowing, bather's trees) offer organic references to oral sex and skinny-dipping. Characteristically, Ashbery stops short of saying that these activities actually took place on the farm. He does, however, refer to himself by his New York School nickname ("Ashes") while recounting these events, just as he takes the opportunity elsewhere in *The Tennis Court Oath* to recast the flowery image of "Little J. A." in compromising positions. The furtive nature of the encounters Ashbery includes in this volume, many of which appear to take place in barns or haylofts, is matched on the linguistic level by the opacity of his wording, which prevents readers from ever fully envisioning sexual scenarios. As Ashbery explains, "the passions are divided into tiniest units / And of these many are lost . . . / In a dumb harvest / Passions are locked away, and states of creation are used instead, that is to say synonyms are used" (CP 85).[11]

Somewhere on the road back to Sodus, Ashbery realized that an elliptical return to native soil, frustrating as it was for conventional understanding, paid its own dividends, and that avant-garde poetry facilitated this venture. A turning point arrives in "Clepsydra," a long poem from *Rivers and Mountains* (1966) inspired by water clocks used to time lawyers' arguments in court (Shoptaw 84). While meditating on his rural upbringing, Ashbery adjudicates the various temporal strategies warranting his attention:

> The past is yours, to keep invisible if you wish
> But also to make absurd elaborations with
> And in this way prolong your dance of non-discovery
> In brittle, useless architecture that is nevertheless
> The map of your desires, irreproachable, beyond
> Madness and the toe of approaching night, if only
> You desire to arrange it this way . . . (*CP* 144)

Proceeding with his "dance of non-discovery," Ashbery learns that cosmopolitan sophistication, identified repeatedly in "Clepsydra" with fanciful architecture, cannot contain his "Former existence," which by virtue of a well-positioned line break remains startlingly "incomplete" and, despite its onrushing proximity, peculiarly elusive:

> It is because everything is relative
> That we shall never see in that sphere of pure wisdom and
> Entertainment much more than groping shadows of an incomplete
> Former existence so close it burns like the mouth that
> Closes down over all your effort like the moment
> Of death, but stays, raging and burning the design of
> Its intentions into the house of your brain . . .

Feeling disconnected after having "Grown up, or moved away," the ruminative city poet decides to recount his rural episodes in vague, evasive language, the better to escape present feelings of entrapment:

> . . . Perhaps you are being kept here
> Only so that somewhere else the peculiar light of someone's
> Purpose can blaze unexpectedly in the acute
> Angles of the rooms. It is not a question, then,
> Of having not lived in vain. What is meant is that this distant
> Image of you, the way you really are, is the test
> Of how you see yourself, and regardless of whether or not
> You hesitate, it may be assumed that you have won, that this

Wooden and external representation
Returns the full echo of what you meant
With nothing left over, from that circumstance now alight
With ex-possibilities become present fact, and you
Must wear them like clothing, moving in the shadow of
Your single and twin existence, waking in intact
Appreciation of it . . . (146)

In this passage we see how Ashbery fashions personal and artistic identities through "absurd elaborations." Again, his imagination is depicted as a building (the "architecture" and "house" of earlier passages replaced by "rooms" and "wooden and external representation"). Within its cerebral corridors there dwell several mysterious phenomena: "the peculiar light of someone's / Purpose," "this distant / Image of you," "the full echo of what you meant," "ex-possibilities become present fact," and most tellingly, "the shadow of / Your single and twin existence." Each represents what Ashbery refers to earlier in the poem as his "incomplete / Former existence," a childhood identity that may be fractured but is still recoverable, given the right conditions. As he puts it in "These Lacustrine Cities," the opening poem from *Rivers and Mountains*, "The past is already here, and you are nursing some private project" (125). Typically, Ashbery's phrasing remains ambiguous, "you" referring to the poet's younger self but also to any reader seeking personal redress with the past. As suggested in "Clepsydra," the task is for all of us to awaken in ourselves an "intact / Appreciation" of our multiple and circumstantial selves.[12]

RETURNING TO AMERICA in 1965 after a decade in Paris, Ashbery analyzed his rural upbringing with renewed vigor. *The Double Dream of Spring* (1970) depicts a bittersweet homecoming. Ashbery laments that his father has just died, the family farm has been sold, and his childhood stomping grounds have undergone transformation. In this excerpt from "Some Words," a translation of an Arthur Cravan poem, Ashbery begins hopefully but concludes anxiously, expressing a prodigal son's fear of abandonment:

When weary henceforth of wishing to gaze
At the sinuous path of your strung-out days
You return to the place where your stables used to tower
You will find nothing left but some fetid manure
Your steeds beneath other horseman will have fled
To autumn's far country, all rusted and red. (*CP* 218)

The erotic imagery of steeds under the reins of multiple horsemen remains available for critics who want to make use of it, though Imbriglio and Vincent steer clear of this poem in their analyses of Ashbery's queer poetics and Shoptaw merely mocks its clunky rhythm. More cogent to my discussion of urban pastoral is the poet's emphasis on "strung-out days," the sinuous trajectory that has taken him from the country to the city. Unfortunately for him, the landscape he has forsaken has grown increasingly unrecognizable. Towering stables have turned to shit. Little else of what the poet remembers remains; time has evidently laid waste to it. "Some Words" is a translation, so we cannot assume it alludes directly to Ashbery's recent trip home. Situated among his other retrospective landscape poems, though, it takes on a quasi-autobiographical character.

A queer perspective becomes useful when we analyze "Fragment," a poem Ashbery began writing in December 1964, when he returned to Sodus to attend his father's funeral. Ashbery has called "Fragment" a "love poem." Shoptaw goes further, insisting that the poem describes "a covert adolescent affair, which the consequent scandal marks as homosexual" (117).[13] Highlighting the erotic indeterminacy he finds in such images as "the volcanic entrance to an antechamber" and the same-sex mutuality embedded in the phrase "either of us" (*CP* 233), Shoptaw seizes upon "necessarily misrepresentative particulars" chosen by a gay poet "suspicious of the myth of a homosexual origin." The overarching tone in "Fragment," Shoptaw argues, is one of incrimination, suppression, and unforthcoming confession. The result is a poem that has "closed more doors than it opened" (117, 124). The scandalous affair hinted at in "Fragment" remains hidden, owing to the lingering effects of rural isolation Ashbery encountered on his return trip to Sodus, and yet an organic subtext pops up through this poem's fractured phrasing, solidifying the poet's allegiances to native landscape. Some of the imagery harks back to "The Picture of Little J. A." In an early section, Ashbery says that "the great flower of what we have been twists / On its stem of earth, for not being / What we are to become, fated to live in / Intimidated solitude and isolation" (*CP* 231). Apparently, Sodus farmland never allowed Ashbery's sexuality to flourish, hampered as he was by the homophobic attitudes of its citizenry. Viewed retrospectively through the prism of avant-garde language, however, sexual secrets are transformed unexpectedly into moments of clarity, episodes the grown-up flower child can memorialize repeatedly in convoluted, nature-based imagery:

. . . Yet the spores of the
Difference as it's imagined flower

In complicated chains for the eyebrow, and pre-delineate
Phantom satisfaction as it would happen. This time
You get over the threshold of so much unmeaning, so much
Being, prepared for its event, the active memorial. (232)

Long ago, Ashbery postulates, the "great flower of what we have been" withered on the vine as it confronted intimidation and isolation, the unhappy
fate of closeted individuals. Years later, though, the experimental writing
of the New York School enables this flower's "spores of difference" to blossom forth in "complicated chains," furrowing the brows of those seeking
conventional understanding. Amid this daisy chain of "so much unmeaning," the poet seems to say, we can safely cultivate our gardens, whatever
our sexual proclivities, and "this time" allow multiple alternate selves—the
flower of "what we are to become"—to grow unabated. Utilizing oddly organic imagery, Ashbery does not offer a confession of past actions so much
as he reconsiders the landscapes framing those actions, cultivating them in
an urban location far from native soil. The key to this linguistic gamesman-
ship, he implies in another passage reminiscent of "Little J. A.," is "to isolate
the kernel of / Our imbalance and at the same time back up carefully; / Its
tulip head whole, an imagined good" (232). Given proper nourishment,
seeds sown secretly in Sodus belatedly give rise to a beautiful bouquet.

"Soonest Mended," a poem that Ashbery says "is about my youth and
maturing but also about anybody else's" (Murphy 25), covers similar terrain. A fragmentary paean to the cliché "least said, soonest mended"
(an unwitting forerunner of "don't ask, don't tell"?), it reveals, in Harold
Bloom's estimation, an "awakening to the haphazardness and danger of
one's marginal situation in early middle age" ("Charity" 61). Yet for me this
poem alludes more directly to the challenge of growing up "different" in
rural America. "Barely tolerated, living on the margin / In our technologi-
cal society," the pastoral man-child in "Soonest Mended" speaks for many
such people, lamenting the fact that "we were always having to be rescued
/ On the brink of destruction" (CP 184). Later in the poem, in an intimate
address intended for his younger and more vulnerable self, Ashbery shifts
pronouns, admitting that "though we knew the course *was* hazards and
nothing else / It was still a shock when, almost a quarter of a century later /
The clarity of the rules dawned upon you for the first time" (185). Assuming
this revelation took place around 1969, when "Soonest Mended" was written, the hazardous events to which Ashbery alludes occurred in the early
1940s, as he left Sodus for Deerfield and Harvard. Only after the dangers of
growing up gay on the farm were safely behind him, presumably, could the

poet avail himself of adulthood's great gift, the healing compensations of time, which for him has meant:

> learning to accept
> The charity of the hard moments as they are doled out,
> For this is action, this not being sure, this careless
> Preparing, sowing the seeds crooked in the furrow,
> Making ready to forget, and always coming back
> To the mooring of starting out, that day so long ago. (186)

Following Shoptaw's "homotextual" strategies, I am tempted to interpret "sowing seeds crooked in the furrow" as a randy sexual euphemism, one O'Hara might have employed while recounting his Grafton childhood. The convoluted syntax and quirky word choice in ensuing lines are more typical of Ashbery's style, however, and do not easily accommodate this critical intervention. Calling this a "one-size-fits-all confessional poem" (Murphy 25), Ashbery, like Emerson, aims to be broadly representative, suggesting that, for most of us, the carelessness of youth presages willful forgetting during adulthood. For those of us possessing childlike imaginations, however, this forced erasure of the past proves neither palatable nor successful, tethered as we are to the "mooring of starting out." As the "fence-sitting" farm boy says earlier in this poem, "time is an emulsion, and probably thinking not to grow up / Is the brightest kind of maturity for us" (*CP* 186). A queer subtext finally emerges when Ashbery asserts that certain details of "that day so long ago," alluded to elsewhere by Shoptaw as the moment the poet's homosexual love letters were discovered, are in fact remembered and serially repeated, albeit in the vaguest, most secretive, and most noncommittal way possible, so as to escape detection.[14]

In "The Chateau Hardware," another poem from *The Double Dream of Spring*, Ashbery offers additional reasons for keeping secrets in farm country:

> It was always November there. The farms
> Were a kind of precinct; a certain control
> Had been exercised. The little birds
> Used to collect along the fence.
> It was the great "as though," the how the day went,
> The excursions of the police
> As I pursued my bodily functions, wanting
> Neither fire nor water,

Vibrating to the distant pinch
And turning out the way I am, turning out to greet you. (*CP* 226)

If the farmland around Sodus was in fact "a kind of precinct," a place where sexual activity and other "bodily functions" were regularly policed, we should not blame Little J. A. for "vibrating to the distant pinch" of big cities, where he was free to pursue pleasure as he wished, to "turn out" (and come out) the way he did. Only after he was safely situated in cosmopolitan havens would his memories of farm life become suffused with a pastoral haze, an atmospheric opacity that, like a "decoy" (to cite another poem from this era), piques the desires of inquisitive readers but ends up frustrating anyone holding up for inspection specific details of the author's life.[15]

IN *THREE POEMS* (1972), Ashbery turns to the prose poem, a genre that allows him to be more effusive, though just as indirect, in his meditations on memory, place, and selfhood. In "The New Spirit," Ashbery admits to intermittent erasures of personal history, the "leaving-out business" he addressed in "The Skaters." "I thought that if I could put it all down, that would be one way. And next the thought came to me that to leave all out would be another, and truer, way." Later, he adds a proviso, explaining that what emerges in this leaving-out business is "Not the truth, perhaps, but—yourself" (*CP* 247). For Ashbery, traveling the road to self-discovery involves clearing certain obstacles from his path, years after they originally appeared. "It is never too late to mend," he surmises, echoing an earlier poem. His goal in looking back to the past is to locate "a prismatic space that cannot be seen, merely felt as the result of an angularity that must have existed from earlier times and is only now succeeding in making its presence felt through the mists of helpless acceptance of everything else projected on our miserable, dank span of days" (273). Positioning personal history in the present time gives the poet a chance to wax optimistic:

One is aware of it as an open field of possibilities. Not in the edifying sense of the tales of the past that we are still (however) chained to, but as stories that tell only of themselves, so that one realizes one's self has dwindled and now at last vanished in the diamond light of pure speculation. Collar up, you are as light as air. . . . The pain that drained the blood from your cheeks when you were young and turned you into a whitened specter before your time is converted back into a source of energy that peoples this new world of perceived phenomena with wonder. You wish you could shake hands with your lovers and enemies, forgive and love them, but they too are occupied as you are, though they greet you with friendly, half-distracted smiles and nods. (273)

"Light as air," pleasurably bathed in the "diamond light of pure speculation," the middle-aged poet enjoys for an instant the unbearable lightness of being. Ghastly childhood anxieties are replaced by a youthful glow that might never have been there. In any event, persecutors and former lovers no longer hold grudges. Involved totally in the transitory present, everyone merrily (and distractedly) goes about his business, free from recurring crises. As Ashbery says in "No Good at Names," a poem written two decades later, "The past recedes like an exaggerated long shadow / into what is prescient, and new— / what I originally came to do research on" (*Notes* 113).

Because his free-floating relationship with the past is exposed as illusory at other junctures of *Three Poems*, Ashbery looks for moments that can stand the test of time, selecting pivotal childhood episodes as exemplary cases. Never one to back away from cliché, he refers in "The System" to the proverbial fork in the road he encountered as a youth. In truth, Ashbery's memory of this moment owes more to Eliot's circuitous "East Coker" than it does to Frost's "The Road Not Taken," since in dialogue with his younger self he realizes that "the two branches were joined together again, farther ahead; that this place of joining was indeed the end, and that it was the very place you set out from, whose intolerable mixture of reality and fantasy had started you on the road which has now come full circle" (*CP* 306). He had said as much in "The New Spirit," arguing that such "paths are not quite parallel and must eventually join in conflict" (266–67). As Herd points out in his reading of "Clepsydra," Ashbery's poetic epiphanies, like Eliot's "still points" and Wordsworth's "spots of time," are always slipping away, though they hold forth the promise of periodic return (*John Ashbery* 108–9). Whereas Wordsworth paints memorial landscapes with a fine brush, Ashbery, like Eliot, veers toward abstraction. What readers encounter, Richard Jackson explains, is a Derridean "crypt," a "figurative monument" full of gaps and occlusions, a face behind the clock that "commemorates not a past but what is hidden by a past." Like Nietzsche's Zarathustra, Jackson asserts, Ashbery is too wily to get bogged down in nostalgia for a Golden Age; his aim, rather, is to deconstruct and thereby "re-create" the historical moments he has selected (157, 161–62). "The phenomena have not changed," Ashbery cannily admits in "The New Spirit." "But a new way of being seen convinces them they have" (*CP* 271–72).[16]

Without a highly selective view of the past, Ashbery realizes, all moments will become equally fleeting, and therefore irretrievable. "What

Ashbery recognizes is that experience is not *necessarily* a poem: it can be a purely linear succession of transient phenomena forever disappearing into the past, leaving behind only faint traces and blurred outlines," Roger Gilbert says. "But that oppressive conception of experience governed by time . . . can under the right circumstances give way to a different mode of consciousness in which space drowns the hum of time" (260). Addressing right measures in "The System," Ashbery casts aspersions upon the "life-as-ritual concept," an unbearable lightness of being in which consciousness has been totally confined to the present moment and "all contact with the past has been severed." In a dizzying passage that would fit nicely in Kundera's novel, Ashbery warns avant-garde types against exclusive engagements with immediacy and weightlessness:

> All its links severed with the worldly matrix from which it sprang,
> the soul feels that it is propelling itself forward at an ever-increasing
> speed. This very speed becomes a source of intoxication and of more
> gradually accruing speed; in the end the soul cannot recognize itself
> and is as one lost, though it imagines it has found eternal rest. But the
> true harmony which would render this peace interesting is lacking.
> There is only a cold knowledge of goodness and nakedness radiating
> out in every direction like the spines of a horse chestnut; mere knowl-
> edge and experience without the visual irregularities, those celestial
> motes in the eye that alone can transform ecstasy into a particular state
> beyond the dearly won generality. Here again, if backward looks were
> possible, not nostalgia but a series of carefully selected views, hieratic
> as icons, the difficulty would be eased and self could emerge with self-
> lessness, in true appreciation of the tremendous volumes of eternity.
> (*CP* 292–93)

Arguably, this meditation on memory has urban pastoral coordinates. The soul's experience of having its "links severed with the worldly matrix from which it sprang" mirrors that of the rural poet who moved to New York City, the "anti-place" that exists in Ashbery's mind primarily as a "loga-rithm of other cities." Life there has its pros and cons. Walled in by abstrac-tion, trapped in an endless succession of New York minutes, the poet often feels "lost." Fast-paced city life might prove more interesting, he speculates, if there existed instead some type of "harmony," a balanced understanding arranged by multiple selves, from different places, who remain in dialogue with each other. Complicating these potential meetings, Ashbery admits in "The New Spirit," is "time's way of walking sideways out of the event, at the same time proceeding in a straight line toward an actual vanishing point" (260). Wisely, Ashbery does not force the issue. "You have to take this as it opens up. There must be nothing resembling a nostalgia for a past which in any case never existed." So anxious is he to avoid grandiloquent Golden Age discourse, in fact, that he admits to being motivated by boredom. As for his occasional decisions to dwell in the past instead of the present: "It is like standing up because you've been sitting all day and are tired of it" (257).

In "The Recital," the conclusion to *Three Poems*, Ashbery's attempts to explain life's trajectory become even more enigmatic. "We have all or most of us had unhappy childhoods," he postulates. "Later on we tried to patch things up and as we entered the years of adulthood it was a relief for a while, that everything was succeeding: we had finally left that long suffering tunnel and emerged into an open place," there to embark on "a series of adult relationships from which the sting and malignancy of childhood were absent, or so it seemed" (*CP* 318). For Ashbery, this "open place" may well be the geometrically contoured city, where childhood troubles "retreated into their proper perspective as new things advanced into the foreground." Immersed in a vibrant arts community and overloaded with sensory experiences, the city poet finds that "the breathless urgency of those black-and-white situations of childhood happily played no part. It became a delight to enumerate all the things in the new world our maturity had opened up for us, as inexhaustible in pleasures and fertile pursuits as some more down-to-earth Eden, from which the utopian joys as well as the torments of that older fantasy-world had been banished by a more reasonable deity" (319). Curiously enough, amid New York's concrete and steel Ashbery finds "down-to-earth" freedom more available than it was in Sodus. Revisiting the themes of "Soonest Mended" and "The Chateau Hardware," he claims that the open city helps him elude the sexual policing that took place in rural precincts: "No more hiding behind bushes to get a secret glimpse of the others; no more unspeakable rages of jealousy or the suffocation of unrequited and unrealizable love" (318–19).

The danger of this approach is that the fleetingness of city life will lead to an endless cycle of becoming. Faced with an onslaught of exciting images, Ashbery initially delights in his artificial Garden of Eden. Before long, though, his contemplative side grows frustrated at time's unrelenting forward march:

[A]s the days and years sped by it became apparent that the naming of all the new things we now possessed had become our chief occupation;

that very little time for the mere tasting and having of them was left over, and that even these simple, tangible experiences were themselves subject to description and enumeration, or else they too became fleeting and transient as the song of a bird that is uttered only once and disappears into the backlog of vague memories where it becomes as a dried, pressed flower, a wistful parody of itself. Meanwhile all our energies are being absorbed by the task of trying to revive those memories, make them real, as if to live again were the only reality; and the overwhelming variety of the situations we have to deal with begins to submerge our efforts. It becomes plain that we cannot interpret everything, we must be selective, and so the tale we are telling begins little by little to leave reality behind. It is no longer so much our description of the way things happen to us as our private song, sung in the wilderness, nor can we leave off singing, for that would be to retreat to the death of childhood, to the mere acceptance and dull living of all that is thrust upon us, a living death in a word. (*CP* 319)

Attempts to capture the pure immediacy of the present are deemed futile, but so too, apparently, is any blind allegiance to the past. The ambiguity inherent in "the death of childhood" suggests that killing off childhood experiences is a dangerous maneuver, but that constantly revisiting those experiences constitutes its own death. More than anything, Ashbery wants to avoid the situation in which continually recounting vague memories relegates his younger self as a "dried, pressed flower," a desiccated version of the flowery head that emerged more colorfully and comically in "Little J. A." As he predicted in "The System," this would result in a "nostalgia whose sweetness burns like gall" (307). Poets must be discriminating when reciting personal histories, yet retrospective voyaging is by no means to be avoided. However much Ashbery's "private song" removes him from "reality," it beats getting trapped in the fleeting realm of the present, enslaved to an unbearable lightness of being, in touch with the energy of the metropolis and yet doomed under these circumstances to suffer a "living death."

SELF-PORTRAIT IN A CONVEX MIRROR (1975) contains fewer memory pieces, although "As You Came from the Holy Land" is notable for lending geographical specificity to the poet's pastoral quest. Modeled on an early modern ballad about the Virgin of Walsingham, this poem has Ashbery addressing questions to a farm boy from "the Holy Land / of western New York state."[17] Engaged in an interior dialogue as he travels life's winding path, the urban poet asks whether forsaken rural traits, rendered here as "signs of the earth's dependency," might become "the magic solution to what you are in now / whatever has held you motionless / like this so long" (*CP* 430). Surprisingly, it is the Manhattan intellectual, not the snowbound Sodus youth, who grows restless and bored. Essentially, Ashbery wants his rural alter ego to invade his urban domain and cure his middle-age lethargy. "The time is ripe now," he insists, for his younger self to make a surreptitious return:

> out of night the token emerges
> its leaves like birds alighting all at once under a tree
> taken up and shaken again
> put down in weak rage
> knowing as the brain does it can never come about
> not here not yesterday in the past
> only in the gap of today filling itself
> as emptiness is distributed
> in the idea of what time it is
> when that time is already past. (431)

Whereas Bloom highlights the "heroic and perpetual self-defeat" and "desperate cheerfulness" embodied in this passage ("Introduction" 6), I see Ashbery outlining an urban pastoral solution, one that is located neither in the nostalgic past nor in the fleeting present, but rather in a complex negotiation of the two, described here as "the gap of today filling itself." Implicitly acknowledging what Paul de Man calls the "rhetoric of temporality," Ashbery dwells in time's disjunction, extricating himself from an unbearable lightness of being while forsaking "nostalgia for a past that never existed." When they were combined, he realized, the past and the present could tell a different story, one that might not have actually taken place but that might nevertheless provide a rudderless writer the grounding he desired. In geographical terms, we might say that the abstract openness of New York City allows Ashbery to insert rural experiences as he sees fit, not in any naïve attempt to escape the ravages of time, but rather to grasp an "idea of what time it is / when that time is already past."

Ashbery revisits his quirky temporal strategy in a poem from *Houseboat Days* (1977) entitled "Crazy Weather":

> I shall never want or need
> Any other literature than this poetry of mud

And ambitious reminiscences of times when it came easily
Through the then woods and ploughed fields and had
A simple unconscious dignity we can never hope to
Approximate now except in narrow ravines nobody
Will inspect where some late sample of the rare,
Uninteresting specimen might still be putting out shoots, for all we
   know. (*CP* 503–4)

Although the exclusive nature of Ashbery's pastoral claim seems far-fetched, we should consider the "unconscious dignity" characterizing his "poetry of mud and ambitious reminiscences." Whatever activities he "easily" enjoyed in the woods and muddy fields near Sodus now take place, in approximate form, in the "narrow ravines" of New York City, which are located between skyscrapers.[18] Here, he happily reports, no one sets out to "inspect" his quasi-erotic activities, including that of "putting out shoots." In the paradoxical workings of urban pastoral, the semiotic openness of the metropolis provides Ashbery the natural lifestyle he was hard-pressed to find on the farm. A similar geographical reversal emerges in "And I'd Love You to Be in It," a poem from *As We Know* (1979) that juxtaposes the attributes of a sleek skyscraper and those of a rude slatted hut. As in "Crazy Weather," the unencumbered protrusions of an organic specimen suggest that sexual arousal and genital penetration go unmonitored in certain urban locations (in this case an apartment): "Today there are tendrils / Coming through the slats, and milky, yellowy grapes, / A mild game to divert the doorperson / And we are swiftly inside" (*CP* 673).[19]

A highlight of Ashbery's middle period is "At North Farm." This poem appears in *A Wave* (1984), a volume that was influenced by Ashbery's near death from infection in 1982 (Ford 62–63). "At North Farm" contains backward glances we would expect from a poet facing his own mortality. It steers clear of nostalgia, however, insofar as it shows the past seeking out the poet rather than the other way around. "At North Farm" was inspired to some degree by *The Kalevala*, a "death-haunted" collection of Finnish myths that alludes to a northern farm "situated somewhere near hell," where heroes search for wives (Shoptaw 12). Ashbery has said that, by describing a messenger of love, an "ambiguous person that everything hinges on," he is sticking to the Finnish script (Munn 63). But Vendler also seems right when she identifies a messenger of fate, a grotesque, goblin-like figure "of whom we always think with mixed feelings" (*Music* 253). In a haunting sequence, fate is personified as Ashbery's younger self, the abandoned country boy who belatedly lights out for the new territory of urban pastoral, leaving Sodus like a stray animal in order to meet up with the adult who, having recently cheated death, secretly calls his name. In my reading, the speaker is the city poet anticipating his alter ego's arrival:

> Somewhere someone is traveling furiously toward you,
> At incredible speed, traveling day and night,
> Through blizzards and desert heat, across torrents, through narrow
>   passes.
> But will he know where to find you,
> Recognize you when he sees you,
> Give you the thing he has for you?
>
> Hardly anything grows here,
> Yet the granaries are bursting with meal,
> The sacks of meal piled to the rafters.
> The streams run with sweetness, fattening fish;
> Birds darken the sky. Is it enough
> That the dish of milk is set out at night,
> That we think of him sometimes,
> Sometimes and always, with mixed feelings? (*CP* 733)

Reviewing this imagery, Bonnie Costello says the poem is "a complex anti-pastoral continually leading to pastoral yearnings," focusing as it does on an "ambivalent homestead in which the prodigal son can never quite settle, which he will not recognize when he finds it" (177). This time, apparently, the prodigal son is the child who stayed home. A mysterious and almost ghostly creature, he leaves Sodus rather late in the game, traveling hundreds of miles to meet the middle-aged man who left upstate New York four decades earlier. Meanwhile, awaiting the arrival of his counterpart, the city poet realizes that a bumper crop of pastoral images is available in his own backyard, a place where "hardly anything grows." Not until he puts out the dish of milk as an enticement to his more creaturely self, however, will he make peace with his past and keep his promise to take advantage of life's rich harvest.

Ashbery complicates his retrospective approach in *A Wave*'s title poem, suggesting that since permanent return to the farm is not feasible, and since the anticipated arrival of his rural self is chimerical, he is better off staying in New York City, letting Sodus orchards filter into his consciousness as they will.

... though there are some who leave regularly
For the patchwork landscape of childhood, north of here,
Our own kind of stiff standing around, waiting helplessly
And mechanically for instructions that never come, suits the space
Of our intense, uncommunicated speculation, marries
The still life of crushed, red fruit in the sky and tames it
For observation purposes ... (*CP* 795)

Vendler, analyzing another image in "A Wave," catches in Ashbery's language a whiff of defeatism: "His poetry is a continual approximation of Zeno's paradox: No matter how you hasten toward your goal, you will always be unable to reach it" (*Soul* 135). Ashbery himself seems untroubled by this dynamic. Indeed, he relishes the fact that the landscape lying between the city and the country remains "Partially out of focus, some of it too near, the middle distance / A haven of serenity and unreachable, with all kinds of nice / People and plants walking and stretching" (*CP* 787).

This blurry middle ground provides a buffer zone for his urban pastoral consciousness, flora and fauna functioning as the natural embodiment of a personal history stretching out to meet him. Unlike Zeno, Ashbery does not have to hasten for an unreachable goal if the desired aspects of an abandoned pastoral landscape hasten after him, assuaging his present anxieties. "The voluminous past," this time-traveler writes, "Accepts, recycles our claims to present consideration / And the urban landscape is once again untroubled, smooth / As wax" (*CP* 797). Later, in a hallway, we see Ashbery's country self, whom he identifies as "the past self you decided not to have anything to do with any more" ("a more comfortable you," he says elsewhere), confronting his cosmopolitan self, asking him to take stock of what he has lost and to envision what he might regain. So much of Ashbery's verse leads up to "moments like this one / That are almost silent, so that bird-watchers like us / Can come, and stay awhile, reflecting on shades of difference / In past performances, and move on refreshed" (798).

THE GEOGRAPHICAL WISH fulfillment Ashbery expresses in "At North Farm" and "A Wave," or in earlier poems like "For John Clare"—the belief that his rural identity can catch up with his urban identity, or at least meet it halfway—manifests itself even more strongly in *Flow Chart*, the autobiography in verse he conceived partly as a memorial to his recently deceased mother and partly as a memorial to his own childhood.[20] Described tantalizingly by Ashbery as "a diagram pointing you in a senseless direction toward yourself" (*Flow Chart* 109), this book-length poem is as complex, convoluted, and misrepresentative as the flow charts he saw in the Iran-Contra hearings on television when he began the project. Locating a unified subject in *Flow Chart* proves difficult, but coherent portraiture has never been Ashbery's goal. "I don't see how / a bunch of attributes can go walking around with a coatrack labeled 'person' loosely tied / to it with apron strings," he declares near the end of the poem (183), adding, "I purposely refrained from consulting *me*, the *culte du moi* being a dead thing, a shambles" (186–87). "Like *Three Poems*," Shoptaw explains, *Flow Chart* presents "a theodicy of an alternative destiny" (301).

Clearly, Ashbery could have stayed in Sodus instead of setting out for the big city, a decision we know he never made. Fortunately, writing poetry allows him to recapture some of that unfulfilled destiny. "It will all flow backwards," he says, positioning journeys he has taken alongside those he has not (*Flow Chart* 15). Likening his poem to "a mammoth postscript / to whatever you thought your life had been before" (97) and rummaging through memorabilia at his mother's house, Ashbery says, "I thought of all my lost days and how much more I could have done with them / . . . Perhaps it's best / this way, and a riper more rounded you could only be the product / of so much inefficiency" (114). "One makes a show of what one rejects, / the better to flaunt what one enshrines," he says at another juncture, "but that / can only happen once in the way of things happening" (135). Kundera's temporal paradox looms large as Ashbery asks himself a fundamental question: how can we revisit watershed moments from our past and lend the choices we made the same urgency, the same recognition that time is fleeting and that we had better make the correct decision immediately? To solve this conundrum, Ashbery searches for a "purely symbolic, anti-functional" mode, defined as a "regulatory system that organizes us in some semblance of order, binding some of us loosely, / baling others of us together like straw." In such a system, "destiny could / happen all the time, vanish or repeat itself ad infinitum," so that "all things would happen simultaneously and on the same plane, and existence, freed / from the chain of causality, could work on important projects unconnected to itself" (199–200). Presumably, Ashbery will locate destiny's child once Sodus ceases to be the referential background for lyrical autobiography and becomes instead the provocative foreground fueling his avant-garde experiments, many of which include hazy memories of adolescent sexual desire.

Toward this end, there appear in *Flow Chart* a number of ambiguously erotic activities ("barnstorming," "juicing the lemon," "horse-trading," encountering a "one-eyed hay-baler") (14, 24, 180) revealing the "launching pad" of Ashbery's pastoral sensibility, "before hunger and fears took over."

Regardless of whether Sodus functions as a site of sexual permission or a site of social exclusion, it looms for Ashbery as a place where "the air was pure and fresh / and I could remember how once all of existence was as painfully expectant, careless of duration / as the mayflies trying to just get by" (197). Does the insouciance of Ashbery's poetry have its basis in natural occurrences taking place long ago, hundreds of miles away? Or is the poet simply being clever, coloring accounts of his upbringing with New York School aesthetics? I suspect he is doing both, enjoying the elasticity of the urban pastoral mode, happy that "Doors are left open / as in spring, and beyond them float tunnel-vision landscapes / brought from somewhere else, and none recognizes the clever substitution" (81). Tellingly, as Ashbery's multiple selves cross paths, they express their collective "wonderment / at how we got from there to here" (4–5)

The "trellised" restrictions hindering "Little J. A." have by this juncture been overcome by a cosmopolitan, lawbreaking self, "immutable as roses." As in previous poems, amorous events from Ashbery's past, including "some episode from your childhood nobody knows about and / even you can't remember accurately," are situated amid unruly organic growth. On several occasions (Rehak 15; D'Agata; MacArthur 153), Ashbery has said that while living in Sodus he and his friends often played in the woods, where he enjoyed an "idyllic" romance with a girl named Mary Wellington. "We had a place where we played called 'the Kingdom,'" he recalls. "We each had a castle, which was usually a willow tree. I made a map of the whole place" (Lehman 123). In an early section of *Flow Chart*, Ashbery taps the awkward thrill of this suspended romance, mentioning "tender shoots of the willow / [that] dry up instead of maturing having concluded that the moment / is inappropriate" (11). This scenario is not unlike the pastoral tryst Aron Trask and his girlfriend Adra enjoyed under a willow tree in *East of Eden*, quite possibly one of the "coming-of-age films" Ashbery recalls viewing (90). He was certainly familiar with Elia Kazan's movie. In *The Last Avant-Garde*, Lehman explains that during an early stage of their friendship O'Hara had equated himself with dashing Cal Trask (played by James Dean) and Ashbery with the meeker Aron, fueling defensiveness in Ashbery owing to his rivalry with an athletic brother and his correspondingly low estimation in the eyes of his father (92–93).[21] Whether the desiccation of the willow shoots in *Flow Chart* is attributable to the restrictive moral atmosphere of Sodus, to some indecision on the part of the young lovers, or to Steinbeck's plot is not clear, given Ashbery's ambiguous syntactical positioning of "the moment." It seems significant, however, that the erotic activity of "putting out shoots," first glimpsed in "Soonest Mended," reappears in *Flow Chart*'s willow tree scene and in several other sections of the poem, heightening the pastoral flavor of Ashbery's amorous escapades.[22]

Ashbery suggests that the willow and other species of trees appearing in *Flow Chart*, while indicative of upstate's natural beauty, offered him safe haven only intermittently. "Forest / dithers protect us a lot of the time," Ashbery says in one passage, "but for those moments when one is thrust willy- / nilly into the spotlight, then oh dear!" (*Flow Chart* 38). Likewise, he alludes to "distant forest" housing his dreams (54) and to "imperfect sympathies" seeking cover in a "tangled forest of misplaced motives," but he seems fearful of divulging the precise coordinates of his woodland meeting places, as though the public's discovery of his adolescent trysts were still an issue. "Am I some kind of freak? No. Am I disingenuous? Maybe, / but the case hasn't been proved" (72). Steering clear of the region's homophobic citizenry after going "astray" (87), the urban pastoral poet talks of leaving the silent forest near Lake Ontario for the welcoming village of adult civilization, hoping to discover in the open environment of the city "a passport to a permanent, adjacent future, the adult equivalent of innocence / in a child, or lost sweetness in a remembered fruit: something to tell time by" (76). Like other émigrés from the hinterlands, Ashbery recalls "trying to disconnect his life and seal it / off" in an attempt to make Sodus just "another place / to take orders in, to be from if convenient" (44). Yet in other sections he fashions an urban pastoral synthesis, transposing onto the cityscapes of Cambridge, New York, and Paris the natural freedoms he had enjoyed in his forest "kingdom." "People would smile at me, as though we shared some pleasant / secret," Ashbery says of a "streetscape" he has bathed in pastoral hues, "or a tree would swoon into its fragrance, like a freshly unwrapped bouquet / from the florist's. I knew then that nature was my friend" (94).

In his attempt to "get together" with his rural alter ego, the urban writer says, "I see you are uncertain where to locate me; / here I am" (*Flow Chart* 27). The most affecting sections of *Flow Chart* are those in which Ashbery clears a mutually agreeable space, "even a negative one" (29), for this reunion of disparate selves. The task proves difficult. "I have to keep fighting / back to find you, and then when you're still there, what is it I know?" one self asks another (22). "Variations don't let you proceed along one footpath normally; there are too many ways to go," the poet complains at another juncture (168). Yet on more propitious occasions Ashbery's younger self is able to seek out his mature self in the latter's urban lair. Once again, the ambiguity of Ashbery's imagery lends an erotic charge to this reunion of forlorn subjects:

> . . . Someone came down
> from upstate to see me, and that was fine. We rummaged in drawers
>   for a spell.
> My, how
> that bush has grown. Aren't you tempted too in the sweet part of the
>   night
> to give up your secret by whispering it and then roll over,
> convinced that nothing can ever repair the climate? (98)

As in "At North Farm," Ashbery plays up the creaturely aspects of his upstate persona, hinting somewhat dizzily that he could have gotten along "without assists from bunnies and wood-sprites if something not of my own construing, / something I had rejected, hadn't interposed a feline quickness and fur just before the fatal / gradient." Under the spell of this cat-like creature, he explains, "I stepped back and stared, and in that moment saw myself on a visit to myself, / with quite a few me's on a road receding sharply into a distance." Following a circuitous path into the past, the city slicker "scoured hills as well as dales in search of the person they / belonged to instead of staying parked under this plain wooden table" (144–45).

Although Ashbery claims that "too much of the city remains standing" for him to speak naïvely of charmed pastoral quests, the truth is that his journey out of Sodus (and back again) informs a great deal of his experimental verse. "I had / many ties to the region," he admits in *Flow Chart* (103). Instinctively wary of the "new age of nothing" that reigned in the New York School's "anti-environment," he gravitates toward palpable natural images, even as he bathes them in abstraction:

> . . . What if [poetry] were only a small, other way of living,
> like being in the wind? or letting the various settling sounds we hear now
> rest and record the effort any creature has to put forth to summon its
>   spirits for a moment and then
> fall silent, hoping that enough has happened? Sometimes we do
>   perceive it
> this way, like animals that will get up and move somewhere and then
>   drop down
> in place again. . . . (145–46).[23]

Near the end of *Flow Chart*, having reached "a hiatus in the manuscript," Ashbery expresses his hope that his "going around in a circle / all the time" will lead to "a place of resolution," envisioned here as an agrarian site, replete with "bored cows and seedlings" (172). "This hiatus is sui generis," he says a few pages later, "and I know not how to read it / like Braille and must forever remain behind in my solicitations, derelict in my duties, / until a child explains it all to me. And then I'll weep / at mountainscapes, if it isn't too late" (176). Freely adopting the perspective of this child, the adult poet immerses himself in native landscape in order to pose a fundamental question: "What passion / brought you to your knees?" The answer to this and other (erotically coded) questions is never fully disclosed, and yet Ashbery's retrospective methodology proves effective. Throughout *Flow Chart*, we find him situating his rural and urban selves in separate spheres but taking care not to "disturb" their fundamental interdependency, their ultimate desire to link up with each other. Doing so, the polyphonic postmodernist insists, "would have been false / to our beginnings" (172–73). The matter is summed up best by one of his questions: "How / can I deny my true origin and nature even if it's going to get me into a lot of / trouble later?" (29).

FOR DECADES, Ashbery has spoken passionately about multiple selves that are always in motion, always in dialogue, constantly measuring themselves against the boy who peeped out in "The Picture of Little J. A.," part of an agrarian landscape he has long since vacated but never truly abandoned. "Perhaps what I am saying is that it is I the subject, recoiling from you at ever-increasing speed just so as to be able to say I exist in that safe vacuum I had managed to define from my friends' disinterested turning away," Ashbery says in *Three Poems*. "As if I were only a flower after all and not the map of the country from which it grows. . . . It does not seem to alter anything that I am the spectator, you what is apprehended, and as such we both have our own satisfying reality" (*CP* 255). Here as elsewhere, the poet who finds a "safe vacuum" in the city indicates that his geographical trajectory has provided him the distance necessary to gauge past episodes with clarity and respect. This means not only refraining from starry-eyed views of rural America but also from glib dismissals of the people whose lives quietly flourish in remote areas. A "satisfying reality" exists in the country and in the city, in the past and in the present, so long as a proper balance is achieved.

Near the end of "The System," having considered the complex relationship of time and place, Ashbery speaks of having achieved this balance, at least momentarily:

> The sadness that infected us as children and stayed on through adulthood has healed, and there can be no other way except this way of

health we are taking, silent as it is. But it lets us look back on those other, seemingly spoiled days and re-evaluate them. . . . [T]hose days are now an inseparable part of our story despite their air of immaturity and tentativeness; they have the freshness of early works which may be wrongly discarded later. Nor is today really any different: we are as childish as ever, it turns out, only perhaps a little better at disguising it. (*CP* 313)

Readers of this passage should not be surprised to learn that, during an address to the Poetry Society of America in 1995, Ashbery cited an aphorism from Auden, explaining that "childhood is all we have" (*Selected Prose* 245), or that in a poem published around this time he maintained that the "children we had lost once / know how to keep on repeating the piece / they learned, knew their way back to us" (*And the Stars* 49).

Given his talents and aspirations, it was unlikely that any set of circumstances could have kept Little J. A. down on the farm once he saw what the big city had to offer. I hope to have suggested, however, the myriad ways Sodus has lingered in his memory. Within the New York School, Ashbery has enjoyed support and camaraderie in the city's studios, clubs, and galleries. But he has also needed to discover who he is and where he comes from. Like Gertrude Stein, whom he praised for creating "a counterfeit reality more real than reality itself" (Ross 197), Ashbery cloaks his landscapes in piebald vestments. And still a serious examination of rural hours emerges amidst his opaque phrasing. "Sometimes one's own hopes are realized / and life becomes a description of every second of the time it took," this former hayseed declares in *Flow Chart* (7). Of course, Ashbery being Ashbery, we are left to ponder whether he is referring to his physical relocation to the city, his imaginative journey back to the countryside, or his ongoing negotiation between the two. Regardless, he has managed to tap into a "defeated memory gracious as flowers / And therefore also permanent in its way / . . . A fortified dose of the solid, / Livable adventure" (*CP* 855). Deftly straddling the urban pastoral divide, opening up his writing to a polyvalent and occasionally erotic egolessness, Ashbery presents us with landscapes that are puzzling and complex, though also distinctly arable and laden with possibility.

3 | FICTIONS DRESSED LIKE WATER
Barbara Guest's Aqueous Imagery

ALTHOUGH SHE was a pioneer of avant-garde pastoral verse, Barbara
Guest was for years conspicuously missing from discussions of
the New York School. Guest's inclusion in Donald Allen's *The New
American Poetry* (1960) and John Bernard Myers's *Poets of the New
York School* (1969) represented a rare exception to this trend. Unfortunately, her exclusion from Ron Padgett and David Shapiro's
An Anthology of New York Poets (1970) left her "suspended," like a
faltering student, from the School (Diggory and Miller 3). It is bad
enough that Geoff Ward, William Watkin, and David Lehman neglect to consider Guest in their critical studies, but more disturb-
ing to learn that her New York School peers may have contributed
to her marginalization. Seeking to justify his exclusion of Guest
from *The Last Avant-Garde*, Lehman cites a 1959 letter that James
Schuyler sent to John Ashbery conveying Kenneth Koch's belief
that no one on the New York poetry scene had much to offer their
new literary magazine, *Locus Solus*, except for O'Hara, Schuyler,
Ashbery, and himself (Lehman 12; Schuyler, *Just* 114). Joe LeSueur
echoes the boy's club attitude exhibited by charter members of the
School, explaining that "no woman besides Jane [Freilicher] was
part of the clique, not even Barbara Guest" (126–27).[1]

Guest's literary reputation received a significant boost with the
publication of *Selected Poems* in 1995, after which she has received
steady scholarly attention. Rachel Blau Du Plessis, Sara Lundquist,
and Lynn Keller, Guest's earliest champions in the academy, have
assessed the difficulties attending this poet's decades-long exclusion. "We don't know her," Du Plessis says in her review of *Selected
Poems* ("Flavor" 23). Lundquist offers a visual analogue, highlighting

Guest's marginal position, her face hidden by hair and turned away from the camera, in a 1961 photograph included in John Gruen's memoir, *The Party's Over Now*. "She is difficult to see, mysteriously not there at the same time that she is ostensibly there," Lundquist opines ("Reverence" 260). Her poetry was every bit as avant-garde as O'Hara's or Ashbery's, yet it suffered from gender assignments Betty Friedan associated with a "Feminine Mystique." Although it stands "as far from New Critical patterns of contained coherence as any other New American work, Guest's writing shows a gentility and civility, a graciousness that I suspect has made it seem less excitingly rebellious than the work of her largely male peers," Keller says ("Becoming" 215).

What makes the scholarship of Keller, Du Plessis, and Lundquist so valuable is that it acknowledges Guest's uncertain position within a male-dominant avant-garde while granting her privileged place within its ranks. Elisabeth Frost and Cynthia Hogue similarly maintain that Guest, like H. D. (the subject of Guest's 1984 biography, *Herself Defined*), was "redolently aware of being both 'object' and peer to her male contemporaries" ("Barbara Guest"). Objectified or not, Guest kept pace with her New York School cohorts, including the hyperactive O'Hara, drinking and talking with him late into the night, lunching with him often (Lehman 176–77), and walking with him through cityscapes he knew she would never spoil with naive commentary (Fraser 126). "She was there," Lundquist says of Guest. "She gave poetry readings; she published; she had her plays produced; she wrote gallery reviews for *Art News* and collaborated with painters (notably Grace Hartigan, Helen Frankenthaler, and Mary Abbott); she served briefly as the poetry editor of the *Partisan Review*; she partied and joked and visited and traveled, corresponded, fought and made up with the other four poets; they admired her work, she admired theirs" ("Fifth Point" 15). Based on this evidence, a photograph of Guest rubbing elbows with O'Hara on the closing night of the Cedar Tavern (McDarrah 73) is more representative than the "loner" photograph Lundquist cites in her earlier essay.

Like the aforementioned critics, Charles Bernstein, Charles North, Marjorie Welish, Kathleen Fraser, and the women poets in the *HOW(ever)* group have claimed Guest as their materfamilias, the intrepid adventurer who paved the way for their own experiments. In the 1980s and 1990s, these poets presented conference panels and wrote incisive essays on Guest's work, some of which were collected in special issues of *Women's Studies* and *Jacket*. Lamenting that she had been "long eclipsed" by other experimental writers, North noted that Guest "has come into her own . . .

partly because the fragmented language and consciousness she has always worked with have become fashionable," going on to explain that "much of the current fashion is uninspired, lacking her artistic integrity, her artistic intelligence, and, to put it simply, her gift" (108). After garnering such praise and winning the Poetry Society of America's Frost Medal in 1999, Guest was no longer a fifth wheel but rather "the fifth point of a star," belatedly recognized alongside O'Hara, Ashbery, Koch, and Schuyler as a charter member of the New York School.[2] Missing in this recent attention, however, is an extended consideration of the natural imagery lending Guest's verse its mystifying beauty and power.

GUEST'S ADMIRERS tend to focus on her penchant for taking risks. Feminist critics emphasize her brave maneuvering within avant-garde communities, highlighting what Keller has called her "profound social disaffection" ("Becoming" 216) with homosocial ideologies and gendered subject positions while praising what Linda Kinnahan has termed her "movement toward variability and ambiguity rather than revelation" (237). Guest became a politically effective writer without resorting to realism, a choice that befuddled 1970s feminists, who excluded her from anthologies (Du Plessis, "Flavor" 23; Kinnahan 231). Illustrating Guest's willingness to dwell in uncertainties, Lundquist mentions her early 1960s collaborations with Abbott and Hartigan, ventures that showed teams of women engaging in heroic gestures heretofore associated with the macho crowd of abstract expressionists. Courageously taking a "voyage into the unknown," Guest and her collaborators showcased instances when "the imagination's at its turning" (Lundquist, "Another Poet" 256, 247), surrealistic moments when surface-level reality becomes intensified by its inherent oppositions or "tensions." Much as painters used abstract techniques to challenge representational modes, Guest suspended poetic syntax so as to disrupt the linearity, subjectivity, and sentimentality of traditional lyric without abandoning the natural beauty associated with this kind of verse.

Indeed, although Bernstein praises Guest for her "aversion to the lyric" ("Introducing"), Welish insists that Guest's approach to language is "more apt to yield to verbal delirium than noise-music," bringing it closer to the beauty associated with a "lyrical impulse" ("Lyric"). North also classifies Guest's verse as "essentially lyrical," albeit in "a post-modern way," identifying her as "something of a hunter/gatherer of poetic materials, restlessly in motion, popping up to surprise, even splitting apart" (153). However atonal her verbal music, Guest's luscious backdrops evoke deep-seated emotion. Her "commitment to beauty," Terence Diggory explains, leads her not merely to suspend art, as Language Poets do, but rather to "assign a positive function to aesthetic illusion, 'semblance' (*Schein*), the locus of beauty in contrast to the sublime." If Guest's "fair realism" reminds Welish and North of traditional lyric, it puts Diggory ("Barbara Guest" 75, 77, 82) in mind of Theodor Adorno, who said that "works become beautiful by force of their opposition to what simply exists."

Navigating a middle path between tension and beauty, intellect and emotion, Guest features natural elements in situations we least expect to find them. Several critics have picked up on her depictions of air, linking these with an array of avant-garde freedoms. Lundquist enthuses about Guest's "aerated poetry" ("Fifth Point"). Ann Vickery, in her article on Guest's "modern pastoral," praises the poet's "adventurous, often airy transpositions—enabling the subject to move across various realities and enter other states of being" (259). Brenda Hillman strikes a similar chord, saying that Guest is "drawn to the increasing freedom provided by light and air, and also to the deepening of a personal style of language that can be inhabited by the reader, the poem and the poet" (208). Anna Rabinowitz explains that "Guest's world is full of light, of human experience, of nature, of evolution and history—and air—air as breath, air as risk and challenge, air as newness wafting." This is especially true of Guest's fragmentary poems, where "space looms large" and "ideas wander in the whites" (105, 101). Arielle Greenberg concurs. "The page looks airy," she says. "Each idea is given room to breathe," owing to "the fresh air [Guest] has breathed into language" (115, 120). Surveying the "great spaces on the page" in *Defensive Rapture* and *Fair Realism*, North assumes that for Guest "the poem was in fact the sky and the fragments of language, now clustering and now breaking apart, were fleeting intrusions on the order of gulls and passing clouds" (154).[3]

Few critics, however, have examined Guest's descriptions of water. Granted, Lundquist notes that the typical Guest persona is a "deep-sea diver" as well as an "aerialist" (among other things), but gives only brief mention to the aqueous images flooding Guest's volumes ("Barbara Guest" 162). Barbara Einzig delves a bit deeper, explaining that, in her best poems, "Guest arrives at a liquid balance. Like liquid inside a leveling instrument that determines our horizon line. The instrument of writing is continually matched against the gravity of 'reality'" (10). But even Einzig fails to investigate thoroughly the aqueous elements lending Guest's poems their suspenseful character. More remains to be said about the way water courses through Guest's imagination, lending her experimental writing its buoyancy and reflective brilliance.

"I BELIEVE that poetic language comes from the same place as experience," Guest asserted in a 1992 interview (Hillringhouse 27). For me, the most important word in Guest's statement is not "language" but "place," namely the geographical coordinates affecting her avant-garde nature writing. The "locale of the mind" Mark Hillringhouse discerns in Guest's work (26), like the "actual location of the mind" Einzig analyzes (9), is based on actual places the poet lived in or visited. Foremost among these are the coastal areas she knew in her youth. Although Guest lists herself as "Resident—New York City" in Allen's anthology (438), she reveals on the jacket of *Poems* (1962), her first major volume, that "I spent most of my girlhood in the seacoast states—Florida and California." Born in Wilmington, North Carolina, she moved to Florida as a girl, settling first in the Miami area, later in Lakeland and other small towns, as her father looked for work. Her family was poor, and young Barbara, who learned to read at age three, was educated in one-room schoolhouses. At age ten, following her father's death, she went to Los Angeles to live with an aunt and uncle, since California had the best public education available in the United States. Guest thrived in the classroom, earning high grades and graduating from Berkeley.[4] All the moving around had a deleterious effect on her psyche, however. She has said that as a young person she "never really had a home" and that this rootlessness led to "unnecessary anxiety." She admitted late in life that "when I say the word 'home' I almost whisper it" (Hillringhouse 26).

Moving to New York in her twenties, Guest finally found a home, telling relatives, "New York is so small, so intimate, you keep crossing and re-crossing the same circles and everyone knows everyone else, so that once you crash the fringes you are to a degree in" (Lundquist, "Fifth Point" 20). As she recalled, "New York had an openness that only major cities have" (Frost and Hogue). Guest is probably referring to the Cedar Tavern and other downtown locations where poets and painters discussed their work, or perhaps to apartment parties, where this "quintessential New York poet" (Lundquist, "Barbara Guest" 160) met other members of the New York School. But her statements are also descriptive of a wider urban topography, one I view as surprisingly bucolic. The "location of things" piquing Guest's imagination involves natural phenomena as well as people, New York's open spaces as well as its open social world. Despite inherent tensions, her poetic experiments are unusually calm and her personae curiously at home in buoyant surroundings. Aqueous elements flood forward in such instances. As Guest "extends Virgil's pastoral to the urban domain" (Vickery 250), she is aided by images taken from the seacoast states she once inhabited.

To gauge water's influence on urban society, consider rain. Impersonal itself, rain alters human relationships, especially in the city, where masses live in proximity. When rain falls in the metropolis, satirists come out to play, splashing around in all that is uncomfortable. Jonathan Swift in eighteenth-century London and Colson Whitehead in twenty-first-century New York delight in describing the bodily aches exacerbated by rain, not to mention the detritus floating in overflowing gutters. But even these cranks admit that rain brings together diverse groups seeking shelter. "Here various kinds, by various fortunes led, / Commence acquaintance underneath a shed / Triumphant Tories and desponding Whigs / Forget their feuds, and join to save their wigs," Swift notices in "A Description of a City Shower" (570). Whitehead likewise marvels that "Underneath the scaffolding the conversations among strangers range from grunts to bona fide connections. Quite serendipitous" (68). "In New York City, rain provides something of a social function," poet Jim Carroll says. "People gather in small places, in hallways and storefronts, and begin to talk. They speak in civilized tones which some of them had all but forgotten. They tell strangers things they would never think of revealing to friends or lovers. During a storm in New York, people actually *agree* with things you say" (*Forced* 139–40).

Urban rainfall is also quite beautiful, in a melancholy way. On pavement or window glass, its sheen reflects artificial lights and poetic thoughts with equal facility, lending the city an ethereal quality. Rain makes the city light up, accommodating private revelations that, curiously enough, seem fit for sharing. In several poems, the rain Guest glimpses from windows and doorways corresponds to an inner climatology known to her and a range of urban pastoral types, from reflective poets like Schuyler to moody musicians like Keren Ann Zeidel.[5] In "Les Réalités," a rainy day prompts Guest to read about Parisian pharmacies. Baffled by a love affair and "overwhelmed by trees" on the previous day's "autumn walk," the poet seeks solace in an imagined storefront, one that is usually grubby but is now glistening with water. "It is as if perpetual rain / fell on those drugstores making the mosaic brighter, / as if entering those doors one's tears / were cleaner." Precipitation provides an ablution more pure than tears. The wistful poet cannot help but want to dwell in it, baptize herself in it, until such spell is ended, at which point "this pharmacy / turns our desire into medicines and revokes the rain." Like the "new shade of powder / orchidee, ambre, rose" displayed on its shelves, Guest implies by means of a Janus-faced simile that the Parisian drugstore in the rain "triumphs as a natural thing" (*CP* 10–11). Like pastoral landscapes Keats includes in his odes, a city building awash in rain has become a perfect place for anyone beset by a melancholy fit to glut her sorrow. Guest's use of a plural pronoun near the end of the poem implies that other city dwellers have access to the drugstore's emotional medicine, provided they share her resourcefulness.

Buildings like the Parisian pharmacy play a central part in Guest's poetic registry, but their edifices are highly mutable. As Robert Bennett says, Guest's architectural spaces are "deliberately constructed both to unsettle conventional expectations about the attire of spatiality itself and to suggest instead intimations of a more complex world in which both 'proofs' and 'illusions' of 'stability' are subverted by a profound awareness of the chaotic contingencies of modern life" (49). And nothing says "chaotic contingency" more than climatologic conditions. Diggory evidently agrees, positioning Guest's architectural genius within the larger realm of nature, noting her ability to eliminate barriers separating buildings from the outdoors, expanding metropolitan views of nature ("Picturesque" 309). Hillman concurs: "Among writers whose central task is to valorize the artist's imagination—Keats, Stevens, Ashbery—cityscapes and landscapes often cross over themselves in the poems, making themselves Everyscapes. Likewise Guest. Her cross-overs are helped by adjective-noun conjunctions, sometimes the hardworking but peculiar adjective with the extraordinarily free-spirited noun, like a ranchhand assigned to a landowner he never meets" (213).

Guest's "Everyscapes" rely on boundaries permeable enough to admit oppositions and playful ironies. An apartment interior portrayed in "West Sixty-Fourth Street" meshes neatly with nearby Central Park, as "candelabra melt into forests / gathering their heartache / into bouquets of grass" (*CP* 26). Guest's use of "melt" indicates the liquidity of thought flowing through her repertoire. Her penchant for fluidly negotiating urban borderlands is also on display in "The Location of Things," a poem in which a rainy Madison Avenue mysteriously extends its reach into a local bar, where the poet enjoys a drink:

> The street, the street bears light
> and shade on its shoulders, walks without crying,
> turns itself into another and continues, even
> cantilevers this barroom atmosphere into a forest
> and sheds its leaves on my table
> carelessly as if it wanted to travel somewhere else
> and would like to get rid of its luggage
> which has become in this exquisite pointed rain
> a bunch of umbrellas. An exchange! (3)

Pressing her head against the bar's window and trying to make sense of "Afternoons / of smoke and wet nostrils," Guest notices that as "The water's lace creates funerals / it makes us see someone we love in an acre of grass." Her delectable feelings of sadness, common among urban bohemians contemplating their fate on leisurely afternoons, are enhanced by aqueous images, which do not seem out of place on a wet city avenue depicted as a "theatrical lake" (4). The special way rain comes into contact with constructed surfaces (windows, streets) has for Guest the ability to alter the "location of things" and with that, our everyday perceptions of reality.

A similar situation exists in "Fan Poems," a sequence from *The Blue Stairs* (1968). The poet tutors a woman named Melissa, pointing out altered reflections in a rain-streaked window so as to nurture her protégé's acceptance of natural heterogeneity:

> Windows, Melissa, they contain what is best
> of us, the glass your arm has arranged
> into crystal by spinning eye, by alarms
> taken when the rain has chosen a form
> unlike the universe, similar to ups and downs
> which vary or change as cowslips
> in the meadow we cross have a natural tint,
> the panes reflect our hesitations and delight. (*CP* 80)

The window glass, the human body, the rain, the cowslips: each of these objects owes its place in the universe, at least in part, to the reflections bringing it to light. That these reflections variously take on physical or mental aspects is axiomatic, as far as Guest is concerned. Of course, it takes a leap of imagination, as well as a trick of light, to see that rain changes as flowers in the meadow change, or to see that a glistening window is rearranged by the arm it reflects. The location of objects refuses to obey calls to reason, since the inner/outer logic of Guest's urban pastoral poetry suspends ordinary categorizations. As she notes in "Landing," another early poem, "The window outscaped / Brings the climate indoors. / The eye is free, adorned / By that which is becoming" (22), the final word referring not only to that which is beautiful and free, but also to that which is constantly undergoing transformation.

In "The Brown Studio" (*CP* 45–46), Guest tests her formula in a less promising space. On this occasion, the duskiness of an artist's studio surprises a persona who has just "spent a night in the grove / by the river," where forms were somber and "even the music was distinctly shady." Yet this empty studio, with its black stove, black chair, black coat, and inky easel, becomes an urban version of the riverside grove, with its starlings and muddy water. Filling in for the absent painter, the poet seizes the opportunity for a pastoral overhaul: "I believed if I spoke, / if a word came from my throat / and entered this room whose wall had been turned, // it would be the color of the cape / we saw in Aix in the studio of Cezanne."[6] Yet only when her voice trails off and the colors envelop her will this ambitious visitor, keenly aware of "the arc from real to phantom" in artistic representation, fully appreciate the studio's "dying brown." Guest is highly conscious of the play of light in this interior, yet she suspects that painters have outpaced poets in this regard. "I don't think writers put enough demands on their surroundings," she has said. "It's almost as if they're afraid to do it, as if it were indulgent and detracts from the mysteriousness of their occupation. . . . Whereas painters demand it" (Hillringhouse 24). Redressing this imbalance in "The Brown Studio," Guest shows how working quarters affect her own aesthetic process.

In her essay on Guest's natural sensibility, Vickery emphasizes her "retreat into the imaginary," arguing that "pastoral, for Guest, is where the imaginary is not only prioritized over the real but informs the real" (251, 254). This relationship is not so easily calibrated, however, for in "The Location of Things" and "The Brown Studio" we find real physical spaces "informing" Guest's pastoral imagination. In "The Screen of Distance," Guest's representation of city architecture contains porosity evident in earlier works. "On a wall shadowed by lights from the distance," the titular screen, "suspended like / the frame of a girder," accommodates the exchange of narratives in an enclosed room.[7] To facilitate the breakdown of artificial barriers, the "worker" constructing this frame fills it with "a plot or a quarter inch of poetry to encourage / nature into his building and the tree leaning / against it, the tree casting language upon the screen" (*CP* 226). Later, this aesthete builder surmises that "To introduce color to form / I must darken the window where shrubs / grazed the delicate words / the room would behave / like everything else in nature." Having created her ideal dwelling, she announces that "Experience and emotion performed / as they did within the zone of distance / words ending in fluid passages / created a phenomenal blush / dispersing illusion" (229). Vickery claims that "the pastoral mood of the poem accentuates the 'distance' between subject and object, the use of language as a frame or psychological screen," citing David Halperin's assertion that "the ideal world of pastoral finds the real world wanting" (258, 259). Yet for me, "The Screen of Distance" shrinks the distance between the ideal and the real, conflating the trappings of urban civilization (buildings, narrative discourse) with their natural counterparts (shrubs, raw emotion), bringing a city poet into intimate contact with her surroundings. Without becoming too literal, Guest implies that metropolitan sites facilitate her abstract imagination, housing the daily mysteries of city living and allowing pastoral wonders to take place.[8]

IN THE POEMS cited above, urban spaces inhabited by open-minded artists are altered by natural surroundings. After perusing Guest's other poems, I wonder whether the seascapes she encountered in Florida and California were responsible for these transformations. Taking an imaginative journey back to childhood scenes, Guest suspends her sense of time as well as her sense of space, tracing a route similar to the one mapped out by Ashbery in his Sodus poems. The abstract dimensionality realized in this poetry of "suspension" dates back to Virgilian pastoral, but it continues to pay dividends in postmodern New York.[9] Instead of fixating on specific times and places, like O'Hara and his acolytes, Guest and Ashbery hold in abeyance life's assumptions, decisions, and judgments, particularly when location and temporality are concerned, revisiting rural landscapes of their youth so as to escape the avant-garde's emphasis on immediacy.

We need look no further than "Parachutes, My Love, Could Carry Us Higher," Guest's most famous poem, to appreciate the suspenseful nature of her work, which although it resists the excess of confessional verse, retains an autobiographical flavor. Kathleen Fraser, who heard Guest read "Parachutes" at the New School in the early 1960s, relishes "the precariousness of emotional suspension and the suggestion of imminent shattering . . . the condition of the tenuous, spoken out of a peculiarly interior experience, yet as far afield as one could imagine from the battering 'confessional' model much favored in certain East Coast poetry circles at that time" (127). Breezy and sensuous, "Parachutes" investigates an environmental indeterminacy felt acutely by those in love:

> I just said I didn't know
> And now you are holding me
> In your arms,
> How kind.
> Parachutes, my love, could carry us higher.
> Yet around the net I am floating
> Pink and pale blue fish are caught in it,
> They are beautiful,
> But they are not good for eating.

Parachutes, my love, could carry us higher
Than this mid-air in which we tremble,
Having exercised our arms in swimming,
Now the suspension, you say,
Is exquisite. I do not know.
There is coral below the surface,
There is sand, and berries
Like pomegranates grow.
This wide net, I am treading water
Near it, bubbles are rising and salt
Drying on my lashes, yet I am no nearer
Air than water. I am closer to you
Than land and I am in a stranger ocean
Than I wished. (*CP* 14)

Because "just" can mean either "simply" or "recently," depending on context, the tone and position of the speaker are immediately thrown into question. Typically, Guest refuses to resolve the inconsistencies lending love affairs their double nature, their wild mood swings, their careening traversals between the poles of allure and torture, passion and ennui. Linguistically, she relies upon clipped rhythms and catchphrases, which help her to reproduce a popular language of love without buying into mainstream ideology. The phrase "My love" joins "my darling" ("Jaffa Juice," *CP* 18–20) and "my dear" ("Nocturne," 42–43) as an assiduously ironic term of endearment, just as "beautiful" and "exquisite," like the words "gorgeous" and "marvelous" appearing elsewhere in her oeuvre, sometimes resist being taken at face value.[10] Similarly, when Guest offers a disappointed lover's by-the-book rejoinder, "How kind," in the poem's shortest line, one can almost hear her mutter the words under her breath.

But natural imagery makes this poem so memorable. While rainy city skies in "Les Réalités" and "The Location of Things" unite bohemian daydreamers, the indeterminate horizon in "Parachutes," hazily situated between the oceanic and the atmospheric, marks more troubling territory. It is hard to know where the persona is positioned, or what her emotional state might be. Initial images suggest airspace. After all, parachutes are devised to bring those falling though the sky to a soft landing. Yet to argue that equipment designed for descent "could carry us higher," as Guest does, is to provide wry commentary on a romantic relationship in free-fall. Suspended in "this mid-air in which we tremble, / Having exercised our arms in swimming," her persona is also "treading water," obscuring her exact location. Her head is evidently above water, since the sea salt dries on her eyelashes. For all her poise, though, she seems imperiled, claiming that she is "no nearer / Air than water," drowning rather than waving. As Guest rewrites the lyrics to Irving Berlin's "How Deep Is the Ocean?" she finds herself "closer to [her lover] than land," leaving her in a "stranger ocean" full of risk and uncertainty.

Moving in a different direction, "The Open Skies" begins with coastal imagery ("mollusks in their shell") but swiftly ascends to the realm of air. Like the ocean, open skies appear indivisible, attracting imaginative types who share their disregard for boundaries. The poem's title, Fraser argues, signals a "horizon of the page where almost anything might conjecture itself into language . . . and leave, as suddenly" (125). "[D]aylight fair / unbreakable you seem," Guest apostrophizes, "Hitched to me as I / window thrust to you" (*CP* 49). As in her city poems, Guest resists arbitrary separations of indoors and outdoors. The "cantilevered" images filling "The Location of Things" are matched in "The Open Skies" by a poetic figure leaning from a window. Suspended thus, she communes directly with airy elements, which have the strange effect of holding her aloft. Speaking directly to the air ("Cloudless / you take // My happiness / rising in the morning"), Guest luxuriates in a weightless atmosphere: "Light descends to me / buoyantly . . . // I pass into your frailness // Noiseless hour / span of float and flight / Sky without lever or stress" (49–50). Giving herself over to "Sky whose fancy / sways and swings above // All quick airiness / and slow guide," pleasurably lost amid her "ecstatic harking to upward dome," she faces the open air a final time to say, "Without you I cannot see" (50). As Kenneth Koch would say, fresh air is necessary not only for subsistence but also for art. Notice, though, that the skies drawing Guest upward are depicted as "buoyant," reflecting the primacy of aqueous language in her poetic register.

"Parachutes" and "The Open Skies" contain their share of ambiguity, and yet their personae seem knowable and their locations, while abstract, accessible on an emotional level. "Biographical details pertaining to the life of Barbara Guest, the person, are not revealed," Lundquist says, "but emotional experience is fully and candidly exposed, without self-pity or narcissism" ("Fifth Point" 24). In "Parachutes," Fraser asserts, "Guest's location of self is disclosed as structural. It is in this uneasy moment that her reader is allowed entry. A recognition takes place. The perception that certainty is contextual, that *un*certainty exists as an authentic condition, hovers in relief" (128). In other words, the suspenseful predicaments faced by Guest's personae remain shareable, a quality that Alpers, in his analysis of singing contests among shepherds, identifies as an important component of pastoral literature. "As opposed to epic and tragedy," Alpers explains, pastoral "takes human life to be inherently a matter of common plights and common pleasures. Pastoral poetry represents these plights and these pleasures as shared and accepted, but it avoids naïveté and sentimentality because its usages retain an awareness of their conditions—the limitations that are seen to define, in the literal sense, any life, and their intensification in situations of separations and loss that can and must be dealt with, but are not to be denied or overcome" (*What* 93).

Confronted with common traumas, Guest's readers can concentrate on linguistic components, as the Language Poets do, or instead on another shareable context Fraser mentions but fails to name, namely the seascapes where her poems are frequently situated. The air and water filling these seascapes are necessary for survival, yet one may suffer from their surfeit as well as from their deprivation. Avoiding extremes, Guest's personae remain suspended in these elements as they seek proper personal attachments. Although they do not always seem very comfortable, they join pastoral shepherds in retaining "an awareness of their conditions," adopting an ironic attitude through various crises and keeping aware of the tensions preventing swift reconciliation.

In Guest's universe, irony emerges as a natural occurrence rather than as a sophisticated literary viewpoint. Einzig says that Guest attempts "to do justice to the tensions of the world, not to fall captive to its beauty, lyricism, music" (10). Unfortunately, Einzig relies upon false oppositions. In "Parachutes," the "tensions of the world" do not exclude the beauty, lyricism, and music of the natural surroundings so much as they indirectly bring them to light. Pink and blue fish are more "beautiful" because inedible, the coral reef more "exquisite" because fraught with danger. Guest's imperiled swimmer blends easily into the dangerous scene, riskily assuming the beauty and majesty of the other coastal creatures. Aided by abstract imagery, quirky phrasing, and a biological sensibility, an ironic New York School poet depicts natural environments where tensions and inequities reveal, rather than obscure, the intimate connections that exist among diverse communities of living beings.[11]

GUEST'S IRONY never retreats to the easy protection of cynicism. Rather, it is bound up with risk. "[B]eware the risky imagination," Guest chides her reader in "Piazzas" (*CP* 4–5), echoing Coleridge's encomium to Kubla Khan, himself a connoisseur of fantastical scenery. Guest's ironic risks facilitate what Lundquist ("Midwestern") and Keller ("Becoming") call her "journeying sensibility."[12] In "Piazzas," for instance, Guest playfully rewrites

Wordsworth's trip across the Alps. Readers of *The Prelude* will recall that England's most renowned nature poet anticipated a daring crossing through the Simplon Pass but faced an anticlimax when he realized that he and his friend, who have become separated from their hiking party, have already (involuntarily and unwittingly) made the crossing. "Lost as in a cloud, / Halted without a struggle to break through," Wordsworth compensates for his disappointment by focusing on mental creativity—"Imagination!"—the "infinite" source of power more sublime than the mountain range inspiring his risky journey (216). Guest, meanwhile, cheekily reduces Wordsworth's moment of crisis to the distracted journal writing of a modern-day air traveler: "Imagination / thunder in the Alps yet we flew above it / then met a confusion of weather and felt / the alphabet turning over when we landed" (*CP* 5). Although Guest uses exclamation points elsewhere in her poetry, her decision to remove Wordsworth's breathy punctuation, combined with her diminishment of his journey to a single line ("thunder in the Alps yet we flew above it"), reflects her wised-up attitude toward Romantic flights of fancy without resorting to caustic put-downs.

Literary seascapes receive the same treatment. Guest's "archaic" poems "In Dock," "Seeing You Off," and "Dido to Aeneas" contain a dizzying amalgamation of ancient and contemporary cartographies. "In Dock" is a poem in which "Atlantic soundings" heard by New Yorkers "living at an embarkation port" herald a classical Mediterranean landscape filled with Virgilian harbors, Thracians, and Phoenicians, along with a "ghost ship from Athens / plying its shuttered bark / crying Zeus! Zeus! / as it shatters this pier" (*CP* 20–21). "Seeing You Off," a river meditation in the tradition of Schuyler's "Hudson Ferry" (*CP* 21) and Edward Field's "A View of Jersey" (Allen 225–26), is shot through with juxtapositions that outstrip rules of decorum but are truthful enough, in the surrealist fashion. It includes a send-up of Matthew Arnold's "Dover Beach," with Guest on a pier, looking out toward the Hudson, claiming to be "ignorant as those armies" of boats passing by. "Send navies out from Jersey / let there be more edens / of soap and fats," she declares in a comical voice alternately haughty and self-deprecating. Later in the poem, looking out on New Jersey's industrial shoreline, she shares a "kiss in the saloon / far above the cries / from plows and auto parts // as ugly as those waifs of paper / on the pier," mocking Arnold's sentimental discourse on the English Channel. The Mediterranean world recorded by Homer and Saint Augustine also makes an appearance in postmodern New York, replete with "moving vans / olympic as dawn" and trucks whose "Departures make disgust into a cartoon / of rose Nabiscos." Inspired by the Hudson's bizarre display, this contemporary ironist in classicist's clothing suggests a journey to Carthage, there to "float on that wine-dark sea" (*CP* 16–17).

"Dido to Aeneas" is a dramatic monologue rife with indeterminacy. Guest may reenact Dido's fabled lament, but echoes of Shakespeare and mention of an auto garage put the scene centuries ahead of ancient times. Meanwhile, the tropical flora Dido describes (palmettos, hibiscus) and the unhappy separation she suffers across "great reaches of wave and salt" fail to distinguish the classical Mediterranean from modern Florida. A "white urn at the driveway" and "plaster flamingos" on "rioting lawns" indicate that Dido is no stranger to Miami Beach kitsch.[13] As in "Parachutes," Guest's declaration of love, voiced faithfully by Dido, is undercut by ironic juxtapositions in ambiguous coastal environments. Yet in neither poem does Guest forsake the human pathos attracting classical or modern readers. Afflicted with yearning, Dido wisely takes instruction from her surroundings, especially from voluble water sources, which tell her that risk-taking is her only option:

> The fountain at noonday cries,
> 'You are not here' and the sea at its distance
> calls to a single path flanked by hibiscus,
> the sea reminds itself each day
> that it is solitary and the bather gambles
> in its waves as a suicide who says 'tomorrow is
> another' an hour in the wrecker foam. (*CP* 34)

If Guest's imagery looks different from that found in most nature poetry, or if her pathos arrives by a more indirect route than that found in most love poetry, it is because she claims to appreciate the "audacious" challenge of fusing the abstract with the concrete, the mysterious with the knowable (*Forces* 21). Her "plasticity," Du Plessis explains, gives rise to "multiple subject positions and viewing positions," with the poet "speaking from the vectors of a site, and not from one voice or any one identity." She explores new ways of being, "favoring the discovery and creation of landscapes in which one could live an emotionally subtle, visually lush, attentive life" ("Gendered" 197, 202, 203). I agree with Du Plessis, though I often want to substitute "liquidity" for "plasticity" and "seascapes" for "landscapes." Guest has asserted that "the person in a literary creation can be both viewer and insider." I glean from this comment her willingness to immerse personae in fluid environments she witnesses and creates. In such instances, Guest explains, "the person is given a place of habitation within the construction and endowed with a knowledge not only of the force of nature, but the aesthetic purpose behind the writer's decision to create this scene. . . . It is the gathering together of varying instructions by the concealed person that presents us with what we may call a 'reliable' landscape" (*Forces* 36, 41–42). Without risk, there is not only no reward but also nothing resembling the natural world.[14]

Seeking immersion in watery environments, Guest indulges her appetite for adventure, which seems to have been a part of her makeup from the beginning. In 1930, when she was ten, a powerful hurricane hit the Florida coast. The costs associated with risk were apparent to the young girl, since curious onlookers wandering out to the beach were swept away by the rising tide. Several poems refer to this event and other episodes of coastal storminess. In "Hurricane," Guest becomes one of those lost in the breakers, accepting the invitation offered by the storm (with "its white cheek and wet arm, / its eyelash curled / and its wrist angry and at last free") to escape her house (which crumbles violently beneath its force) and other trappings of civilized existence (*CP* 50–51). The danger is real, and yet the allure of putting oneself at the mercy of nature's swirling forces is undeniable.

A similar sense of foreboding imbues "Timor Mortis, Florida," a poem in which borders of blue and white shift violently during an "odd winter" spent on subtropical shores. During a cold snap, "Risked sails" move on a "Gulf whose eye is bluest screen." The calmness of the scene serves as a prelude to disturbance, however, since the "threshing sea," provoked by strong winds, changes color, distributing "silt light as dawn" (*CP* 52–53). Once more, a tempestuous coastal scene filled with displaced objects beckons to a woman enamored of adventure:

> Desire at the stake of palmetto
> Desire the empty marina   tideless
> Sands
>   Oars in the fronds
> through bullrushes
> Sunset the backland washes   gates (53)

The oars are found among palm fronds, not in a boat, implying that they have been strewn by powerful forces. Guest surmises that "desire" is at the root of such transformations. Hoping to escape the dullness of her Florida girlhood, she peers out from "backland washes" to observe the transcendental "gates" accommodating her flight.

In "Saving Tallow" and "Colonial Hours," poems from *The Blue Stairs* (1968), Guest extends the childhood memories sketched in previous works. The first poem describes the resourcefulness required to ride out tropical storms. In lieu of kerosene, the tallow found in candles offers the best available fuel for hurricane victims who want to find their way in the dark. Recalling the "Visible tallow of the hurricane night," Guest manifests the inside-out dynamic shaping her urban pastoral meditations, drawing herself closer to the elements raging outside her window. As it burns and drips, the "thin fair candle" in her room resembles a number of coastal objects, including "a yacht cradling / the room's deep water," a "lone palm tree," and a "lonely diver / covered with sea lice." Possessing a sovereignty admired by creative writers, this "most vertical" taper survives the swirling chaos that surrounds it. Firing the homebound girl's imagination, the candle assimilates natural energy, not unlike the way Wallace Stevens's jar tames the wilderness of Tennessee, though Guest assiduously avoids Stevens's solipsism.[15] Guest's avant-garde aesthetic involves relinquishing authorial control, not only to her wild imagination but also to the wild landscapes influencing that imagination. In "Saving Tallow," she tells the candle that "the room dedicates its curves to you," but she is quick to snuff it out at the end of the poem, having become enchanted by "diving fish" and other varieties of marine life frolicking near the shore. "Take me on your dolphin skin! / I shall be absent soon!" she cries, abandoning herself to the stormy sea (*CP* 71–72).

"Colonial Hours" is set in the same time and place: "The year of the hurricane / (we are speaking) / bay roadway / the drenching / leaves flattened to echo / dry velvet before / hush" (*CP* 68). The movement from drenching wetness to velvety dryness, from loudness to softness, turns a climatologic catastrophe into an aesthetic opportunity. A hibiscus plant, like the one flanking a pathway to the sea in "Dido and Aeneas," announces a subtropical setting, identified here as "Land in wake of Prospero // with splayed tendrils / washed" (69). With the mention of Shakespeare's character, the storm takes on new resonance, as does the poem's title.[16] Since the advent of "postcolonial" criticism, *The Tempest* has been read as an allegory of European imperialism. In addition to tropical storms, America's East Coast weathered wave upon wave of colonists, who came by the boatload, with each group claiming the newfound land as "ours," a dubious designation Guest acknowledges in her title's homophonic pun. She aims for something rather different: a daybook of coastal "hours," a littoral version of the "rural hours" projects composed by Susan Fenimore Cooper and other nineteenth-century naturalists.

Though it contains echoes of "On the Way to Dumbarton Oaks," an early poem that contrasts the "colonial air" of a museum's holdings with the writer's "aborigine sights" (*CP* 12), "Colonial Hours" functions primarily as Guest's *tristes (sub)tropiques*. Looking back on her days in Florida and California, she remembers "Night temples of palms / the rain blows *tropique* / as ceiling fans / you go in your orphan feet / crossing the tiles." Guest was not an orphan, but she was shuttled among relatives whenever financial circumstances dictated. Accordingly, the uprooted persona in "Colonial Hours" whispers to herself in the midst of "remembering the prisons from which you sprang / the machinery of coral walls / your bamboo crest / the stockade that encircles you," as well as the time "you are released / to the jointure of others." The seascape mirrors her predicament, as the coral reef, positioned underwater in "Parachutes," is suddenly transmogrified into imprisoning walls. Overcoming the emotional trauma of childhood becomes Guest's mission many years later, yet there comes a time when accepting the past also seems wise. Lacking the Ivy League pedigree of her New York School cohorts, Guest makes a virtue of necessity, claiming tropical bamboo as her family crest, her special talisman. Equally symbolic is "an amulet that is a beetle / to be fed by palmetto and cane // cherished by the thrice blue seas." Emboldened by her rediscovery of coastal charms and the roar of ocean waves, she stakes out her natural legacy, telling herself, "you shall reconnoiter // As a shell your dynasty" (69–70).

Above all, Guest wants a place to settle, if only in her mind. In her nomenclature, "colonial" settlement takes on a bioregional rather than a political meaning. Colonizing, moving alongside others of the same species in order to survive and prosper, was a practice adopted by wild animals and insects long before humans got into the act. Homing in on her native landscape, the poet takes instruction from birds, seeking to learn "the colonial language / of tern sibilancy" (*CP* 70). Glancing at a map, repeating an activity she had first described in "Geography" (57–58), she pauses in an awestruck manner (represented here by a "blink"), reflecting upon a "Magnified world / my education / my craft // My fruit my oranges" (70). If her gradual shift to smaller frames of reference reverses the process adopted by Stephen Dedalus in Joyce's *Portrait of the Artist as a Young Man*, Guest's movement from abstract to organic realms suggests that she received her first "education" in subtropical environments, quietly honing her "craft" by revisiting these scenes of plenty. Establishing a connection with effulgent warm-weather landscapes makes Guest a unique presence among first-generation New York School poets.[17] With the inclusion of "my oranges," she claims as her possession a crop of images harvested in Florida while differentiating herself from O'Hara, whose collaboration with painter Grace Hartigan on the "pastoral" sequence *Oranges* was famous for avoiding all reference to the fruit.[18]

ALTHOUGH GUEST attends closely to natural facts, her repeated encounters with Florida assume a mythological aspect, not unlike that found in the poetry of H. D. In "Cape Canaveral," for example, the chilly seascape Guest described in "Timor Mortis, Florida" now features an anthropomorphic creature enamored of her supernatural gifts:

> Fixed in my new wig
> the green grass side
>   hanging down
> I impart to my silences
>   operas.
> Climate cannot impair
>   neither the grey clouds nor the black waters
> the change in my hair.
>
> Covered with straw or alabaster
> I'm inured against weather.
> The vixen's glare, the tear on the flesh
> covered continent where the snake
> withers happily and the nude deer
> antler glitters, neither shares
> my rifled ocean growth
>   polar and spare. (*CP* 12–13)

Elsewhere in "Cape Canaveral," Guest refers to "Nose ridges / where the glaciers melt / into my autumnal winter-fed cheek / hiding its shudder in this kelp," strengthening a connection between bodily features and offshore influences (13). Similarly, the sea goddess appearing in "From Eyes Blue and Cold" delivers "a far off coastal lithesomeness / when she awakes / with seaweed in her arms" (33). In "The Return of the Muses," written a bit later, Guest calls out to the sea creatures drawing her attention, named here as "you who had vanished / . . . [with] salt in your mouth / where the sea was whipping itself up in a corner / and foam falling like ash." She privileges liquidity over solidity, allowing herself to become drenched by a rainstorm "sluicing / about in memory, fishing up" images from her past. Shifting the scene from a rainy valley to a "new perspective"—the "fresh horizon line" of the sea—Guest rejects the mantra of "strict discipline, continuous devotion, / receptiveness" taught in writing workshops in favor of the magical evocations supplied by birds and ocean muses, conspiring with these creatures to usher forces of nature headlong into her working space (73–74).

"Sand" celebrates the limitless seascapes where poets "Rejoice / in ancient nothingness" (*CP* 55). Echoes of O'Hara's James Dean elegies emerge in one passage: "Poets walk across you their footprints / cannot shock your softness, on you / shells, pearls, weeds / discards as on a mountain top / is found record of horizon" (54). Like O'Hara, who traced a "leaving word in the sand" at Fire Island to pay tribute to the deceased Hollywood idol, knowing his lines would be washed away (*CP* 231), Guest is poignant in her appraisal of human impermanence. The pliant sand readily accepts her imprint, only to swallow it up moments later. Linguistically mirroring this process, Guest's connective syntax disappears like footprints in a rising tide, yet she is able to locate amid ocean debris a means of amalgamating beauty and death. Various gifts from the sea, including a storm-tossed pearl, reveal the "record of horizon," a Heideggerian euphemism for history. Writers hoping to leave their mark need to realize that the tide of history is filled with transitory images that are only belatedly translated into words. They should therefore tread lightly, with humility and wariness, across any landscape or seascape, the shifting surface ("surf face") of which is always subsuming them into its own text, as though writing their epitaphs.[19]

"Wave," a pendant piece to "Sand," continues to survey the borders separating sea, sky, and land. Adopting the guise of a daredevil swimmer (O'Hara again comes to mind), Guest seems willing to risk everything in order to commune directly with the ocean's treacherous power, boldly announcing, "Wave / whose arm is green / your / half-wayness I, too, would meet you there / in foam." A few lines later, she issues another boast: "we cry deepest and turn not daring to spy / full-face on ocean crest that carries on / on / space now azure fullest where the depth / is danger" (*CP* 55).[20] I can imagine brave but ill-fated onlookers uttering these words during the 1930 hurricane. Then again, these words resemble those uttered on Mediterranean shores in "Dido to Aeneas." As she is apt to do, Guest dots modern seascapes with classical figures. Matching the allure of the open ocean, tempestuous mythological beings overwhelm anyone dreaming of gentler waters:

>   Triton's throng appears
>   where zephyrs
>   cast skyward by the spume glance down

on islands of the deep mermaids
we'll never see   or hear   yet each
wave rolling brings in brightest
phosphorescence their hair
                    a lyre
sweet voice of brine
              other secrets
in the tease and stress of wave song (56)

With its indented and fragmentary lines, "Wave" locates beauty amid "the tease and stress of wave song." The sea's tumult and anger are touted as passionate manifestations of an ecological imagination, to be sought after rather than avoided by stalwart swimmers and adventurous poets alike.

"A HANDBOOK OF SURFING," a long poem from *The Blue Stairs*, represents the high-water mark of Guest's coastal writings. Although it was written in Greece, this poem is a fascinating portrait of California beach culture in the 1960s as well as a secret commentary on the Vietnam War raging on the other side of the Pacific. In this poem about risk, based in part on a real handbook, a surfer becomes an inspirational figure for the writer, much as the daredevil swimmer did in "Wave," with Guest again finding her way in the blue element. According to Hillman, "A Handbook" shows us an "unconscious mind at play in oceanic language" (208). I agree, since the "wave wilderness wily wild" draws the poet together with "surf kindlers in the riddle splash," who like her possess an "ocean plan for a soupy ride" (*CP* 85–86).[21] When Guest confronts the ocean's "eyewash of roar speech saltness" (85), her "wavering" syntax reminds me of Lorine Niedecker's unconventional descriptions of water. Yet "Handbook" is informed just as much by pop culture, its fragmented form mimicking the turnabouts and other hotdogging techniques perfected by California surfers. "I remark your courage / when you decide the form is exactly at its crest of / sequence," the poet gushes (87). To register these quick transitions, Guest fills her left-hand column with various surfing activities—"Paddling out" and "Rolling through"—much as she consigned images associated with risk to a right-hand column in "Safe Flights." Failure is acceptable in this marine environment, she implies, since "'All can transform the ugly wipeout / into a thing of beauty' / can save face even in oceanic pratfall" (89). As she reports, "it's only / a quaint mishap to be thrown by the imagination" (87). Yet even the most daring riders ("writers") will avoid certain scenarios, a fact made clear when Guest says: "'In closeout conditions no one surfs.' / *There is a point beyond which big storm surf is unrideable"* (emphasis in the original). Throughout the poem, the authoritarian tone of the handbook—*"Nobody rides in closeout!"*—is matched by Guest's own sense of urgency, her fear of warmongers targeting the Pacific Rim as their eminent domain (90). There is more to this poem, in other words, than merely the fundamentals of surfing.

Conflating carefree escapades of California youth culture with military maneuvers taking place in Vietnam, Guest recounts "daily decisions both / politic and poetic" (*CP* 86).[22] Her task is made easier by clever word choices. "Changing directions," "closeout," "pullout," "wipeout," "wing position," "hotdogging," and "turning about" were phrases uttered on both sides of the Pacific in 1968. Of course, context meant everything. "Wave strength" might provide a good ride on a surfboard, but it could also mean the advance of guerillas in Indochina. One rider's pursuit of pleasure signals another man's peril. Thus, films like Bruce Brown's *The Endless Summer* (1964) and Francis Ford Coppola's *Apocalypse Now* (1979) celebrate surfing while showing it to be an extension of Ugly Americanism. In Brown's campy "surfari" documentary, young Californians in search of the perfect wave make their way to Africa, lightly mocking native customs while basking in the sunny adulation shown them by various tribal people, who naively yet charmingly make their own "primitive" attempts to scale breakers on their "underutilized" shoreline. In *Apocalypse Now*, the character Lance Johnson, a renowned surfer from San Diego, is urged by a deranged army colonel to surf an imposing break off the Vietnamese coast, even as the North Vietnamese strafe the waves with machine guns and American forces drop napalm on the nearby jungle. The risks of surfing are concomitantly linked with the risks of warfare, with Americans claiming primacy in each category. As Johnson's commanding officer shouts gleefully, "Charlie don't surf!"[23]

In "Handbook," Guest beats Coppola to the punch, emphasizing the nefarious link between boards and bombs, subtly at times, mock-heroically at others. Prophecies of violent aggression abound. Philomela appears at one juncture, straight from Ovidian legend, the memory of her brutal rape by Tereus juxtaposed with the contemporary image of "cuckoo strength bearers as rapists" fulfilling their mission in the Pacific (*CP* 85). Steering her argument in a feminist direction, Guest associates 1960s beach "bunnies" wearing wraparound beachwear or "glossy tunics" with ancient "statues on the hill stanced seaward sunstruck / withered frequently headless only the bosoms / upholding strict maidens courageous" (88). Sadly, these beautiful women, whom "surf horses" (91) and soldiers with "warrior torsos" endeavor desperately to impress, have witnessed in contemporary California what women in ancient Greece once witnessed: fatal macho posturing on the high seas done in the name of honor. Across the ages, women have seen on seacoasts "so many storms and tribal wars so much murder / to remain unburied" (88).

Underscoring classical contexts, Guest depicts California surfers as "oracles . . . en route to wave line-up," awaiting word from the ocean breezes about "flat or uncommon sea surf down or up." In 1968, the year of the Tet Offensive and the My Lai massacre, America's military outlook was less than rosy. By saying "we'll know soon enough when the obituaries are out," Guest provides veiled reference to the body counts reported on network broadcasts, indicating the farsighted sobriety of her poetic enterprise. Looking west from American shores, this coastal soothsayer suggests that she be "called Cassandra in these summer days / when in the soft illness of heat I'm ready / to talk of battles" (*CP* 90). Tapping dire geopolitical trends, she laments that the loopy fun of the Endless Summer has given way to an endless conflict in which young men are sent beyond the blue horizon to wage war. With its "associative, lateral *combinatoire* of surrealism" (Du Plessis, "Gendered" 194), "A Handbook of Surfing" stands as one of America's most fascinating war poems, for it is at once contemporary and classical, lyrical and fragmentary, lusciously decadent and deadly serious, lightly comical and eerily prophetic.

In "Handbook" and other early poems, Guest accedes to what Nathaniel Mackey calls a "coastal way of knowing," defined in his essay on H. D. as a "dissolute knowledge, repetitive, coastal knowledge, undulatory, repeatedly undone and reconstituted." Availing herself of the ocean's "insular drift," H. D. sought a special variety of coastal knowledge that "seeks to seal itself against antinomies of totality and dissolution, eternity and time, through recourse to a prolonged, rapaciously finite moment." With their "tidalectical swing between annunciative ebb and annunciative flow," her Imagist poems exhibit "no desire other than that of maintaining oneself within the limits of this zone for the longest possible time, in free orbit" (Mackey 62–63). Guest's fascination with littoral zones is based on the same dynamic. "Ideally a poem will be both mysterious (incunabula, driftwood of the unconscious), and organic (secular) at the same time," she writes in "A Reason for Poetics" (*Forces* 20). Juxtaposing aleatory poetic form (pictured here as movable type), sea drift, and the free play of the mind, Guest remains faithful to modernist experimentalism while reaching back to natural sources for inspiration. She implies that the "plasticity" for which her avant-garde work is admired "cannot be achieved through language alone, but arrives from tensions placed on the poem's structures" (22). Most prominent among these tensions, though she does not say so specifically in her essay, is the interplay between air and water and the "special language" she uses to represent them, described as "a pull in both directions between the physical reality of the place and the metaphysics of space." She says "this pull will build up a tension within the poem giving a view of the poem from both the interior and the exterior" (20).[24]

In city-based poems, Guest's emphasis on "tension" lets her deconstruct confining architectural spaces. In poems about Florida and California, it reveals a suspension between natural and imaginative forces. One does not need to be an aerialist or a swimmer to acknowledge the suspension felt by those who make their way through air or water, just as one does not need to be an avant-garde poet to realize that suspension of disbelief leads to creative moments. But one must possess a good deal of talent if she hopes to translate feelings of buoyancy into abstractly intelligible verse, which is precisely what Guest does in her early work.

In the 1970s, Guest began to explore the attributes of water in other environments, including lakes, rivers, and sloughs. Her aqueous imagery is not as concentrated, though it figures prominently in *The Countess from Minneapolis* (1976) and *Seeking Air* (1978), which incorporate urban rivers into disjointed prose narratives. In her essay "The Midwestern New York Poet," Lundquist praises *The Countess from Minneapolis* for its "awareness of nature," and rightly so, since Guest herself alludes to "elemental understandings" "corresponding to hemispheric requests of flatness" (*CP* 149). Guest chooses as her protagonist a nineteenth-century European noble, who like the poet feels displaced in the contemporary Midwest (Guest was visiting painter Mary Abbott, who was then teaching at the University of Minnesota). The Countess eventually learns that "separations begin with placement" (145). "Within her limited mathematics she comprehended space" (156), Guest reports, even if her comprehension does not come easily. In the end, she joins a select group of New Yorkers (Washington Irving, William Cullen Bryant, Caroline Kirkland) and Europeans (Karl Bodmer, Madame de Stael, Alexis de Tocqueville) who toured the Midwest during the nineteenth century, reporting how bewildered they were by its open expanse.

True to form, Guest concentrates not merely on the region's flat horizon and big sky, but also on the water that exists there, or once existed. Guest initially approached this topic in "Nebraska," a poem included in her 1973 volume, *Moscow Mansions*, referring to an ancient inland sea believed to have covered the Great Plains (Everhart). Although it seems strange to associate landlocked Nebraska with the sea, several writers (Bryant, in "The Prairies," most effectively) have likened the wavelike undulations and endless vistas of Middle America to oceanic horizons. Guest takes the extra step of imagining today's Great Plains completely underwater, its "Climate succumbing continuously as water gathered / into foam or Nebraska elevated by ships" (*CP* 101). In the mind-bending passage bringing "Nebraska" to a close, Guest portrays Middle America as a sea of joy, altering an equation so that contemporary Nebraska becomes the vehicle and the ancient inland ocean the tenor of a long-standing metaphor:

> Hallucinated as Nebraska the swift blue
> appears formerly hid when approached now it
> chides with a tone the prow striking a grim
> atmosphere appealing and intimate as if a verse
> were to water somewhere and hues emerge
> and distance erased a swan concluding bridge
> the sky with her neck possibly brightening
> the machinery as a leaf arches through its yellow
> syllables so Nebraska's throat (102)

Guest hints that the inland ocean "formerly hid when approached," but that "now it chides." The tides of history no longer recede beyond the feet of contemporary observers but instead flood their minds, mocking all disbelievers, erasing temporal and spatial distances, and ultimately causing the shimmering surface of ocean water to reflect against the vast prairie sky a most glorious mythological image. That image appears rather magically when the "swift blue" of sea and sky is transformed by the "yellow / syllables" of Guest's language into the arching neck of a swan. John Bernard Myers likened Guest's landscapes to surrealist writer Andre Breton's "sense of the marvelous," which for Breton "included besides the magical and the whole rich drama of the unconscious, everything in nature that revealed her strangeness: caves, volcanoes, moths with fabulous markings, fish that lived in the deepest waters, minerals, grotesque beasts and reptiles, weird birds, carnivorous flowers, insects expert in camouflage" (*Poets* 12–13). One can see at the close of "Nebraska" just how marvelous, how strange and yet how utterly organic, are Guest's own landscapes, which take their cue from the liquidity of their surroundings, "as if a verse / were to water somewhere."[25]

In "Nebraska," Guest regards America's vanished inland sea as "a city in our mind we called silence" (*CP* 102). In *The Countess from Minneapo-*

lis, she turns to consider an actual city haunted by the water remaining. Throughout the volume, Guest suggests that the Mississippi causes artists "riven by the river" (154) to commit "spiritual suicide" and call it triumph (147), implicitly commenting on the fatal leap John Berryman took from a Minneapolis bridge in 1972. Getting "high on Mississippi rock water" in a section entitled "Eating Lake Superior Cisco Smoked Fish" (146), Guest's Countess says that "reasonable" rivers in Paris and New York simply do not inspire the kind of "river worship" (147) she has discovered in the "Myth-West" (154). Crossing a footbridge near Minneapolis's Minnehaha Falls, the mercurial Countess resists her own impulse to jump into the drink, claiming that "the unappetizing swell of the muddied water could appeal only to the truly desperate" (148). Yet she remains conscious of the river's melancholy beauty, its dangerous allure, its aesthetic undertow, offering in tribute this nocturne:

> There was a poem with
> A moon in it travelling across the bridge in one
> Of those fragile trains carrying very small loads
> Like moons that one could never locate anywhere else.
> The Mississippi was bright under the bridge like a
> Sun, because the poem called itself the Sun also;
> Two boxcars on the bridge crossing the river. (160)

Calling to mind James Wright's Ohio poems and Allen Ginsberg's "Sunflower Sutra," Guest pays witness to the loneliness of grimy industrial landscapes and still manages to find beauty, solace, and inspiration amid the smoke and rust. The Mississippi River does its part as well. Just as the moon reflects the sun's light, so too does the river reflect the moon's, allowing the water and Guest's language to share a complementary luminosity. Like the boxcars transporting the moon as cargo, this poem's words would be like anonymous vehicles traveling through a modern wasteland if not for the reflective capacity of natural phenomena, which physically and intellectually bring pleasing images to light.

Water views allow portions of *Seeking Air*, an experimental novel Guest wrote in an "apartment in the E. 90s overlooking the East River" (*Seeking* 1), to shimmer with the same type of urban beauty. *The Countess from Minneapolis* has its share of stunning landscapes, but the aqueous imagery in *Seeking Air* seems more poignant given Guest's extended residence in New York City, where most of the novel takes place. In her analysis of *The Countess*, Lundquist associates Guest's avant-garde writing style with the unfamiliar challenges she faced in the Midwest: "Unlike the regional writer, whose first mandate must be 'write what you know' (with its corollary 'write where you know'), Guest as outsider can only write in order to know, and in order to grasp the self as it shifts in relation to unfamiliar place." In *Seeking Air*, I find Guest taking the same approach in her evaluation of New York City. The urban pastoral subgenre depends largely on the process of de-familiarization. Members of the New York School regarded their adopted hometown as beautiful and peaceful because they took the time to notice phenomena that other city dwellers overlooked or took for granted. In *Seeking Air*, familiar haunts in New York are as uncanny as unexplored spots on the Minnesota prairie. The trick involves searching out the city's interstices, which exist in time as well as space. Throughout the novel, Guest refers to these interstitial moments as "intervals," passing on their aesthetic challenge to readers. As we do when viewing Cubist paintings, Fraser surmises, "we must put together a 'meaning' via the subject's angles, materials, functions, and planes; we must read the gaps, the overlapping clues" (172).

As his name implies, the novel's protagonist, Morgan Flew, is a lost soul taking flight from his claustrophobic Upper East Side apartment. Desperately "seeking air," he looks out upon buildings, streets, and the East River as "life's cinema aspect" rolls by (*Seeking* 62). Stereotypically neurotic, and faced with what he calls "another urban scene requiring my 'relating' to," this New Yorker attains solace by slowing down the pace of city life. "Out on the street pushed east and west by the unflagging noise of machinery, I felt a desperate need to observe slow moving objects," he explains. "It was the 'intervals' I wished to celebrate. As anyone knows there are few intervals in New York City. They must be carefully uncovered, their rhythms caught in the moment of surrender" (112).

Throughout the book, Morgan's troubled relationship with a woman named Miriam is countered by his intimate attachment to Dark, an allegorical figure representing his melancholy creativity and his need for pastoral refuge. Discovered by Morgan during a tropical storm at his family's beach house when he was fifteen (94), Dark is constantly sending this nervous New Yorker into a trance, causing him to slow things down, changing his perspective, throwing up "barricades" and "secret directives" that tempt him "to discover here in the city a variation of haven" (48), in the pastoral fashion. Morgan's mission, as he understands Dark's message, is "to make a small countryside within New York City" (42).

Fittingly, the interstitial havens Morgan locates are laden with moisture. In Guest's early poems, rainfall introduces the city to a whole new rhythm, one that is conducive to reflection. Similarly, in *Seeking Air*, Morgan notices that water in all its forms makes the city glisten and pause. "Losing sight of the freighter as it cruises under the bridge and rounds the bend," and subsequently welcoming its reappearance, Morgan comes to appreciate the calm, steady flow of the East River (114).[26] During another interval, he marvels at "how orotund [is] the city voice in the spring rain," noticing as though for the first time miscellaneous objects the precipitation sanctifies, including an "orange firescape penetrating the exposed side of the Synagogue whose stained glass windows had formed prayer wheels all the winter long" (134). The air Morgan seeks is almost always heavy with liquid. Over time, he notices that a humid climate has the pleasing effect of softening the hard lines of urban architecture and muffling the sounds of traffic and machinery. "Cloudy days and fog produce concertos of intervals, like those of John Cage. Snow, as I have pointed out, is perhaps the ne plus ultra. Simply having the noise dimmed creates a false watt as the tires crunch silently through the snow carpeted streets. One may close one's eyes and relish the interval, knowing that sometimes nearly a minute will pass before the scene again becomes blurred with other categories of movement" (113). That the music and poetry of Cage get linked with suspended water droplets suggests that avant-garde writing sometimes takes its cue from natural surroundings, as Lundquist intimates in her study of *The Countess*. I would simply add to Lundquist's thesis the possibility that metropolitan New York—every bit as much as Minnesota, Florida, Nebraska, or California—accommodates Guest's fortuitous encounters with nature, many of them associated in some way, shape, or form with water.

IN "TWILIGHT POLKA DOTS," a poem from *Fair Realism* (1989), Guest offers a cautionary tale for nature writers. Two human figures approach a "curious lake," a body of water that tries "to set a tone of solitude edged with poetry," since "duty suggested it provide a scenic atmosphere / of content, a solicitude for the brooding emotions" (*CP* 237). At first, the lake performs its role quite admirably, offering the couple "a picture appealing both to young and / mature romance," and becoming "the visual choice of two / figures who in the fixity of their shared glance were / admired by the lake." Containing exotic "fish with . . . lithesome bodies," "bugling echoes and silvered laments," this watery environment is indeed rather "marvelous." "The scene supplied them with theatre," Guest says of the couple who wander the shore, so long as they "referred to the lake without speech." But inevitably, "the letter fell." Ostensibly, this "letter" is the kind that comes in an envelope. The man tears it into pieces and throws it into the lake, stippling the water with polka dots, which in turn cause a "superannuated gleam like a browned / autumnal stalk" to pursue (or "stalk") the couple back into the shallows, where they huddle frightened, "like two eels who were caught."

But the tumbling letter also announces the couple's fall out of natural Eden into artificial language. Humans frolic freely in the beauty of the scene until the letter enters the picture, after which point their linguistic separateness becomes exposed, spoiling the landscape they innocently enjoyed but are now fated to describe. Granted, Guest compares the couple to eels, which like the other lacustrine creatures swim a "conscious" body of water without apparent self-consciousness. But her comparison is intentionally misleading, since it is accomplished with the poem's only simile, a bold exception meant to highlight the referential imprecision the lovers must endure. The lake has offered its own warning, having presented the couple "an appeal . . . to meditation and surcease" (*CP* 237–38). Knowing how and when to refrain from meddlesome language so as to let the natural elements speak for themselves is a goal Guest shares with other eco-friendly writers. Of course, as a poet, she must rely on the linguistic medium, constantly tweaking her phrases to make it appear as though water is doing the talking.

I began this chapter by mentioning Guest's exclusion from anthologies and critical studies of the New York School. Unfortunately, one also looks in vain for her name in books on contemporary nature writing. I believe that there should be a space reserved for Guest in books like *Writing on Water* or *Shorewords: A Collection of American Women's Coastal Writings*. Yet nature writers remain as wary of avant-garde writing as avant-garde writers are of nature writing. Clearly, reading the work of Barbara Guest is not the same experience as reading Mary Oliver, for as Hillman notes, "we must push out into the places we don't understand, trying to decide how much to extend ourselves into the silences." For a writer such as Guest, "the landscape is disordered and the observing makes it more so" (209, 214). Lundquist also speaks to this issue, reminding us that in her "alert, casual, tender descriptions of the natural and social worlds," Guest prefers "her own sense of the mystery of things, the way people and objects occupy space, of gorgeous surfaces, and suggestive depths" ("Fifth Point" 20). Admitting Guest into nature anthologies or journals like *Interdisciplinary Studies in Literature of the Environment* would expose her work to a larger audience and benefit the field, merging the natural complexity cherished by eco-critics with the literary experimentalism attracting avant-garde types.

As I hope to have shown, Guest's mysterious accuracy, her attention to surface detail, and her sympathetic approach to the natural world are most apparent when she is "afloat with the telling" (*CP* 432), when she is composing "fictions dressed like water" (188). As Schuyler disclosed in an admiring letter he sent Guest in 1955, reading her poetry is like encountering "an irregularly swelling cascade over which slides a slightly rippling sheet of water" (*Just* 24). In Guest's most provocative writings, natural images and avant-garde language flow together in an aqueous confluence, shaping poetry notable for its daring and its uncompromised beauty.

4

NEW WINDOWS ON NEW YORK
The Figurative Vision of James Schuyler and Jane Freilicher

WRITERS AND ARTISTS associated with the New York School are renowned for their abstract experiments, their edginess, and their brave ambitions. Realistic, intimate, or small-scaled representations of nature are not what most readers or viewers expect of them. We have seen traditional pastoral themes (catalogs of flowers, leisure bordering on languor, an elegiac sense of something lost and retrieved) make effective appearances in the verse of Frank O'Hara, John Ashbery, and Barbara Guest. Still, the turbulent surface of their work confounds most nature lovers. Poet James Schuyler and painter Jane Freilicher deviate slightly from this trend. They were no less experimental than their New York School peers, yet their easygoing approach to representation lent them an accessibility not often associated with the avant-garde. Working separately, but remaining aware of what the other was doing, they abandoned abstraction for a more figurative artistry, intriguingly described by Ashbery, in a review of Freilicher's paintings, as "slightly rumpled realism" (*Reported* 243). Quietly, somewhat magically, Schuyler and Freilicher managed to shed new light (soft and various in hue) on the realities of city living. Viewing their work from a pastoral perspective, I am awed by their ability to make a rural-urban synthesis seem as natural as a flower, as sturdy and shareable as an apartment building.

Schuyler did not publish a major volume of verse until 1969. Although he won the Pulitzer Prize in 1980, he did not give a public reading until 1988, just three years before his death. His earliest public exposure was in Donald Allen's *The New American Poetry* (1960), to which he contributed four poems and a statement on poetics, "Poet and Painter Overture," perhaps the most concise explanation of the aesthetic alliances New York poets forged with visual artists. "In New York the art world is a painter's world," Schuyler says. "Writers and musicians are in the boat, but they don't steer" ("Poet and Painter" 418). Schuyler knew whereof he spoke. Like O'Hara, Ashbery, and Guest, he wrote a substantial body of art criticism (for *Art News* and *Art and Literature*). He also worked at the Museum of Modern Art (MoMA). He was immersed in postwar America's most prominent avant-garde milieu, writing, drinking, carousing, arguing, cohabiting with poets (O'Hara and Ashbery) and painters (Fairfield Porter), loving all that New York City had to offer. Yet something set his work apart.

To me, the interchange Schuyler achieved between his everyday activities in the New York arts community and his writing has always seemed more fluid than that of his peers. With his witty, conversational tone and his eye for colorful detail, Schuyler avoided the ekphrasis favored by Ashbery and Guest, opting instead for offbeat epiphanies of urban wonders. Although he seems to have fully absorbed the aesthetic theories of his time, he wore his learning lightly, rendering marvelous aspects of New York City casually and intimately. To pick up Schuyler's *Collected Poems* is to find oneself gazing distractedly out an apartment window and focusing intently on what one sees (the flip side, I suspect, of an art connoisseur walking though a museum exhibit and falling prey to distraction). Schuyler's subject matter is the daily: he concentrates on everyday events city dwellers experience but often fail to notice.

Like Schuyler, who is known for his "poetry of quirks" (Ward 17), Jane Freilicher combines exquisite attention to urban detail with a decidedly offbeat romanticism, fusing oppositional viewpoints in order to bathe New York City in an uncanny pastoral light, a hazy atmosphere full of color and possibility. In a 1971 review aptly titled "Urban Pastorals," Peter Schjeldahl called Freilicher's paintings "an ambiguous enterprise of painting after nature," arguing that her work is "about New York, but not about the way one sees New York when one is merely looking." For Schjeldahl, the "casual distortions" we see in her cityscapes "owe not to carelessness but, if anything, to an excess of care in a certain direction, [which] curiously enough may profit more than most avant-garde art of the day from the sense of Man Ray's brag that he created not out of necessity but out of desire"; as a figurative artist, Freilicher possesses a "romantic (approved-by-desire) dream of what reality may be" (32, 62). New York's gritty environment never had it so good. Viewing Freilicher's paintings, Schuyler told Ashbery, was "like strolling into the Vale of Sunshine" (*Just* 232). As we shall see, vastly different life experiences did not prevent Schuyler and Freilicher from sharing a luminous vision of the city.

THE SHEER DELIGHTFULNESS of Schuyler's urban pastoral verse belies the difficult circumstances he faced during his life. By many accounts, including his own (see his posthumously published *Diary*), he was a shy, secretive, and insecure man. From the time he entered New York City, an inferiority complex dogged him mercilessly. A graduate of Bethany College in West Virginia, Schuyler did not share the educational pedigrees of O'Hara, Ashbery, and Koch (whom he called "the Harvard wits") or Guest (a Berkeley graduate). Despite his apprenticeship to W. H. Auden in Italy in the 1940s, he did not have the same access to Europe as did Koch and Ashbery. Public recognition of his talents was also a loaded issue. In the 1950s and 1960s, Schuyler complained in personal letters about his lack of publishing opportunities (*Just* 138), and he seethed when O'Hara turned to him and said, "Let's face it, John's the poet," elevating Ashbery's reputation while relegating Schuyler to second place (Lehman 71).

Compounding Schuyler's professional disappointments were the delusions and nervous breakdowns he suffered throughout adulthood. Although his writing proceeded apace, these jarring episodes compromised his moneymaking opportunities. Fortunately, he had friends there to support him. The most loyal was Fairfield Porter, a highly regarded painter. After suffering a major emotional collapse in 1961, Schuyler saw his relationship with O'Hara cool significantly. Porter, by contrast, gave Schuyler the attention he required, offering shelter at his homesteads in Southampton, New York, and Great Spruce Head Island, Maine. "I'll never let you down, Jimmy," Porter said when he picked up Schuyler at the hospital and spirited him off to Maine. Porter held fast to his promise. His Southampton home was like an "enchanted planet," art world denizens have said (Ashbery, *Fairfield* 316), for it was far enough removed from the breakneck pace of Manhattan to seem like a real retreat. Anne Porter, the painter's wife, took to labeling it "Porter's Rest Home for Broken-down New Yorkers" (Spike 107), while Freilicher called it a "crash pad" (Spring 196).[1] It clearly functioned that way for Schuyler, who lived there until 1973. "Jimmy came for a visit and stayed for eleven years," Anne Porter recalled (Spike 120).

Schuyler composed many poems on Long Island and in Maine, his writing time enabled by Porter's hospitality and his love of nature reinforced by the painter's approach to art. Over time, the two became best friends and, according to Porter biographer Justin Spring, secret lovers. In a 1960 letter, O'Hara told Ashbery that the troubled Schuyler seemed much improved since Porter "more or less officially adopted him" (Spring 252). In truth, the aesthetic partnership between Porter and Schuyler was more equitable than O'Hara's admittedly ill-tempered missive would have it. In typical New York School fashion, the painter completed several portraits of the poet (most of which show him reading or lounging) and designed some of his book jackets (including *Hymn to Life*, which depicts the pear tree and forsythia bush visible through Schuyler's bedroom window in Southampton). In turn, Schuyler dedicated several poems to Porter and wrote enthusiastic reviews of his exhibits, admiring his refusal to follow prevailing aesthetic trends when abstract expressionism and pop art held sway.

A 1972 catalog essay by Schjeldahl praised Porter's ability to subdue "the merely intellectual" in favor of the sensual and the personal (Spring 321), and a 1986 retrospective at Boston's Museum of Fine Arts proclaimed him a "realist painter in the age of abstraction" (Ashbery, *Fairfield*). But it was Schuyler who emerged as Porter's earliest champion and most sympathetic explicator. In a 1967 article entitled "Immediacy Is the Message," Schuyler marvels at Porter's ability to "paint air as light," arguing that his figurative art provides us with "an aspect of everyday life, seen neither as a snapshot nor as an exaltation. . . . Their concern is with immediacy. 'Look *now*. It will never be more fascinating'" (*Selected Art* 14, 16–17). In a letter sent to Joe Brainard two years later, Schuyler lauds Porter's avoidance of flashy expressionist brushstroke, preferring his shimmering surface of color. He describes it as "the look of there not being much there, as though there were barely enough paint to get from one edge to the other, a look some might call thin and which seems to me marvelously so" (*Just* 249).

The appreciation cut both ways, for Porter saw a lot that he liked in Schuyler's verse. Although it is routinely overlooked, one of the first critical pieces to recognize O'Hara, Ashbery, Koch, and Schuyler as a school of poets (Guest again goes missing) was authored by Porter in 1961. Entitled "Poets and Painters in Collaboration," Porter's essay explained that, though they formed a school, the four writers "differ more than they resemble each other," especially in their modes of address. O'Hara's rambunctious prophecies are "an outpouring in first person," Porter argues, whereas Koch's ironic verse is "addressed to a second person as though part of a dialogue." Schuyler, by contrast, is "contemplative and compressed; even when he says 'I,' the 'I' is a third person, as though he were invisible in the presence of his object." Rounding out the quartet, Porter explains that Ashbery's "stiff lucidity of words . . . constitute[s] a fourth, an impersonal person" (*Art* 221). Following this flowchart of voices, we see how the temperaments of the New York School poets align, overlap, and eventually diverge. Porter's most interesting juxtaposition pits the invisible (but still personal) third person in Schuyler's poetry against the impersonal fourth person in Ashbery's verse. Porter clarifies his distinction later in the article. "Ashbery's language," he surmises, "is opaque; you cannot see through it any more than you can look through a fresco" (224). Schuyler, on the other hand, "tends toward a deceptively simple Chinese visibility, like transparent windows on a complex view" (223). Though brief, Porter's analysis is incisive. Schuyler does provide readers a great window on New York. Less abstract than Ashbery or Guest, he refuses to obscure the cityscape he frames, beholds, and ultimately cherishes. In this light, it seems significant that a visual artist, not a literary critic, was the first to appreciate Schuyler's objective romanticism, the operative mode of his urban pastoral project.[2]

By focusing on his window poems I do not mean to suggest that Schuyler possessed a magic casement allowing him to eradicate the difficulty, entrapment, and anxiety that are part and parcel of city life. On the contrary, what makes his work so fascinating is the combination of tension and ingenuity lurking beneath its shimmering simplicity. As William Empson famously noted, the pastoral mode involves "the process of putting the complex into the simple" (22). Yet that complexity inevitably makes its reappearance, for nothing that is repressed can be contained for very long. In every pastoral dream, Frederick Garber asserts in his study of Empson, there is a melancholic subtext marking the absence upon which that utopian fantasy is built. The pastoral landscape is an "inner geography" that may align with the writer's wish fulfillment, but it is always undercut by the reality principle of the civilization he can never fully forsake (Garber 440–41). Even Golden Age landscapes contain "faint traces of our former wickedness" (Virgil 55), reminders of the contemporary society framing our backward glances to utopian loci.

Understanding Schuyler's role in pastoral tradition is tricky, not only because so much of his verse is situated in the metropolis, the hot zone of civilization's ills, but also because it was written in a postmodern era when nature was increasingly regarded as a linguistic construction or simulacrum. Nevertheless, this talented poet was able to enjoy solace amid New York's hectic environment, and he did so with little of the backsliding irony O'Hara, Ashbery, and Koch employed in their more abstract experiments. At the same time, Schuyler's work never comes across as precious or overly earnest. Blessed with a savage wit and an eye for the unusual, he managed to balance his love of pastoral themes against the tumultuous subtext of life in the city.

SCHUYLER'S COMBINATORY REGISTRY has proved attractive to literary critics, even as it befuddles them. Helen Vendler calls Schuyler "that unlikely writer in contemporary New York, a pastoral poet," explaining that his work "values leisure, the sexual life, the 'trivial' (as in Herrick), and retirement from the active life" (*Soul* 62–63). Implicit in her argument is a distinction between Schuyler's "wistful and atmospheric" (62) nature poetry and the "full assent to city life" she locates in O'Hara's verse ("Frank"). David Lehman concurs, maintaining that Schuyler, "so attentive to flowers and trees, had the most pastoral and least urban sensibility" in the New York School. Lehman admits that Schuyler "wrote . . . affectingly of New York City" (260) but claims that as a city poet he was no match for O'Hara, purportedly the only member of the School to write about New York with "incessant exuberance" (19). Tom Clark is another who links Schuyler to rural literary traditions, British writings in particular, revealing that Schuyler based his poems named after months ("February," for example) on John Clare's "Shepherd's Calendar," at one time planning a sequence for each month (7).[3] My concern with these analyses derives from the hard distinctions they draw between the country and the city. Losing myself in Schuyler's poetry, I am more interested in his ability to fuse urban and rural atmospheres, despite his recurring personal crises.

It is true that Schuyler's relationship with New York City ran hot and cold. Though he knew nothing of the spotlight that followed O'Hara to his grave, Schuyler often felt trapped in the city and longed to escape it. Because Schuyler shared O'Hara's propensity for "ceaseless self-chronicling" (Lehman 267), readers of his poetry know that the circumstances giving rise to his urban pastoral fusion were not always happy, particularly during the summer months (the city's off-season). Much of his sadness stemmed from separation anxiety, which was based not so much on a separation from people as from the tranquil rural locations they inhabited. While spending the summer of 1954 in Connecticut with Arthur Gold, Schuyler returned briefly to New York and reviled what he saw. "I suppose one has to be out of [the city] a while to feel its size and self-absorption, its peculiar toughness," he told Porter (*Just* 7). A few years later, working at MoMA and feeling abandoned by friends vacationing in the Hamptons, he wrote dispiritedly to Ashbery in France, complaining that "weekends have taken on their summer vacuum" (78). Schuyler's poetry echoes these sentiments. In "Thinness," the melancholy poet recognizes that while friends have gone to upscale country retreats, he has been left behind in the "drawn-outness" of Manhattan, joining "the sick, the slothful, the bemused / [who] make the most of town and its unusual / silent state, no trip hammers, no gas buggies, / no old Indian woman selling wild flowers" (*CP* 20). He claims to "like" the listless summer atmosphere, but New York does not resemble the urban oasis appearing elsewhere in his work.

Schuyler's loneliness abated somewhat in the 1960s, when he lived with the Porters in Southampton and shuttled between the country houses of other New Yorkers. But it reappeared with a vengeance upon his permanent return to Manhattan in the 1970s. Diaries from this period show Schuyler struggling to reacclimate himself to city living as he moved from one run-down apartment to another. At other junctures, though, he seems surprisingly resourceful, especially when he is writing. Subject to impecuniousness, sloppiness, and fits of emotional imbalance, he finds recompense in quickly sketched pastoral solutions, plotting the coordinates of his "inner geography" against a harsher reality with subtle shifts of rural and urban imagery. Consider "Afterward," in which Schuyler recounts his return to New York City after a visit to Kenward Elmslie's house in Calais, Vermont:

> . . . In
> the valley, the snow
> was already gone. Now,
> New York, in a tempest
> of rain, stalled cabs
> and cars, neon re-
> flected on asphalt:
> I like that, too.
> Dreaming of a white
> Vermont, scratched
> by alders and firs. (*CP* 205)

In this slightly surreal take on organic urbanism, Schuyler again claims to "like" the city, sounding more convincing than he did in "Thinness," in part because he adapts himself to New York as readily as snow changes to rain. There is a resemblance here to Barbara Guest's dazzling poems about rain, which cast the city in a favorable light. The stunning beauty of "Afterward" arrives when the reflection of neon lights on wet streets throws forth an image in the poet's mind of a white Vermont valley, its melted snow reconstituted with the unlikely aid of asphalt, stalled taxicabs, and a rich imagination. The dual nature of this "re- / flection," both in Schuyler's mind and on the streets he takes as his object of inquiry, is heightened by the line break separating the related actions of vision, memory, and revision.

Heading in a different direction from Wallace Stevens's "The Snow Man,"
Schuyler's urban idyll manages to make something out of nothing.[4]

The same resourcefulness emerges in "Thursday," a poem in which
Schuyler, left alone again in the city during the summer, ponders the day's
options. The poem begins inauspiciously:

> A summer dawn breaks over the city.
> Breaks? No, it's more as though the night
> —the "dark," we call it—drained
> away into the sewers and left transpicuity.
> You can see: buildings, dogs, people,
> cement, etc. The summer city, where,
> I suppose, someone is happy. Someone.

Yet as the poem continues, the forlorn poet learns how to make do, initially
by detailing the natural abundance other cosmopolitans tend to rush by
and eventually by conceiving of a "fifth season," a way of looking at New
York that is "his secret." The revelation arrives as the poet peers through
the window of a taxi:

> The other bright evening cabbing
> down Fifth Avenue past the park I
> saw all the leaves on all the trees
> and counted them: not one by one, in
> bunches. I forget precisely how many
> there were: quite a few. Oh yes, more
> than you could count. Not me, though.
> I counted them, bunch by bunch.
>
> As I said above, it's summer: not
> my favorite season. I prefer the spring,
> when leaves bud and unfurl, or
> autumn, when the leaves
> color and fall. Or winter, when
> the leaf-bearers stand naked,
> flexing their triceps like bodybuilders
> exhibiting their charms.
>
> Then there is a fifth season,
> called—but that's my secret.

Yes, my secret, and I'm going
To keep it that way. Yes, my secret. (*CP* 311–12)

Schuyler's ability to access "fifth season" heterogeneity in New York provided necessary solace after Porter died, but it was there from the beginning of his career. In "Freely Espousing," his debut's title poem, Schuyler speaks of a "commingling sky" and "marriages of atmosphere," indicating his love of oppositional unions, which rely upon elemental aspects like the weather. Viewing refracted angles of light in the city fog, he tells himself, "You are experiencing a new sensation" (*CP* 3). Other poems from *Freely Espousing* follow suit. "A White City" (13), a Zen-like meditation on long-distance friendship that focuses on city snowfall and apartment steam pipes, anticipates the teasing secrets of "Thursday." Meanwhile, the radically indented "Flashes," with its changeable sky and "puddles / on a tar roof" (23), foreshadows the urban impressionism we see in "Afterward." Likewise, in beautiful seasonal pieces like "February," "April and Its Forsythia," and "Roof Garden," Schuyler would set the terms for his urban pastoral project.

Of these, "February," included in Donald Allen's anthology, is probably the best known. City dwellers accustomed to limited views from apartment windows might marvel at the easy expansiveness Schuyler achieves through his observation of swirling colors:

A chimney, breathing a little smoke.
The sun, I can't see
Making a bit of pink
I can't quite see in the blue.
The pink of five tulips
At five p.m. on the day before March first.
The green of the tulip stems and leaves
Like something I can't remember. (*CP* 4)

Notice that the "marriages of atmosphere" influencing Schuyler's urban pastoral poems are composed of everyday city objects: chimney smoke, tulips on a sill, a winter sunset. At least nine different colors appear in the poem, modifying the viewer's appreciation of urban objects while indirectly tracking the sun's westward course. The appearance of certain colors sends Schuyler back in time and to places far removed from Manhattan. He has said he wanted to write about Italy but reports that "looking out the window I saw that something marvelous was happening to the light, transforming everything. It then occurred to me that this happened more often than not . . . and that it was 'a day like any other'" (*Just* 240). Bathed in Schuyler's colorful palate, New York's daily occurrences seem like little miracles. After extolling "A gray hush / in which the boxy trucks roll up Second Avenue / into the sky," and marveling as the green from his tulips blends with "a green copper steeple / and streaks of cloud beginning to glow," the poet is prompted to exclaim, "I can't get over / how it all works in together." The kicker for city dwellers is his depiction of "a woman who just came to her window / and stands there filling it / jogging her baby in her arms." Suddenly, all window views are interconnected. "She's so far off," Schuyler says of this woman he does not know. She is no doubt busy attending to her own routine across the way, but that does not prevent the poet from surveying all available angles, searching the winter twilight for blurred realities. "Is it the light / that makes the baby pink?" one apartment dweller speculates while watching another (*CP* 5).

Schuyler realized that his conceits were stretches, but he knew they helped him see the city in its best light, literally as well as figuratively. Thus, in "Hudson Ferry," another poem from *Freely Espousing*, a fawning metaphysical compliment from the pen of Shakespeare (Sonnet 130) is recalled, retracted, but eventually offered in loving praise of a New Jersey sunset:

> . . . Like the April weather
> you can't talk about the weather
> it's like saying my lady's damask cheek
>
> look at the smoke blazing over Jersey
> the flats are on fire it's like a flushed cheek
> and nearer a smokestack blows a dense dark blue
> smoke is hot it looks cold trailing like hair
> the bite-me kind springy or flung about
>
> you can't get at a sunset naming colors
> the depth the change the charge deep out of deep
> the flaring upward what it nails on houses
> the smoke swiftly pouring at the stack
> hangs lazy wide and scarce dispersed . . . (*CP* 21)

The harbor in "Hudson Ferry" is an uncanny seascape of dreams, recognizable but sadly unfamiliar to New Yorkers too busy to look. Despite his rhetorical assertions, the poet hedges his bets before settling on an atmospheric mood, a word-picture in which Jersey's industrial shoreline is luminously transformed. A diary entry from 1988 implies that Schuyler carried the lesson of "Hudson Ferry" with him: "The sun coming up turns the fragmentary cloud cover the colors lingerie—ladies' delicate unmentionables—used to be: peach, Nile green. But when the sun goes down, it sets New Jersey on fire and lights up the western flanks of Manhattan's ugliest buildings in beauty" (*Diary* 239). Schuyler emerges as a superb colorist on each occasion, perfecting the painterly sensibility for which New York School poets are celebrated.

In Schuyler's art criticism there are hints of his poetic approach. Going beyond the figurative realm, Schuyler claims to have heard "fifth season" secrets whispered in abstract paintings by Mark Rothko and Joan Mitchell. In a 1958 review, Schuyler praised Rothko's large moody canvases for their "culmination of the inner seasons, just as at times it is not the passage of a swift dawn or a prolonged sunset that is so deeply stirring, but its palpability: the concretion of flux." In a Rothko painting, he noticed, "nature images gave way to the joy of seeing the purely opposed, the purely related, the so-closely and dramatically distinguished" (*Selected Art* 135). Mitchell was another kindred spirit. "I am very much influenced by nature as you define it," Mitchell explained in a 1958 interview. "However, I do not necessarily distinguish it from 'man-made' nature—a city is as strange as a tree." Fittingly, in the 1970s, Mitchell composed a series of color abstracts to accompany three of Schuyler's most atmospheric poems (Nelson 14, 18). Even though Rothko and Mitchell were abstractionists rather than figurative artists like Porter or Freilicher, Schuyler's attraction to their work makes sense, since figurative artists themselves work somewhere between the poles of abstraction and realism. Theirs is an objective romanticism, "neither snapshot nor exaltation" (to cite Schuyler's praise of Porter's paintings), in which physical reality is heightened by imagination though never obscured by it. By the same measure, abstract artists have relied upon realistic natural phenomena to quicken their aesthetic vision (Jackson Pollock was inspired by the Atlantic Ocean, David Smith by the woods around Bolton Landing, and so forth). Schuyler prized such aesthetic "commingling." Frequently in his poems, an unexpected abstraction, of the kind Rothko or Mitchell employed, comes to complicate his view of a natural scene, until he realizes that abstraction is just another part of nature.[5]

AMONG THE PAINTERS routinely grouped alongside New York School poets, few have understood the interchange between abstraction and figuration better than Jane Freilicher. Born in Brooklyn, Freilicher studied with Hans

Hofmann, who used abstract expressionist techniques in his art but let his students follow their own path, so long as they put in serious studio time. "Hofmann's genius had everything to do with pushing artists to go into the studio and find, there, the world outside," Jed Perl says (9). Hofmann's tough-minded dialecticism, particularly his emphasis on push and pull, resonated clearly with Freilicher, even though she has opted for a softer line and lighter palate. Her work thrives on a heightened tension between representational and natural modes, tending toward playful juxtapositions of framed realities, which the artist puts into conversation with each other. Her 1954 portrait of Ashbery provides one example. Although the apartment wall behind the poet looks like it contains two windows opening out to a view of the city, what we really see are two of Freilicher's cityscape paintings. Transparency and opacity thus trade places, the lack of cohesion becoming more palpable, a *New York Times* reviewer noted, when one discovers Ashbery's "Foujita gaze following one about the room" (Lehman 180). In other paintings, Freilicher added a mirror to her mix of window frame, canvas, and vista. The inherent confusion implies that desired views, reflected views, and created views are all of one piece at some psychological level.

Freilicher had her debut at Tibor de Nagy in 1952, the year the gallery published O'Hara's first book. By this point she was already quite popular in the New York literary scene. Shy but witty, she was, in John Bernard Myers's estimation, "a sybil who seemed to draw poets around her" ("Frank" 34). She let the keyless Ashbery into Koch's apartment when he arrived in New York and corresponded with him regularly during his sojourn in Paris. She went to Ann Arbor to paint O'Hara's portrait prior to his arrival in Manhattan and remained his muse for several years. In poems such as "Chez Jane" and "Interior (with Jane)," O'Hara celebrated an artist who transformed her cluttered East Village apartment into a magical realm of possibility. Emanating from her paintbrushes, O'Hara breathlessly remarked (in what amounts to a pretty good definition of figurative art), was "the eagerness of objects to / Be what we are afraid to do" (*CP* 55).[6] Schuyler was just as smitten. He met Freilicher the year of her gallery debut and wrote a play about her (*Presenting Jane*) shortly thereafter. According to Koch, whose aesthetic criteria were known to be stringent, Schuyler "passed one test for being a poet of the New York School by almost instantly going crazy for Jane Freilicher and all her works" ("James" 21). Only Porter expressed reservations. "I also like Jane's wit," he divulged in an undated letter to Schuyler, "but I don't feel the necessity of flipping every time she opens her mouth" (*Material* 217).

Throughout her career, Freilicher's affinity for New York City has been tempered by her love of greenery and open landscape, and vice versa. After visiting the Porters in Southampton in the mid-1950s, she and her second husband, Joe Hazan, decided to buy a home in nearby Water Mill (Doty, "Interview" 49). Since then she has split her time between Long Island and Fifth Avenue, drawing inspiration from both spots. Interviewed by CNN reporter Elsa Klensch at her Water Mill studio, Freilicher described what it is like to shuttle back and forth between the country and the city. Surrounded by her floral paintings and a beautiful view of Long Island's green meadows and tidal inlets, she offered a confession worthy of any urban pastoralist: "I'm out here for four months straight. By the end of September I don't want to see green!" New York, by contrast, provides her a "cooler urban light, a whole other tonality and excitement—a different arc. I think New York is more beautiful than the country," she told Klensch, her voice trailing off with choked emotion, "the sky and the buildings—sheer poetry."

Like Schuyler, though, Freilicher has been known to reverse direction, describing traces of the city visible in the countryside. In her 1981 painting, *The Changing Scene*, she stands with paintbrushes in hand near the window of her Water Mill house. Looming outside are a bulldozer and the heaped-up soil of a construction site. The message is clear: developers have invaded her pastoral retreat. In a characteristic teaser, the pushed-out window frame in her Water Mill home resembles an easel, so that it is unclear whether we are viewing a real scene or an already painted scene. In *Landscape with Construction Site* (2001), Freilicher revisits the topic of Hamptons' development. Viewing this painting led Ashbery to remark that "Nature is both pretty and ugly, and happens to include backhoes as well as jacaranda trees" ("Works" 9). Just so, Freilicher's paintings suggest that an urban pastoral synthesis is more environmentally friendly in New York City than in the Hamptons, where multimillionaires have taken to "improving" the land with large-scale earthmoving projects.[7]

As her primary means of negotiating rural/urban dialectics, Freilicher began placing flowers in front of her studio windows, which in lower Manhattan give way to a dense, low-rise cityscape. The result was a panorama of natural and man-made images. Ashbery called *Early New York Evening* (1954), an early window painting of hers, "one of the most magical artworks I know" (*Reported* 243). It is easy to see why. Windowsill and rooftops exist in a precarious horizontal balance, their parallelism thrown slightly askew by the painter's inconsistent obedience to rules of depth perception.[8] Meanwhile, the vertical elements—a green vase filled with irises, a few rooftop chimneys, and a distant set of smokestacks—force the viewer to scan what is near, far, and for one brief moment, connected. We notice, for instance, that the smoke from the stacks is nearly as purple as the irises, and that a snatch of hazy sky appearing among the fumes throws their color into relief, just as the yellow stamen breaks up the purple petals of the flowers. The purple smoke drifts to the left, in the direction the irises themselves might have swayed if they were on the other side of the glass pane. But they are not. They remain in the artist's studio as one more tool she uses to create a beautiful picture.

As Freilicher told Robert Doty, "I like to play still life or architectural elements of the studio against the landscape, maybe as a way of asserting control—maybe also to indicate another subjective level, the simultaneous experience of an interior and outside world, closure and openness" ("Interview" 51–52). In *Early New York Evening* and similar paintings (*12th Street and Beyond*; *Red Velvet Marigolds*; *February*; *When It Snowed in April*; *At Night*; and *Summer Flowers, Urban Dusk*, to name just a few), a window view allows us to appreciate urban beauty even as it separates us from that beauty. An inner/outer tension emerges, as it does in Guest's architectural poems. Freilicher's competition between interior and exterior views ends up "creating a sweetly wry but also intensifying plenitude of 'favorite things,'" Schjeldahl astutely remarks ("Urban Pastorals" 60).[9]

Freilicher's technique of grafting an organic foreground onto an urban background is not unprecedented in American art. In *Pastoral Cities*, James Machor lists several eighteenth-century painters who "placed in the background of their work a panoramic view of the city done in soft shades. In the foreground, framing the canvas in richer, darker tones, was a bucolic scene of grazing cattle, stacks of hay, tall trees and open fields." The illusion, Machor explains, was of "the city nestling in the natural setting as though growing from it" (88). During the early years of the republic, such pictures were used to draw people to New York, Philadelphia, or Baltimore, where ostensibly they could enjoy an urban pastoral balance. Freilicher's paintings have no obvious ideological purpose, though they too soften the edges of urban architecture, making the city seem like a more peaceful place. The major difference is that her flora are cut flowers placed in a vase perched on a windowsill, not rooted plants in semirural city outskirts. By the 1950s, she would have had to go far beyond city limits to find open fields, cattle, and hay, yet her work displays the creative resourcefulness I associate with Machor's version of urban pastoral.[10]

SOME MIGHT find Freilicher's work too pretty, too exquisite. This seems to have been O'Hara's judgment, for he began to withdraw from her in the mid-1950s, fearing her marriage to Hazan had made her too bourgeois in her painting and her lifestyle (Gooch 253; LeSueur 128). Schuyler had no such reservations, even as he watched Hazan "raise the roof" to give Freilicher studio space in their posh Fifth Avenue penthouse (*Just* 19, 78). He was completely won over by her decision to paint the everyday miracles she glimpsed. In a 1961 *Art News* review, Schuyler claimed that "Jane Freilicher has abandoned motif and taken beauty for subject matter, a brave and winning choice; and a rare one in New York" (*Selected Art* 26). He liked that she did not follow the crowd or make a big deal of exhibiting her work. Her "courage to experiment," he noted in a 1966 *Art and Literature* feature, "had the effect of making a good part of the gallery-going public wary. A Jane Freilicher show signally lacked that authoritarian look, public-spirited and public-addressed, stamped on so much post-war work like a purple 'OK to eat' on a rump of beef. The big cold dramatic gesture may be welcome, but can't tell us much about the distinctions and nuances that most delight and sharpen apprehension. The reward of not painting shows was learning to paint her own solutions" (30).

Freilicher's admirers have often highlighted the suggestive quality of her work. In "Jane Freilicher Paints a Picture," a 1956 installment of the popular *Art News* feature showing artists at work in their studios, the artist let Porter in on her secret: "When a painting suggests, it seems to be thought to have greater virtue than when it states clearly. Why can't you be just as suggestive when you present fully—for often the more you see, the more you can imagine" (47). A painter need not feel bound to nature, she implies, nor should she feel the need to escape it.[11] Speaking at the Fischbach Gallery in 1995, Ashbery used similar language, noting Freilicher's "determination to impose her own revisionist light on what was after all a mere suggestion in nature." Her figurative approach to painting, he said, is a "kind of advanced realism, which hasn't congealed on the canvas but is still alive and thrashing, almost but not quite pinned down" ("Introduction"). On another occasion, Ashbery noted that she did not try to generalize or "correct" nature, that she merely let things be, with the understanding that no image was better than any other (*Reported* 242, 244).

Similarly, Schuyler recognized that Freilicher shared with postimpressionists such as Bonnard an "affective alertness . . . to the witty subjects constantly presented to the eye, along with the means to make something of them." Above all it was her "inconsistency," the quirkiness that distinguishes a figurative painter from a strictly realist painter, that allowed her

to "create exactly New York as it is" (*Selected Art* 29). I cannot help but notice that Schuyler's curiously positioned adverb, "exactly," foregrounds the
artist's act of creation rather than the city she takes as her subject matter.
As Freilicher herself says in her *Art News* interview with Porter, "a realist
painter doesn't copy forms from nature anymore than an abstract painter"
("Jane" 49). Every artist takes an active role in shaping her environment,
which is always less exact than her perception of it.[12]

Like O'Hara, Schuyler saw his passionate response to Freilicher's art
make its way into his poetry. With its harried-sounding title, "Looking Forward to See Jane Real Soon" betrays the excitement of a New York School
writer discovering a kindred spirit. In this poem, Schuyler re-creates the
colorful communion the painter enjoyed as she gazed out a studio window
framed with fresh flowers. In Freilicher's version of urban pastoral, he suggests, a fresh beauty, properly nurtured, lasts throughout the city year:

> May drew in its breath and smelled June's roses
> when Jane put roses on the sill. The sky,
> in blue for elms, planted its lightest kiss,
> the kind called a butterfly, on bricks fresh
> from their kiln as the roses from their bush.
> Summer went by in green, then two new leaves
> stood on the avocado stem. The sky
> darkened the color of Jane's eyes and snow
> wrote her name in white. Such wet snow, that stuck
> to the underside of curled iron and stone.
> Jane, among fresh lilacs in her room, watched
> December, in brown with furs, turn on lights
> until the city trembled like a tree
> in which wind moves. And it was all for her. (*CP* 73)

Thoroughly inspired by his friend's window paintings, Schuyler continued the sensation gathering he began in *Freely Espousing*. With swirling
phrasing reminiscent of Freilicher's figurative distortions, his poem "An
East Window on Elizabeth Street," from *The Crystal Lithium* (1972), portrays a city teeming with life and littered with detritus:

> Among the silvery, the dulled sparkling mica lights of tar roofs
> lie rhizomes of wet under an iris
> from a bargain nursery sky: a feeble blue with skim milk
>   blotched

on the falls. Junky buildings, aligned by a child
("That's very good, dear") are dental:
carious, and the color of weak gums ("Rinse and spit"
and blood stained sputum and big gritty bits
are swirled away). (*CP* 84)

Notwithstanding O'Hara's periodic antipastoral boasts, Schuyler knew
how crucial it was to appreciate greenery in New York, where city planners
relegate nature to parks, parkways, and squares (Page 48). To do so, he adopted an unusual perspective. At the end of "An East Window on Elizabeth
Street," he takes flight from New York's "junky" streets, assuming the viewpoint of a bird looking down on a polluted but still beautiful city,

burgeoning with stacks, pipes, ventilators, tensile antennae—
that bristling gray bit is a part of a bridge,
that mesh hangar on a roof is to play games under.
But why should a metal ladder climb, straight
and sky aspiring, five rungs above a stairway hood
up into nothing? Out there
a bird is building a nest out of torn up letters
and the red cellophane off cigarette and gum packs.
The furthest off people are tiny as fine seed
But not at all bug like. A pinprick of blue
Plainly is a child running. (*CP* 85)

This high-flyer is not like Keats's nightingale or Shelley's skylark, nor is the
scene it surveys traditionally romantic or pastoral in its makeup. Even so,
this resourceful bird, making do with found objects, promotes a unique
way of sorting through and unifying city images. In its own fashion, this
bird stands as a figure for the urban pastoral poet.[13]

Beholding New York from his apartment windows, Schuyler discovered
that strange transformations could, and often did, take place. In "Blue,"
a white coffee cup falls upward and splits into two clouds that rest on a "blue
pressed / tin ceiling sky" (*CP* 81). The lack of gravity Schuyler depicts here
recalls O'Hara's "Sleeping on the Wing" and Guest's "Parachutes," even as
it heralds the weightlessness made popular by Jim Carroll and other members of the Warhol underground. Like Ashbery and Guest, Schuyler liked
to mix landscapes. In "Pastime," a traffic cop directing stalled cars becomes
a cowboy, "herding the big machines / like cattle" (257). In "Buildings,"
concrete corridors morph into coral reefs. Taking nature where she can get

it, a solipsistic female figure not unlike the one in Stevens's "Idea of Order at Key West" emerges in this poem, "striding the ragged grass / her fixed stare devouring the restless river / striding on the far side of the parkway / all those cars / all those millions of windows" (87). Schuyler admits earlier in "Buildings" that his surreal distortions of the city are attributable to "morning light on dirty windows," so it makes perfect sense that his female persona pays homage to the millions of windows in New York, each one of them a realm of imaginative possibilities. A similar motif appears in "A Sun Cab." On a sunny day, as a yellow cab "goes by below / reflected across the street / in a window / four stories up," the poet peers down from his own apartment, taking in all the reflections and reverberations at play in the busy city. Noises peel and fade, sunspots and shadows find their mottled balance, and the sharp angles of the city round off into something more delightful, described mysteriously by Schuyler as "a fluent presence" (90–91).

The most magical window of all was located in Room 625 of the Chelsea Hotel, where Schuyler spent the last twelve years of his life. According to Eileen Myles, who helped take care of the ailing poet during this period, 625 was a "messy, beautiful room" (260).[14] French doors led out to a balcony bordered by a wrought iron balustrade. The soft northern light that filtered through these doors allowed Schuyler to do his reading, as depicted in the luminescent Darragh Park painting gracing *Collected Poems*.[15] Although he initially dismissed the balustrade as "the Victorian fancy of chrysanthemums crudely reduced to iron" (*Diary* 175), Schuyler came to admire its union of pastoral beauty and urban craftsmanship. He wrote three poems about the balustrade, each of which strikes a note of reconciliation, as the hotel-bound poet, like the bird in "An East Window on Elizabeth Street," makes peace with his rundown surroundings, building a nest with accessible materials.

In "The Morning," the first of the balustrade poems, Schuyler's enjambed lines are as restless and cramped as the walks he took on the Chelsea's tiny balcony. An ordinary city day

breaks in splendor on
the window glass of
the French doors to
the shallow balcony
of my room with a
cast-iron balustrade
in a design of flowers,
mechanical and coarse

and painted black . . .
 . . . I
almost accept the fact
that I am not in
the country, where I
long to be, but in
this place of glass
and stone . . . (*CP* 320)

The ailing poet remains confined in a city apartment, and yet he is "almost" content. A poem entitled "Beaded Balustrade" surveys the same location, with even better results:

The balustrade along my balcony
is wrought iron in shapes of
flowers: chrysanthemums, perhaps,
whorly blooms and leaves and
along the top a row of what look
like croquet hoops topped by a
rod, and from the hoops depend
water drops, crystal, quivering.
Why, it must be raining, in Chelsea,
NYC! (323)

Schuyler secretly acknowledges William Carlos Williams, the modernist poet who in his own enigmatic pastoral piece told us that "so much depends / upon / a red wheel / barrow / glazed with rain / water" (56). Outside the Chelsea Hotel, raindrops "depend" on a wrought iron chrysanthemum, apparently reversing the process by which living plants rely on water, until we take into account the alternate definition of "depend," which is to hang suspended, as these raindrops surely do.[16] In either case, the rain prompts Schuyler to daydream of time spent in Southampton, even as he realizes those days are long gone. By poem's end he finds solace right in front of him: "Oh well, if / I haven't got that, at least I've / got a beaded balustrade." The poet's compensatory leave-taking suggests that if the rain depends upon the urban variety of floral beauty, he should too.

Schuyler's reward for cultivating urban pastoral reversals arrives in "Three Gardens," for he notices that the dianthus flower and herbs in his balcony window box have intertwined, and that a morning glory has wrapped itself around the wrought iron railing:

Drawn by the sun,
woven by the wind, they
intermingle: the herbs flower
unexpectedly with rose-red lights.
Behind,
up in the 1880s iron balustrade, twine
a few implacable thin tendrils
of morning glory. (*CP* 397)

In Freilicher's most affecting window paintings (like *Harmonic Conver-gence*), distant city lights appear as delicate dots, effectively approximating the flower petals in the studio foreground and ultimately competing for the viewer's attention. Schuyler achieves a similar effect in "Three Gardens." It is unclear whether the "rose-red lights" he mentions belong to the dian-thus on his balcony or to automobile taillights flashing six stories below on Twenty-third Street. No matter. The fact that the morning glory has wound itself around his floral balustrade implies that the organic and the inorganic were bound to meet anyway. With both beauties now entangled, the urban pastoral vision is complete, and the glory of this city morning is his (and ours) to relish.

IN 1988, Schuyler gave a long-awaited public reading at the Dia Art Foun-dation. Ashbery introduced him, remarking that in forty years of writing poetry Schuyler had "managed to draw on the whole arsenal of modern-ism, from the minimalism of Dr. Williams to the gorgeous aberrations of Wallace Stevens to the French surrealists and still write what Marianne Moore calls 'plain American which cats and dogs can read.'" Like Elizabeth Bishop, Ashbery went on to say, Schuyler was on "such intimate terms with [nature] that he can afford to give it a slap on the wrist when it tends to run on, as it so often does" (*Selected Prose* 209). I find it interesting that Ashbery uses similar language to praise Freilicher's art, discovering in her canvases "a democratic urge to avoid the solemnity of 'privileged moments' in favor of a feeling for how nature and objects just keep plugging along" (278–79). For all devotees of the New York School, the pairing of Schuy-ler and Freilicher makes perfect sense. Their figurative works recognize normal geographical and natural categorizations, but they are not above messing around with them in order to reach higher ground. Whenever the country or the city edges toward excess, the creative artist intervenes, admonishing all of us for our expectations and providing a little something from the other locale as a form of restraint or countermeasure. Describing her affinity for Schuyler's poetry, Freilicher told me she liked his "concatenation of natural images," which like a Schubert piano composition starts off in one direction and arrives unexpectedly at another place.

The response Schuyler received at the Dia reading was overwhelmingly positive, causing the normally reticent poet to write in his diary that he was a "sensation" (*Diary* 242). At the end of the reading, Joe Brainard turned to Ann Lauterbach and said, "Don't you want to rush home and write Jimmy Schuyler poems? He makes it seem so easy" (Lauterbach, "Fifth" 70). The catch, both knew, was that Schuyler's urban idylls, for all their simplicity of tone, were not at all easy to write. John Yau once called Freilicher "a virtuoso who never showed off" (45). The same could be said of Schuyler. We should hail both for introducing the city to its long-lost relative, its country cousin, and for doing so in a manner that is surprisingly natural and breathtakingly beautiful.

5 FUN CITY
Kenneth Koch among Schoolchildren

IN 1973, a child from the inner city wandered into my rural community to demonstrate the powers of imagination. I was only nine years old and he appeared to be even younger. He was alone, kicking cans in a trash-strewn lot before venturing out onto a busy street, the shadows of tall buildings obscuring his movements, until at last he hit an open stretch of pavement and faced the glare of sun-bleached sidewalks. Harried passersby paid him little notice, but a voice told of his predicament: "To a child who can't read, the world is a closed book" ("Shadows"). For a long time the boy seemed forlorn and downcast, anonymous amid teeming crowds, but then he spotted a Bookmobile across the street. Curious, he decided to pop in and browse the selections, eventually choosing *I Am Somebody*, a book whose title echoed the self-empowerment messages Jesse Jackson and other activists were disseminating to urban youth during this era. Book in hand, the boy ran down to the banks of the East River. Before he disappeared, I saw him with his new prize open on his knees. He was smiling and mouthing its words in an open air library, his back propped up against a pier stanchion. A few feet behind him, a murky waterway rippled and glistened in the sunshine.

Actually, millions welcomed this child into their homes. He was the subject of a successful television advertising campaign for Reading Is Fundamental (RIF), an educational outreach initiative based in Washington, D.C. Like the vacant lots and polluted waterways he encountered, this boy's prospects suffered from societal ignorance and condescension, a trend reinforced by Daniel Patrick Moynihan, who recommended a governmental policy of "benign neglect." RIF redressed cultural imbalances by giving underprivileged city children free books ("for keeps," their commercial promised), thereby providing a boost to Great Society programs like Head Start. When RIF organized in the mid-1960s, mainstream media were becoming interested in exposing the harsh plight of inner-city kids. Memoirs by Claude Brown and Malcolm X detailed the challenges their protagonists endured in New York and Boston. Songs by James Brown, Curtis Mayfield, the Spinners, and even Elvis Presley (aided by the equally unlikely Mac Davis) examined the harsh conditions ghetto children suffered on a daily basis. *Sesame Street*, the juggernaut launched in 1969 by Children's Television Workshop, shifted attention to the untapped intellect of urban preschoolers.[1] Three decades before "No Child Left Behind," children residing in decaying cities were challenged by an intrepid corps of progressive educators to pursue their interests and talents. Although I was young, one geographical irony hit me hard. When they were encouraged to express themselves, I noticed, city kids found in their gritty environment a pastoral peacefulness missing from my rustic perch in western New York. At the very least, they displayed a greater capacity for creating beauty playfully, spontaneously, pragmatically.

I realize that to write glowingly about the artistic aptitude of underprivileged children is to risk sentimentality and exploitation. Phillip Lopate, a key player in the progressive arts programs making inroads in New York City schools in the 1960s and 1970s, was among the first on the scene to indict the self-serving motives of liberal educators. He lambasted elite society's "ghetto sensationalism" and the bad faith of grandstanding teachers ("Issues" 113). Although he published a reminiscence of teaching in public schools (*Being with Children*), Lopate reviled stories that "corresponded to a momentary hunger on the part of people, mostly white people, to hear deprived schoolchildren expressing—deprivation. Drugs, roaches, and muggings—what had seemed at first like a breakthrough in honesty, became in time a mannerism: was this all there was in these children's minds, or was it what we are asking of them?" (112). He also castigated lenient teachers whose reliance on "metaphorical thinking and sensory sensitivity and affective expression and so on" led them to believe every child was a natural poet. The unintended result, Lopate said, was a "nauseating sort of professional flattery," and ultimately the manipulation of innocent children ("Conclusion" 332).[2]

Anyone who recoils at self-congratulatory narratives of middle-class instructors charging into city classrooms with the intention of rescuing recalcitrant students from lives of ignorance and misery (consider Hollywood schlock like *Dangerous Minds* or *Freedom Writers*) likely shares Lopate's concerns. It makes no sense, however, to impugn a few misguided messengers of educational reform if in the process we diminish the achievements of the kids they teach. This is especially true if children demonstrate their ability to move beyond messages of empowerment that have become shopworn injunctions and intellectual dead ends; if instead of ingratiatingly attempting to "keep it real" or "represent," they defy patronizing expectations, making their work surreal and misrepresentative, as avant-garde writers do.

In this chapter, I maintain that notebook poems written four decades ago by students attending a Lower East Side elementary school are worthy of sustained critical attention, insofar as they take inspiration from, and in some cases rival, the innovative poems published by that era's avant-garde elite. Their creative writing teacher was Kenneth Koch, a charter member of the New York School known for his comic sensibilities. With his high profile, Koch ended up stealing the limelight from other poets visiting public schools, but that should not blind us to the fine writing he elicited from kids at PS 61, a generous selection of which made its way into the education books he published. Edgy and honest, yet also whimsical and full of fun, this student poetry proves especially attractive to devotees of urban pastoral, an aesthetic mode cataloging the diverse landscapes to which metropolitan nature lovers direct their attention. In the resourceful minds of children, the Lower East Side takes on a magical cast, particularly as the arbitrary categorizations organizing adult society (rich/poor, smart/dumb, organic/inorganic, bright/shadowy, real/fantastical, country/city) drop away.

Some will say that I am bringing the high culture of Koch and his peers down to the level of elementary school students, or alternatively that I am elevating the latter's notebook jottings to intellectual heights they would never have achieved otherwise. We should acknowledge, though, that New York School poets cherished the variety of metropolitan life, and that they had little problem accommodating the observations of everyday New Yorkers. We should realize too that postmodern poetry's topsy-turvy nature, however bizarre it may appear to the uninitiated, had its corollaries in the socioeconomic realm these children inhabited. Looking back at this era, I am struck by the carnivalesque aspects of New York City culture that exist alongside troublesome images of squalor and decay. *Herald Tribune* columnist Dick Schaap captured the spirit of the age when he coined the moniker "Fun City," in part to describe Mayor John Lindsay's enthusiastic display of civic pride, which included sponsorship of a "Be-in" in Central Park.

During its heyday, Fun City was less a physical place than a social happening, a continuously unfolding event ripe with possibility. Candy-colored images persist whenever we think of pop art, Jackie O, or the Miracle Mets. Contemporaneously, the city was sliding into economic despair and social unrest, trends announced when teachers and garbage workers went on strike, and when the Oscar-winning film *Midnight Cowboy* put the sleaziness of Times Square on the big screen for all to see. The desperate situation came to a head in the 1970s when Gerald Ford refused to save New York from bankruptcy, or told it to drop dead, depending upon which headline you read. A decade after Fun City had its coming out party, aerial shots of Yankee Stadium, broadcast nationwide during World Series games, showed the South Bronx on fire, its crumbling tenements sacrificed by greedy slumlords seeking insurance payoffs.[3] As usual, children stood to suffer most from ongoing crises. But as kids playing stickball in adjacent streets could have attested, in lean times you make your own fun. Out of the rubble of demolished apartment buildings you build stadiums of epic proportions. Out of trash-strewn alleys and fouled waterways you create pastoral gardens fit for frolic. To young New Yorkers staking a claim for innocence in the midst of troubling experiences, Fun City was never a policy initiative. It was a state of mind.

Like his New York School cohorts, Koch was adept at finding fun and beauty in unlikely places. Among schoolchildren, however, he recognized as never before the city dweller's need for pastoral solace. "It is possible to live without ever having seen mountains / Or the ocean, but it is not possible to live without having seen some / Beauty," Koch opined in a poem written shortly after his elementary school teaching stint (*CP* 275). Even if you were only ten years old and confined to your block, he realized, your creativity was unlimited, since "a rock / Picked up in the street contains all the shape and hardness of the world. / One sidewalk leads everywhere" (331). A world-in-a-grain-of-sand romanticism infuses such passages, as it does in city poetry by Blake, Wordsworth, and Whitman. Koch introduced PS 61 students to the work of these writers and to his own. The benefits cut both ways, prompting students to envision themselves within a community of writers and Koch to revisit childhood for more immediate renderings of life. Judging by his books on teaching poetry to children—*Wishes, Lies, and Dreams* (1970), *Rose, Where Did You Get That Red?* (1973), and *Sleeping on the Wing* (1981)—this highly regarded poet may have learned as much from his time at PS 61 as did the pupils he served.

IT SEEMS APPROPRIATE that kids in Fun City affected Koch so powerfully, for among the members of the New York School he did the most to cultivate playfulness in his work (and that is saying something!). Nicknamed

"Doctor Fun" by John Ashbery at Harvard, Koch lived up to his billing, whether that meant donning a gorilla mask to surprise passengers on the Third Avenue El (which ran outside Koch's apartment) or writing parodies of modernist masters such as Williams, Frost, and Lawrence.[4] In short order, Frank O'Hara noticed, "excitement-prone Kenneth Koch" became "the backbone of a tremendous poetry nervous system" (*CP* 331). Like his friends, Koch brooked little pretension in his work. The studied seriousness characterizing the high modernist mode of T. S. Eliot was anathema to his comic vision. "So many poets have the courage to look into the abyss," Koch explained in an appreciation of Saint-John Perse, a French poet who balked at convention, "but Perse had the courage to look into happiness" (Lehman 40). Had they read this analysis, the fifth graders who laughed at Koch's classroom antics would have caught his drift, since "looking into happiness" was their way of keeping sane on city streets.

Liberating the imaginations of city kids with unconventional assignments, Koch noticed that their wily toughness ran counter to the saccharine palaver they had come to expect from schoolbooks. Clearly, they had a different story to tell. In Koch's classes, their street swagger gave way to expressions of serenity and harmony, though rarely to vapid sentimentality, which tends to have a short duration in their neighborhood. Above all, PS 61 students liked playing the literary game on their own terms. If their sense of wonder was tempered by the city's concrete and steel, they nonetheless refused to become constrained by the physical spaces they inhabited. Instead, they tapped into New York's hardness, moving adventurously and unself-consciously through its byways, adhering in some way to the tradition of Rudy Burckhardt, Joseph Cornell, and other flaneurs whose casual gathering of urban images blazed a new path to transcendence.[5] Mixing seriousness with play, these fledgling writers scouted the city's gray areas, seeking places where blight and beauty merged, combining various environmental perspectives until a garden of verses blossomed forth on treeless streets.

Koch joined PS 61 in 1968, but his teaching and writing were already bound together. He began teaching at the New School in the 1950s and shortly thereafter joined the faculty at Columbia University, where he spent four decades training an impressive group of second-generation New York School poets (including David Shapiro and Ron Padgett). Despite his lofty credentials, Koch's relationship with academia was stormy. In his best-known poem, "Fresh Air," he launches an uproarious attack upon formalist poetry and New Criticism, which were entrenched in American colleges at midcentury. Literary study of this sort was not only rearguard, Koch suggests in his hilarious poem, but painfully boring and harmful to young minds:

> Where are young poets in America, they are trembling in publishing
>   houses and universities,
> Above all they are trembling in universities, they are bathing the
>   library steps with their spit,
> They are gargling out innocuous (to whom?) poems about maple trees
>   and their children,
> Sometimes they brave a subject like the Villa d'Este or a lighthouse in
>   Rhode Island,
> Oh what worms they are! they wish to perfect their form. (*CP* 123–24)

The remainder of "Fresh Air" shows Koch refusing to swallow T. S. Eliot's literary castor oil. Anticipating the cartoon images handed him by school-children a dozen years later, he introduces us to "the Strangler," an antihero he has commissioned to kayo the smug pretenders occupying university department chairs and holding forth at the Poem Society. "Here on the railroad train, one more time, is the Strangler. / He is going to get that one there, who is on his way to a poetry reading. / Agh! Biff! A body falls to the moving floor" (124). Several writers in Donald Allen's *The New American Poetry* rail against academia, but Koch is the only one to use sound effects ordinarily reserved for comic books.

To the high-toned literati, Koch's playfulness rendered his work hopelessly juvenile. Alison Lurie said that "everyone has an ideal age" and that "in Koch's case that age is 19" (Lehman 216). "He is precious and puerile when he is not merely futile and noisy," Harry Roskolenko complained in a *Poetry* review of Koch's first volume, raising the ire of O'Hara, who fired off a response praising Koch's "vivacity and go, [his] originality of perception and intoxication with life" (*Standing* 60). "Poems are not mature, nor are they childish," O'Hara reiterated in a follow-up letter (62), which *Poetry* declined to publish. As O'Hara saw it, critics like Roskolenko failed to acknowledge the whimsical nature of fringe literary movements in the twentieth century. As Ashbery's critical writings have illustrated, poets of the New York School, long drawn to "other traditions," had specific predecessors in mind when they took their collective leap into serious silliness. It was after reading French writer Alfred Jarry, for instance, that Ashbery turned to Koch and said, "I think we should be a little crazier" (Koch, *Art* 159).[6]

The experimental proclivities of children proved just as influential to New York School writers. Ashbery wrote often about his rural childhood and Schuyler wrote a novel (*Alfred and Guinevere*) about precocious kids. Second-generation poets Jim Carroll and Victor Hernandez Cruz rose up from New York's mean streets to publish widely as teenagers. The frequency with which the word "playful" appears in *What Is Poetry*, a collection of interviews Daniel Kane conducted with avant-garde poets (Ashbery and Koch among them), indicates that an unbridled freedom, of the kind children know, continues to open doors of perception. To play at something is to enjoy an original relation to the world, regardless of one's age or station. "If a poem exists, what difference does it make how old its poet is?" O'Hara asks in his letter to *Poetry*. "The whole conundrum about children's art is completely passé—in the other arts Satie, Dubuffet and many others have accepted spontaneity and freedom from formalistic constraints to their benefit, basing their works in some cases on children's drawings, the work of the insane or visual accidents. The public is far from lax in appreciating the special qualities this liberation has permitted. . . . Infantilism has many forms" (*Standing* 63). Far from being puerile, Koch and his peers are simply avoiding the staleness suffusing the literary establishment.

In Koch's best poems, seriousness and frivolity are set on a collision course. Readers are invited to survey the damage done to the vehicle of language, reassessing their attitudes toward conventional written expression as Koch throws himself headlong into the crash test. In "Where Am I Kenneth," the poet's discordant and competing selves search disingenuously for whatever it takes to "Nail Kenneth down." The inconsistent point of view reveals an adult calling after his irrepressible inner child, who roams mischievously from pleasure to pleasure, ignoring all reasonable advice. Yet Koch never strays too far from recognizable fact. Instead of having his protagonist disappear down a rabbit hole, Koch brings Wonderland to the surface of midcentury Boston in an effort to wake up that city's narcoleptic student population:

> Nail Kenneth down
> For I fear the shades have gone to sleep
> Throw the windows, and hey!
> Grace comes, it is a rabbit
> A rabbit discovers the triumph's lips
> And a tuneless campus is deader than ships. (*CP* 26)

Despite its welter of obscure images, the educational message of this poem is clear. Whenever a classroom becomes unbearably stuffy due to too much professorial blather, it is best to throw open the window and breathe some fresh air. Like the triumphant rabbit he glimpses through the window, this Harvard graduate would rather cast his lot with the musical breezes of open field poetics than become trapped behind walls on a "tuneless campus."

The same restlessness pervades "West Wind," a sly update of Percy Shelley's paean to poetic inspiration. The message is reminiscent of "Fresh Air" and "Where Am I Kenneth." For too long, poets trapped in airless classrooms have waited for an animating breeze to arrive from the west. Taking a proactive approach, Koch employs convoluted language to stir up his own whirlwind:

> It's the ocean of western steel
> Bugles that makes me want to listen
> To the parting of the trees
> Like intemperate smiles, in a
> Storm coat evangelistically ground
> Out of spun glass and silver threads
> When stars are in my head, and we
> Are apart and together, friend of my youth
> Whom I've so recently met—a fragment of the universe
> In our coats, a believable doubling
> Of the fresh currents of doubt and
> Thought! A winter climate
> Found in the Southern Hemisphere and where
> I am who offers you to wear,
> And in this storm, along the tooth of the street
> The intemperate climate of this double frame of the universe. (*CP* 173)

Here as elsewhere, Koch's natural imagery is filtered through an avant-garde lens, rendering his location indeterminate. With his harum-scarum delivery of words, he abandons conventional modes of expression to go with the natural flow, which in turn seems like a product of his "unsyntactical" linguistic style.[7] The poem's first line break tempts readers to regard "western steel" as a modifier of "ocean," not of "Bugles," instruments whose brassy sound contemptibly mimics the high-toned trumpets making clarion calls in "Ode to the West Wind" and Ralph Waldo Emerson's "The Snow-Storm." A disagreement between subject and verb disabuses us of this notion, but the image of a gray metallic ocean lingers nonetheless, rendering the natural scene "intemperate," though hardly uninviting. As in "Where am I Kenneth?" the situational aspect of "where / I am" has become Koch's obsession, and he tends to seek all available guides. In this case, he is aided by a "friend of my youth / Whom I've so recently met." Could it be that for Koch, as for Ashbery, forgotten childhood allegiances rush forward to reorient the mature poet, guiding him back to a lost landscape? Regardless, the fantastical "storm coat" Koch's persona dons, together with the stars crowding his head, suggest that his playful excesses mirror those of the natural scene. Perhaps, like Shelley, Koch is submitting to impetuous forces he has had a hand in creating. Eliot castigated Shelley for his solipsism (*Selected Prose* 81), but that no doubt confirmed Shelley's genius in the mind of Doctor Fun. It remained to seen how the educational system Koch was in the process of joining would react to his creative impulses.

As a rambunctious poet launching his career, Koch opposed an overly strict literary establishment. As Koch got set to teach in public elementary schools, he discovered that progressive educators were on the same wavelength, ushering in a more relaxed approach to student writing. Just as the "open field" poetics developed by New American Poets granted writers license to publish unorthodox renderings of contemporary life, an "open education" movement encouraged American schoolchildren to explore favorite themes and topics uninhibited by adult expectation. By the time Koch wrote *Wishes, Lies, and Dreams*, top-down methods of instruction featuring an authoritative teacher and passive pupils were being replaced by spontaneous learning models in which teachers "facilitated" intellectual discoveries children made on their own. "Child-centered education," as it was known, derived from a model of "natural development" outlined colorfully in Jean-Jacques Rousseau's novel *Emile* (1762). The model was later popularized by John Dewey, who promoted a "reverence for childhood," arguing that kids benefited from firsthand experiences in classrooms that felt less like school and more like home (Ravitch, *Left Back* 169, 172, 174). Subsequently, any curriculum based on the logical organization of disciplinary subjects was labeled puritanical and discarded in favor of student-centered activities. Harold Rugg, coauthor of *The Child-Centered School* (1928), embodied the new spirit, naming "child interest as the orienting center of the school program." In Rugg's "Garden of Eden," Diane Ravitch explains in *Left Back*, the emphasis was no longer on books and rules so much as it was on the genius of children, those romantic "artist-philosophers" innately attuned to "the rhythm of life" (194, 225–26).

Not every educator was pleased with open education methodology. William Bagley, Dewey's most vociferous critic, called the child-centered movement "glorified hedonism," useful for teaching animals perhaps, but not for meeting geopolitical challenges in the modern world. Not all classroom activities could be "fun," he warned. Carl Joachim Friedrich voiced similar concerns. He proudly recalled having shocked a patron of New York's progressive Lincoln School, telling her that "happy" students were being outfitted for a life of leisure in "a golden pastoral age" rather than being prepared to face modern life. Howard Mumford Jones likewise lamented that progressives "have in fact substituted an adolescent wish fulfillment for that rigorous discipline which alone will permit modern man to survive." Boyd Bole joined the attack, calling the "reverence for childhood" passed down from Rousseau "superstitious." Modifying his thinking in the face of such criticism, Dewey admitted that children who were asked pointblank what they wanted to do in open classrooms tended toward artificial responses and bad habits. Operating in revisionist mode in *Education and Experience* (1938), he agreed to abandon Rousseau's laissez-faire approach after hearing children ask progressive instructors, "Do I have to do what I want to do today?" (Ravitch, *Left Back* 234, 246, 289, 308, 311–12).

After weathering these attacks and surviving a period of retrenchment during the early years of the cold war, child-centered education made a comeback in the 1960s, fueled by the widespread loosening of cultural mores and the eradication of authoritarian organizational models. During this period, A. S. Neill's *Summerhill* (1960), which took its title from an innovative British grade school, became required reading among progressive educators. Like Rousseau, Neill took a libertarian approach, asserting that children were "innately wise and realistic" and therefore able to discover truths for themselves without the unnecessary intrusion of teachers and books. Shortly after Neill's book appeared, American teachers latching on to its message implemented the new methodology and rushed to tell others of its success. Herbert Kohl's *36 Children* and Jonathan Kozol's *Death at an Early Age* stressed the feasibility of open education in the inner city, where too many kids were forced to endure the condescension of teachers, the ignorance of administrators, and the irrelevance of assigned textbooks (when books were available). Essentially, open education advocates wanted to make students full partners in the learning process. Kohl, for instance, noted how underachieving Harlem students came alive when asked to develop their own course of study.

In ensuing years, a host of books—including George Leonard's *Education and Ecstasy* (1968), Neil Postman and Charles Weingartner's *Teaching as a Subversive Activity* (1969), Charles Silberman's *Crisis in the Classroom* (1970), and Ivan Illich's *Deschooling Society* (1971)—sought to transform the way schoolchildren acquired knowledge.[8] Leonard believed learning should happen in an "ecstatic moment," free from claustrophobia (the school as prison) and standardization (the school as factory). For this new generation of students, the process of learning would take precedence over the content of learning. Reading assignments were deemed retrograde. Grades, tests, and "right answers" were abandoned in favor of the affective expression of personal concerns. Philadelphia's Parkway Program did away with the structure of the schoolhouse, becoming one of America's first "schools without walls." For children in this program, the streets of Philadelphia functioned as their classroom, their teacher, and their text (Ravitch, *Left Back* 388–98).[9]

Granted a radically different intellectual environment, urban schoolchildren in open classrooms seized the chance to share their perspectives of city life, particularly in creative writing contexts. In an era when expository writing instructors were privileging fluidity of expression over logic or correctness, poems and stories allowed students an even better opportunity to overcome perceived disadvantages and simply write what they felt. Avant-garde poets entered into an easy alliance with these budding writers, eliciting their unself-conscious renderings of experience and using these as an antidote to the stilted pap filling their literature textbooks.[10] Though he knew little of the innovations spearheaded by educational reformers, Koch adjusted easily to open classroom settings, having developed a fluid pedagogical style at the New School. Former New School pupil Lewis Warsh recalls that under Koch's tutelage "it was more important to look out the window, to feel the light coming in, or the way the whole world seemed to collapse around you and rearrange itself as you stepped off the curb, than to think about poetry in a way that might improve people's lives." Thus inspired, Warsh realized that any person, at any given time, could be a poet (xxv).

Koch's contributions to elementary education were made possible by the popular "poets-in-the-schools" program. Academy of American Poets director Betty Kray, who began the program in 1966 with grant money from the National Endowment for the Arts (NEA), eventually partnered with Teachers and Writers Collaborative, the New York City Parks Department's Cultural Affairs Division, and various state arts councils (to which the NEA transferred authority in 1970) to procure the funding necessary for expansion. The first year, Kray placed poets in forty-seven of New York City's public high schools, with stunning results. Flipping through teacher diaries and field reports written by Harvey Shapiro, Paul Blackburn, Ishmael Reed, and other visiting poets, Kathleen Norris (soon to join their ranks) learned that children embraced poetry when it was made relevant to their daily lives. Encouraged by the intellectual potential of kids in the city's poorest districts, program participants agreed that poetry instruction should no longer be reserved for students on an "academic" track. Leading the charge, Kray made sure vocational high schools were among the first places her poets visited (Norris, *Virgin* 35, 98–99).

Reports from the field were illuminating. In March 1966, Kathleen Fraser visited a vocational high school whose students had been deemed "deficient in literary training." Although most were training for jobs as cosmeticians or dress-pattern cutters, these students listened intently to a writer whose purpose, she said, "was to make them understand that poets were human beings who felt many things in common with [them] . . . and that poets simply tried to put these deep feelings into words" (Norris, *Virgin* 100). The hurdles inner-city students faced became clear to Fraser when she visited a junior high in a slum area. Sadly, one instructor's imperious attitude had left the kids feeling as though their own thoughts had absolutely no validity or merit. As Fraser recalls, "I felt so demoralized by the atmosphere in the rooms and the teacher's treatment of the kids (as she turned to me smiling and preening) that I wanted to reach out to them and let them know they counted for something and that the way they saw things and felt things counted." To attain her goals, she adopted a method picked up from Koch at the New School. "I talked about city imagery, about the things I'd seen on their block, walking from the subway to their school, and tried to encourage them to look at things in new ways. They didn't really know what to think. But they were sweet afterwards and had me autograph their hands" (101). Reading Fraser's reports, Norris liked that she "addressed each of these students as one human being to another, offering herself as a listener and a friend" (102). David Henderson also tried to erase the "antipodal relationship" between instructors and students, telling Lopate, "I tried to be the exact opposite of what a teacher is to them" (Lopate, "Attitude" 193).

Like Fraser and Henderson, Koch discovered that the children society had cast aside as "disadvantaged," "disabled," or "deprived" were rather talented when it came to imaginative expression. "The power to see the world in a strong, fresh and beautiful way is a possession of all children," Koch writes in *Wishes, Lies, and Dreams*. "And the desire to express that vision is a strong creative and educational force" (45). Reading the student poetry gathered in *Wishes*, we can assay the latitude creative writing offers kids whose "incorrect" language was heretofore subject to condescension or penalty. We notice, for example, how the repetition of linguistic modifiers, routinely forbidden in expository essays and other rhetorical exercises, accurately limns the character of a misunderstood outsider, whether that person is a canonized intellectual like Gertrude Stein or an unknown sixth grader like Gloria Peters, whose poem "Really" is noteworthy for its revelation of hidden personal traits:

I seem to be so dumb to my teacher, it seems.
But he really doesn't know me, really. . . .
To the students of the class I seem to be kind of dumb, I seem to be
But really, I'm kind of smart, really. . . .
To other people I seem to be a stranger
But really, I'm their sister, really. (254)

Writing down her thoughts in a poem, Peters becomes the "sister" of Koch and of her student peers, not only in the humanitarian sense but also in the literary sense. Admittedly, that relationship remains somewhat tenuous, at least from Peters's perspective. Her sense of empowerment rises to the surface of her poem, but so too do the obstacles she faces in the realm of public perception. Miguel Ortiz, who ran workshops in the South Bronx and East Harlem, remarks in his reminiscence of the open education movement that literature and art are things "poor people are not supposed to have" (293). Students like Peters possessed demonstrable talent, Ortiz and other writers realized, but they struggled to convince people with elitist attitudes of this reality. Responding to backhanded compliments paid to Koch's "slum children" by a feature writer at *Newsweek*, another PS 61 student wrote mockingly, "I used to be a slumchild, but now I am a poet" (Lopate, "Interview with Kenneth Koch" 277). However facetious her tone, we can see how liberating it is for young Eliza Bailey to forge her own identity on the written page, there to escape the tags placed on her by out-of-touch adults.[11] When Emily Dickinson wrote "I'm Nobody—Who are You?" she was an outsider challenging the literary establishment to regard her as a somebody. A century later, New York schoolchildren displayed the same moxie. Koch's decision to reprint their poems in his books not only validated their efforts but also introduced readers to fresh viewpoints on rapidly changing cityscapes.

IN *WISHES, LIES, AND DREAMS*, Koch talks about change being a common experience for young writers and about crafting assignments based on this dynamic. "I had forgotten that whole strange childhood experience of changing physically so much all the time," Koch writes. "It came very naturally to the children's poems once I found a way of making it easy for them to write about change" (16). The physical aspect of change was particularly important to city kids. According to Jane Jacobs, cities are "thoroughly physical places" in which "we get useful information by observing what occurs tangibly and physically, instead of sailing off on metaphysical fancies" (95–96). As a lifelong city dweller, Koch knew this instinctively, and yet he also wanted to accommodate the escapist impulses prompting urban children to stray beyond their immediate surroundings, be they a dreary classroom, a rundown apartment building, or a stark city block.[12]

In 1994, Koch told educators at Teacher and Writers Collaborative that during his childhood "the whole idea of writing poetry had a lot to do with escaping, escaping from the bourgeois society of Cincinnati, Ohio, escaping from any society of Cincinnati, Ohio, and escaping from any society anywhere. The first thing I had to find out to be a poet at all was that there was a bigger world, a bigger world than that of my school and my parents and their friends. I had to find out that there was a world where people talked to the moon or said, 'O wild west wind'" (*Art* 157). Writing became his form of adventure. "I needed people to help me get away from making sense in the usual way, because if you make sense the usual way, it's like an asymptote, the thing in mathematics that gets close to a line but never gets all the way to it. You never escape from the rabbi and your parents and your teacher if you go on making sense in the usual way because they're all making sense in the usual way, and they're older than you are, and they can do it better. So I had to make some other kind of sense" (159). When it came time to teach, Koch emphasized poetry's ability to call into being these new perspectives, to cross spatial barriers, "to see beyond reality" (*Sleeping* 65).

Once the PS 61 kids latched onto Koch's message, they learned that negotiating the space of a poem was not unlike negotiating the space of the city: you feel where you are within a given form, abiding by some rules and breaking others, altering the terrain as you go. "When you write a poem," Koch told Teachers and Writers, "it's as if you are saying how you feel on a grid, and you are hanging flowers everywhere on it" (*Art* 156). Analogously, when you walk down the streets of Manhattan, the world's most famous grid, you are free to adorn that space with your imagination, "hanging flowers everywhere on it" if you choose, turning all that rectangular concrete and steel into something soft and beautiful. Michel de Certeau highlights such transformations in "Walking in the City," arguing that the spatial practices of mobile city dwellers "follow the thicks and thins of an urban 'text' they write without being able to read" (93). Physical movements ("forests of gestures," de Certeau calls them, in pastoral fashion) "make some parts of the city disappear and exaggerate others, distorting it, fragmenting it, and diverting it from its immobile order" (102). Instead of stratified or hierarchical structures, "there is only a pullulation of passer-by, a network of residences temporarily appropriated by pedestrian traffic, a shuffling among pretenses of the proper, a universe of rented spaces haunted by a nowhere or by dreamed-of places" (103).[13]

William Watkin explains that de Certeau "accepted no normative categorization of everyday existence" (41). Koch and his peers likewise sought new conceptualizations of city geography as they launched their careers. Koch's urban pastoral impulses appear to have kicked in rather early, when he was a child in Cincinnati, as evidenced by his long-standing pride in that city's hills, parks, and waterways. In early poems, we witness a Japanese baseball player's appreciation of Cincinnati's organically named Vine Street, which with its "grand / Bravura and agility, seems to run / Irrespective of the way the town was planned" (*Seasons* 92), and an avant-garde sculptor's decision to install his grand work, the *Magician of Cincinnati*, "in the Ohio River, where it belongs, and which is so much a part of my original scheme" (*CP* 117). In each instance, shifting emotions color the locations Koch's protagonists observe or create, until urban objects take on a markedly different cast. Long after a town is laid out, its streets and rivers run this way and that, according to the moods of people navigating them, whether it is a baseball pitcher named Ko or a deranged sculptor, an established writer like Koch or a beginning reader like the kid in the RIF commercial. As Koch sees it, "You are born in a place, you have all your strongest feelings associated with a place, with the way streets look, with the way things smell, with the way things are packaged, and you almost have to love it. It appeals to you, it arouses you, it moves you. At the same time, you can feel that sometimes it's stupid and empty and dopey. But I think these things can be expressed simultaneously" (Spurr, "Interview").

Countering conventional wisdom, David Spurr says it was Koch's lifelong intention to move "beyond irony toward an attitude of genuine innocence" ("Kenneth" 355). If so, Koch was aided by the PS 61 kids, whose wonderment challenged myopic perceptions of inner-city space.[14] Koch reveled in their flights of fancy, realizing that their mixed metaphors and misspellings led readers down some interesting avenues. Students who described a "swan of bees" or asked "What shall I chartreuse today?" (*Wishes* 154–55, 210) probably would have had these lines thrown out before Koch arrived on the scene ("Kenneth Koch Tribute"). Koch viewed these unlikely combinations as magical, yet he felt he must provide some guidance. He could not rely solely on the instinctive ability of elementary school kids to produce great art. Reviewing a draft of *Wishes*, James Schuyler pressed

Koch on this topic: "I think it would be worth spelling out that you aimed to get the children freer, wilder, more open; but that you never said so in so many words to them." Wary by nature, Schuyler detected disingenuousness in open education methodology. "I've met the kind of teacher who wants to make anything a command: 'Be free! Soar, damn it, soar!'" (*Just* 279).

Addressing the problem Schuyler identified, Koch offered students direction in the form of prompts, or "poetry ideas." Facing an audience of eleven-year-olds, Koch was careful not to make these ideas overly elaborate, and in the end he found that the simplest instructions brought the most nuanced responses. Essentially, Koch freed children from the burden of expressing some inner reality, urging them instead to put funny things together. His call for personal wishes, for instance, prompted students to describe a series of urban events, some of them fantastical, others based on more mundane things, such as schoolyard jealousy: "I wish when Superman flies over New York he would turn green with envy" (*Wishes* 60); "I wish the street was ice cream" (67); "I wish a boy in my class would jump in the Hudson River" (82). Students responding to comparison exercises created the kind of surreal juxtapositions beloved by New York School poets. To say that "the cat is as striped as an airplane take-off" (95), as fourth-grader Tara Housman does, is to utter a phrase worthy of O'Hara's exotic urban meditations.[15] Other comparison poems, like those written about springtime, recall the topsy-turvy epiphanies influencing Schuyler and Guest: "Spring is like a paper bag / (Always busting in the air)" (187); "Spring is like a plate falling out of a closet for joy" (188); "But best of all spring is part of nature, like the baby next door / She's grown so big" (182).

Students who shared darker visions of the city, whether out of anger or some other motivation, may have achieved success on their own terms, but their work resembles that of other accomplished writers. Responding to a call for "sound comparisons"—an exercise that tended to put "a certain zip into children's work," according to Koch (*Wishes* 126)—Evan Steinberg crafted vitriolic scenarios reminiscent of Bob Dylan's noisiest revenge songs:

> The wind coming out of your mouth
> Is like the wind in a dark alley
> When you hear older people talking
> You hear groaning
> Hitting a chair with a ruler
> Is like hearing a machine gun fire

Hearing a dog whine
Is like a fire truck's siren
Seeing two boxers connect with a punch
Is like a bullet hitting a tin can. (123)

When Ron Padgett, who succeeded Koch at PS 61, asked fourth-grade
students to write a comparison poem about spring, he received a blast of
incongruous images from Henry Ponce, who in some respects sounds indistinguishable from Arthur Rimbaud:

The spring is like polluted air.
When spring comes the flowers die.
Spring is the ugliest season there is.
In spring a tornado comes.
In spring the ice cream man faints.
In spring everybody turns into stamps.
In the spring rotten birds fly for air. (182)

Ponce's phrasing is clipped and his wording deliberately anaphoric as he
sets out to follow Padgett's prompt. His tone, too, is rather matter-of-fact,
until the final lines, when his imagery turns strange and his message gathers strength. Armed with little more than a pencil, notebook paper, and his
own imagination, an unknown kid from the Lower East Side is encouraged by an established poet to let fly his secret thoughts, to register his
true feelings about springtime, regardless of whether they reflect conventional attitudes. That Ponce does so haltingly at first cannot obscure his real
achievement at the end of this poem, which like Steinberg's recalls surrealism's darkly enchanting verse experiments. Ponce's sense of empowerment
is undeniable. Who among New York's eight million citizens can say that
birds that "fly for air" are not "rotten"? During the moment of composition, this fourth grader travels the city without meddlesome interference
from adults. Like the hero of Paul Simon's contemporary song, he is for
that instant "the only living boy in New York." The rest of us just happen
to reside here.

NOTWITHSTANDING THE PROMISE shown by PS 61 kids, Koch wondered how
much better their writing might be if they were introduced to canonical
poets and inspired to imitate their techniques. He therefore began to introduce readings of Whitman, Stevens, and Lawrence in conjunction with
his regular writing prompts (*Wishes* 37–42). In *Rose, Where Did You Get*

That Red? Koch describes more fully than he does in *Wishes* the balance he wanted to achieve between reading famous poets (Shakespeare, Blake, Stein, Williams) and nurturing one's own visions, jettisoning authoritarian models while establishing equitable exchanges between novice writers and more practiced hands. "The important thing," he notes, "is to keep the atmosphere free, airy, and creative, never weighed down by the adult poems. Once they are too grand and remote, their grandeur and remoteness will be all they communicate; and children, in the classroom and elsewhere, thrive on familiarity, nearness and affection, and on being able to do something themselves. What matters for the present is not that children admire Blake and his achievement, but that each child be able to find a tiger of his own" (*Rose* 27).

Blake's antinomian spirit proved popular with young writers, but his songs of innocence and experience were a bit too imitable. Poems by Shakespeare, Shelley, and Whitman, by contrast, showed students "how to float things," how to suspend mundane occurrences, or at least make them sound more exciting, and to do so in their own voices (*Art* 161–62). Shakespeare, in particular, elevated students to a new level of engagement with pastoral themes. Citing three Shakespeare songs that "appeal to children's sense of fantasy," Koch reports that children responded positively to "the magical places and the wonderful creatures so small and light that they can sleep, like Ariel, in the cup of a flower. Along with fantasy there is a fresh and sensuous feeling for nature, especially for its colors and sounds. The cowslips and bluebells are real, fresh flowers, yet invite the wildest imaginings. The bird, animal, and object noises (Bow-wow, Cock-a-diddle-dow, and Ding, Dong, Bell) give a freedom and craziness to the poems which add to the feeling of gaiety and escape from restrictions and rules." In student poems inspired by the songs, "the most noticeable theme is desire for a place where one can be free—free from school, free from being forced to live in the city and to stay indoors, free to kiss and to love, free to do exactly as one likes" (*Rose* 92).

Later, Koch invigorates Shakespeare's pastoral message by giving it an urban twist. After introducing students to "Over Hill, Over Dale" from *A Midsummer Night's Dream*, Koch says:

> Imagine you are very, very small, and you have a special job to do in nature every day. Think about the way something is in nature and imagine that it would only be that way if some little person did something to it every day. There would be a little person, like the one in this poem, to put dewdrops in flowers every morning, one whose job was

KOCH AMONG SCHOOLCHILDREN | **139**

to keep the grass green, one to make the leaves stick to the branches in summer and make them change color and fall off in autumn, others to do all kinds of things. One could imagine little people doing things in a city too—changing the colors of traffic lights, making sure revolving doors go around, putting pretty pictures on stamps in the post office. To have any of these jobs, you would have to be able to move very, very fast and be very active. Imagine you are one of these little people and write a poem about it. (*Rose* 226–27)

Notice the canny shift in this prompt from organic to inorganic imagery. As soon as the writer's imaginative ability to effect change in natural environments is deemed acceptable, the teacher asks that this agency be allowed to modify various city objects (traffic lights, revolving doors, postage stamps). For the novice, as for the expert, conflating natural caretaking with urban engineering offers rich rewards. A child who envisions traffic lights as flowers can travel far in his or her imagination without losing sight of what is right there in front of him or her. Sensationally altering his or her surroundings, the child can have the best of both worlds, identifying with gardeners, school crossing guards, or postal workers, as he or she likes. Russian critic Victor Shklovsky called this process "defamiliarization." For Shklovsky, "the purpose of art is to impart the sensation of things as they are perceived and not as they are known. The technique of art is to make objects 'unfamiliar,' to make forms difficult, to increase the difficulty and length of perception because the process of perception is an aesthetic end in itself and must be prolonged. Art is a way of experiencing the artfulness of an object; the object is not important" (12). Similarly, Koch urges children to reconsider their familiar knowledge of place with imagery that dislocates that territory. If city kids want to see faeries haunting traffic lights and revolving doors, they should endeavor purely to perceive their "home geography" without any sustained attempt to know it.[16]

Urban pastoral poetry by Walt Whitman and William Carlos Williams likewise exhorts children to alter relationships with familiar habitat. Although Koch recommends that teachers assigning "Song of Myself" include sections "suffused with Whitman's big breezy sensuousness," he favors sections composed on an intimate scale, closer to what we find in Shakespeare's songs. Crucial here is Whitman's "claim to have important secret knowledge." According to Koch, this poet's confidence derives from his sense of "how to be close to animals and other creatures and to nature, [of] how beautiful the world is, and [of] how exciting and endless it is to be alive in it" (*Rose* 104–5). Just the same, city kids can stay on their block and enjoy an original relationship to the universe. As Whitman advises, "You shall no longer take things at second or third hand / . . . You shall listen to all sides and filter them through your self"(30). Citing Paul Valery's evaluation of Whitman for emphasis, Koch wants children to see that "greatness in poetry can come not from difficulties overcome but from—and this is better in French, *facilités trouvées*—easinesses found. Whitman shows you, why not do what is easy?" (*Art* 162). We appreciate Whitman most when we abandon attempts to sound literary and simply write what we believe is true.

Even more than Whitman, Williams prompts children to recast familiar environments in bristling, unpretentious language. If dealing with change comes naturally to city kids, Williams sanctions their lightning-fast responses in his writing process. As Victor Hernandez Cruz, a high school dropout who ended up teaching poetry in New York City schools, has said of Williams, "I love the quality of the / spoken thought / As it happens immediately / uttered into the air / Not held inside and rolled / around for some properly / schemed moment" (149). Cruz's early poems about "floating" around Manhattan on buses and subways attest to this feeling of lightness and spontaneity. Recalling his own discovery of Williams at age nineteen, Koch says, "I realized then that I could write about what I was really doing. All these vacant lots in Cincinnati, those suburban houses, the gutters, the automobiles, the schoolyards were things that I could write about. . . . I hadn't been able to use words like *dog, parking lot*, and *sidewalk*, and from Williams I learned that I could" (*Art* 163). When Koch began teaching, Williams's easy way of relating to his surroundings became a benchmark against which he judged promising writers, including Joseph Ceravolo, his student at the New School. In the work of both poets, Koch noticed, "there is a blurring expansion of identity, a sort of giving oneself completely to a tree, an insect, flowers. . . . It is a quality rare among poets, a combination of clear down-to-earthness with the sort of wild dreaminess of Lorca or Rimbaud" (47). Williams's pragmatism had a major influence on PS 61 students as well. Children who imitated the choppy line breaks of "The Locust Tree in Flower" and the pithy tone of "This Is Just to Say" reportedly enjoyed "asserting the importance of their secret pleasure against the world of adult regulations" (*Rose* 130–31). Equally influential was Williams's prosodic ability to proceed agilely, line by line and word by word, in any direction.

My favorite among the Williams-inspired poems collected in *Rose* is "Love." Composed anonymously, "Love" shows how unadorned language, when presented in an unusual way, can capture elusive subjects. Using the

sparest possible lineation, the student writer throws into relief the indeterminacy of ten everyday words, all of them monosyllabic, many of them
functioning dually as verbs or nouns, depending on contextual shifts the
reader makes:

Love
sex
mouth
touch
dream
wink
smile
peek
rose
feels
good (*Rose* 149)

As in verse experiments by Williams or Stein, the ambiguity of isolated
words conceals the writer's secrets and at the same time reveals quite a
bit about the type of pleasure he or she seeks. Armed with avant-garde
techniques, streetwise kids can articulate personal passions without giving
away too much in the process.

Students also responded well to Williams's "Between Walls," a poem that
does not talk about the physicality of urban beauty so much as it rubs up
against its jagged, glistening edges. Simplicity and serendipity merge in an
antiformalist dance that is severe yet welcoming, inorganic yet decidedly
pastoral:

Between Walls
the back wings
of the

hospital where
nothing

will grow lie
cinders

in which shine
the broken

pieces of a green
bottle (*Rose* 129)

Forging a link between Williams and Whitman in his reading of this poem,
Stephen Tapscott explains that "the joy of surprised recognition in perception is qualitatively the same whether one observes grass or glass, pastoral lushness or urban grit" (103). Koch convinced students that "Between
Walls" had "an appealing idea—something supposed to be ugly which really is beautiful—but [that] the children would get more out of it if I could
connect it to their feelings as well. I did that by using the words *really* and
secretly, which I found as helpful here as, in other lessons, appealing to
the children's senses and asking them to think of colors and sounds. My
suggestion was, 'Write a poem about something that is supposed to be
ugly, but which you *really secretly* think is beautiful, as Williams thinks the
broken glass shining in back of the hospital is beautiful'" (*Rose* 15). Asked
to defamiliarize "ugly" neighborhoods, sixth graders Marion Mackles and
Andrew Vecchione produced nuanced appraisals of discarded items:

Goldglass
In the back yard
Lies the sun
White glass
Reflecting the sun (152)

Nothing Made to Something
The garbage I saw was like millions of crayon marks on paper.
It looks like the fire crackers of the world being shot off,
But the best thing was it looked like itself—ugly, but nice in a way.
  (152–53)

In Koch's estimation, "Goldglass," the poem by Mackles, "shows not only
Williams's attention to the beauty of small and supposedly unbeautiful
things, but also his way of making the poem, as it goes along, a physical experience of discovery for the reader" (23). I like how the white glass that reflects the sun is initially mistaken for the sun itself. For a moment, the glass
orders everything in the backyard, much as the light it reflects serves as the
centripetal force of the solar system. Besides honest perception (what she
really or secretly sees), this student's most important means of discovery is
her pruned-down diction. For Mackles and others inspired by Williams's
minimalism, selecting words is like choosing pieces for a mosaic or fitting

patterns for a crazy quilt: it is best to pick from what is immediately available, juxtaposing a few odd shards or scraps, finding beauty where others find none.

Befitting its subject matter, Vecchione's poem about trash is rougher in style and texture, though it too celebrates overlooked treasures. I have heard of stray crayon marks on paper ("scribble scrabble" in preschool parlance) likened to garbage, presumably to be thrown away, but never have I heard of garbage likened to crayon marks, although Vecchione's inversion makes perfect sense to anyone who has looked closely at the hopper of a sanitation truck.[17] Then again, the best thing about this rubbish is that it "looked like itself." Verlyn Klinkenborg, in a luminous piece published in the *New York Times Magazine,* refers to windblown bags caught in the fence at Staten Island's Fresh Kills landfill as a "mosaic of trash," prompting viewers of an accompanying color photograph to regard garbage as an urban art form, strangely beautiful in itself, though also useful to New York's debris artists.[18] Combing the city for raw material, acclaimed artists like Joseph Cornell and Robert Rauschenberg saw that discarded items possess their own splendor. The novice poets at PS 61 are extending this tradition.

IN *SLEEPING ON THE WING*, Koch (with coauthor Kate Farrell) continues to stress poetry's ability to focus on real objects and at the same time "see beyond reality" (65). An anthology "written specifically for high school students, though it will also be useful to students in college—and beyond" (the jacket copy tells us), *Sleeping on the Wing* features poets who are complex yet also accessible. In *Rose,* Koch equated elementary school students' encounters with difficult poetry with living in a big city: at first you feel overwhelmed, but over time your immersion in its aleatory atmosphere expands your capabilities and enriches your sense of self. Having city kids implement avant-garde techniques in their own writing was not as impossible as some experts feared, Koch explained, since "children aren't bothered by the same kinds of difficulties in poetry that adults are bothered by and aren't bothered in the same way. Along the way, they may even be intrigued by certain kinds of strangeness. . . . They have an advantage over some more educated readers whose fear of not understanding every detail of a poem can keep them from enjoying it at all" (*Rose* 209). In *Sleeping on the Wing,* Koch elaborates on this interchange, introducing adolescent writers to masters of the craft while highlighting the childlike curiosity lending modernist poetry its experimental sinuousness.

Koch was bolstered in his latest project by antididactic poets whose bizarre visions nevertheless drew on accessible objects. A poet like

Rimbaud, Koch claimed, filled his work with the kinds of colors, tastes, textures, and fragments recognizable to anyone taking a random walk on the Lower East Side (*Sleeping* 67). Koch encouraged students to build a new city out of these kinds of images, and to do so in piecemeal fashion, engaging in a style of writing in which "the plot is less important than the beauty of the details" (67). "You can't see a whole city while you're still in it," he says in his discussion of Yeats, but you can provide clues of its existence (77). Koch cites Guillaume Apollinaire as an exemplary city poet, one who made the mundane marvelous simply by paying attention. "Walking around Paris, as he does in his poem 'Zone,' inspired him in the way poets have usually been inspired by walking around in nature," Koch says, citing as evidence the prosaic phenomena the French poet encounters: airport hangars, newspapers, billboards, new industrial streets (133). Beguiled by "pretty industrialism" in writings by Apollinaire and Vladimir Mayakovsky, Koch wants young poets to become invested in their immediate surroundings, to "let the different parts of the city get into your poem as you come to them in your walk" (136).[19]

Koch had a ready audience for such techniques in public schools, for as Jane Jacobs notes, city kids are drawn by playful instincts to transform everyday objects into something marvelous. "A lot of outdoor life for children adds up from bits," Jacobs explains, especially in the city. "During such times children have, and use, all manner of ways to exercise and amuse themselves. They slop in puddles, write with chalk, jump rope, roller skate, shoot marbles, trot out their possessions, converse, trade cards, play stoop ball, walk stilts, decorate soap box scooters, dismember old baby carriages, climb on railings, run up and down. It is not in the nature of things to go somewhere formally to do them by plan, officially. Part of their charm is the accompanying sense of freedom to roam up and down the sidewalks, a different matter from being boxed into a preserve" (85–86).[20] Channeling Jacobs's "street ballet," Koch solicited provisional poems based on free play with found objects, insisting that students cast their nets wide and not get hung up on what is expected of them. After all, Koch maintained, Williams proved that although "people are moved by things that are officially beautiful, like roses and the moon, they are also moved by things that aren't usually considered beautiful—neon signs, old stairways, yards, rusty bicycles" (*Sleeping* 147). Jacobs, with her grassroots understanding of urban density patterns, likewise asserted that "right amounts are right amounts because of how they perform" (209). Koch believed young poets should adhere to similar principles, both qualitatively (in terms of subject matter) and quantitatively (in terms of metrics, rhyme, and form). "Just say what seems and sounds right to you," he advises. "Try not to plan much in advance, maybe no more than one line at a time, and be as free in thinking as you are in feeling. You may find, when you read the poem over, that this freedom has given it an interesting kind of logic" (*Sleeping* 224).[21]

Turning to the New York School, purportedly a place-based milieu, Koch equates the process of writing with the vertiginous experience of traveling, implying that imaginative urbanites need not leave familiar stomping grounds to experience the thrill of transport. "The Instruction Manual," an Ashbery poem about a daydream, stands as proof. Composed while Ashbery was working on an actual instruction manual at McGraw-Hill's midtown headquarters, the poem whisks the reader off to Mexico for an exotic interlude. Despite its abundant detail, the poem's travel scene is witnessed from a hazy remove. Ashbery writes vividly about Guadalajara but later admits to never having visited that city during his 1955 trip to Mexico. Anchored initially by facts, the truant technical writer gradually allows his thoughts to drift, much as travelers sometimes abandon itineraries to follow adventurous detours. Ashbery's pursuit of indeterminacy in the face of quotidian entrapment is the message embedded ironically in his title. "Discover the place as you write," Koch urges those who would take instruction from Ashbery. "Talk about anything you want to, and in any order, as if there is nowhere in particular you have to get to, nothing of great importance to see" (*Sleeping* 265). Koch repeats this footloose advice when commenting on his own poem "Lunch," telling fledgling writers, "I never knew what was going to come next in the poem. I wanted to let myself be surprised by what I was writing—this, too, was a little bit like travel, like being in a strange city and, for no reason, deciding to walk down a particular street or go into a certain doorway" (291).

O'Hara's "Sleeping on the Wing," the anthology's title piece, strays in the same wayward direction. A New Yorker's dreamy transport (beyond a "shoreless city" to the Atlantic Ocean) is hastened by his imagination but is actually made possible by the claustrophobic physicality of the city. Not until a "car honks or a door slams" does O'Hara, inspired by pigeons, acknowledge his desire to take wing, as though the city had to envelop him before it could reveal a way out. As Koch explains, a spontaneous evasion of routine expedites this poet's flight. "To get to the brilliant, concise, honest kind of sense there is in 'Sleeping on the Wing,' you probably have to give up advance planning and logic and restraint, and trust your nerve," he advises students (*Sleeping* 251). The payoff for O'Hara was clear. In the free space of a poem, a writer renowned for celebrating New York City says goodbye to all that, eschewing the social and professional commitments that, in real life, kept him trapped in fame's fishbowl. But beginning writers also stand to benefit from O'Hara's approach. Based on what he saw in public schools, Koch believes that any writer possessing sufficient "nerve"—the street-smart quality O'Hara trumpeted in "Personism" (*CP* 498)—has the opportunity to escape environmental troubles, whatever they may be, even if he or she never strays beyond city limits.

AT THEIR MOST POIGNANT, Koch's education books move beyond the classroom to showcase the idealism fueling participatory urban society. Jane Jacobs says that "cities have the capability of providing something for everybody, only because, and only when, they are created by everybody" (238). Koch shared Jacobs's equitable vision, ushering into his elementary classroom the vibrant egalitarianism of city streets, locating lyric potential in every shouting voice, honking car, or wailing siren, as Whitman and Williams had done. Introducing students to these innovative poets, Koch sought to make them creators of urban culture rather than passive observers. His efforts were rewarded when the poems he received so vividly expressed what it was like to find one's way in Fun City. Koch's books on education still inspire me—as a teacher, a parent, a writer, and a New Yorker—four decades after he walked through the door at PS 61. Schuyler, responding to the first draft of *Wishes*, spoke for countless readers when he told his friend, "My emotional cart has become hitched to a horse of grade-school poets" (*Just* 280).

For a while, Koch felt the same way, telling Lopate that teaching children influenced his poems in *The Art of Love* (1975) ("Interview with Kenneth Koch" 276). In "The Art of Poetry," "On Beauty," and "The Art of Love," readers discern the mutual benefit of Koch's classroom exchanges, learning that "one most grow and develop, and yet stay young" (*CP* 254). Above all, the children persuaded Koch not to be overly cerebral, to delight instead in palpable discoveries, to tap into immediate surroundings without completely abandoning whimsical flights of imagination. In "The Art of Poetry," Koch adopts the declamatory tone of a teacher, but his seat-of-the-pants wisdom likely comes from his students:

> Your poetry, if possible, should be extended
> Somewhat beyond your experience, while still remaining true to it;
> Unconscious material should play a luscious part
> In what you write, since without the unconscious part
> You know very little, and your plainest statements should be
> Even better than plain. A reader should put your work down puzzled,

Distressed, and illuminated, ready to believe
It is curious to be alive. (263)

The vital curiosity steering the childhood intellect is indistinguishable from practical matters, the adult teacher has learned. Beauty means little to children if they cannot enter into it, experience it for themselves, and draw their own conclusions. Kids are great students, Koch implies in "On Beauty," because they take nothing at face value:

> Birds are something I was told
> Were "beautiful" when I was a child. Flowers also were, and
> Especially roses. I am still slightly uncomfortable with
> Roses. The moon and the stars were also on my parents' and
> Teachers' list of what was beautiful. It has been
> Hard for me to love them (stars and moon, I mean) but I have,
> Despite this early "training," which may be injurious to beauty
> In some cases, in others not. In raising your child,
> You should share your feeling with him of what is beautiful,
> But do not expect a child to respond to it that way.
> He or she is likely to respond more like a poet or an artist,
> By wanting to "do" something with it—to run
> Through it, or eat it or tear it apart. It is in later life perhaps
> Precisely the suppression of these feelings, or some of these feelings,
> That results in our feeling of beauty, which we are merely to contem-
>   plate. (270)

Before you learned to appreciate a beautiful object, you did something to it (or with it). The concept of beauty—which like innocence, wonder, or any number of sentimental notions, belongs to the nostalgic realm of adult consciousness—is worlds away from the instinctive responses fueling childhood behavior, not to mention the best poetry. Reflecting upon *The Art of Love*'s "instructional poems," Koch told Lopate that "some [were] meant very seriously, some more lightly" ("Interview with Kenneth Koch" 270). Years later, he told Jordan Davis that "the instructional dry sound tends to make anything plausible—'You may wish to fire ten cannons at once'—It was another way to bring everything I wanted into a poem" (*Art* 206). The spirit of PS 61 lingers in either case, for it was there Koch saw how to disentangle poetry from complicated aesthetic discourse and act boldly, like a child, showing his readers, instead of telling them, how magical are the contours of his expanding universe.

Sadly, Koch felt his achievements in elementary education obscured his accomplishments as a publishing poet and a university professor. He won a Bollingen Prize in 1995 and continued to teach at an Ivy League school, but that is not how he is remembered in most people's minds. The media onslaught surrounding the publication of *Wishes* had a lasting impact. Back then, PS 61 kids not only read their poetry at New York's 92nd Street Y and on national television (David Frost's show; *Good Morning America*) but also were featured in the *Wall Street Journal*, *Newsweek*, and *Life*. The NEA dispatched filmmakers to the Lower East Side to capture Koch in action. As he went on lecture tours and conducted demonstration classes, and as *Wishes* continued to sell (xvi–xvii), Koch received so much mail he had to hire a secretary (Lopate, "Interview with Kenneth Koch" 277). By the end of the 1970s, it became easy to lump his education books with Carole King's *Really Rosie*, Marlo Thomas's *Free to Be . . . You and Me*, and other mainstream learning tools. "For those of us whose tie-dyed, early-child-rearing years happily coincided with the first printings of Koch's popular books about teaching children to write poetry," Jeredith Merrin explains, "it's natural to associate him with Fisher-Price Ferris wheels and Kermit the Frog. Sitting cross-legged with our five-year-olds, pens in hand, we prompted our young according to Koch and proudly recorded their responses. I used to be . . . 'What, honey?' 'A wave,' she replies. But now I am . . . 'A brick.' 'Wow'" ("Poetry Man").

As Koch's widow, Karen, reminded me, the writers he taught at Columbia (including filmmakers Ric Burns and Jim Jarmusch) have achieved notable success. The legacy of PS 61 kids has been more modest, but their classroom writing has paid its own dividends, long after the crescendo of open education has faded. The "great and terrible onslaught of self-consciousness" hit many of these kids in junior high school, as Koch predicted, and thereafter most either struggled mightily with writing or gave it up entirely. But not all of them did. Jeff Morley (the student who likened spring to "a plate falling out of a closet for joy") landed a position at the *Washington Post*. In 1983, he sought out his classmates and discovered that many had left the Lower East Side. Marion Mackles (author of "Goldglass") graduated from New York's High School of Performing Arts and earned a drama degree from Ohio University. She was back in Manhattan, acting and specializing in sign-language performance, continuing to draw on the practical good-heartedness she displayed in her girlhood poems. Vivien Tuft ("But best of all spring is a part of nature, like the baby next door") was at a Park Avenue advertising agency. Others worked across the United States and the Caribbean as astrophysicists, secretaries, servicemen, telephone operators, and energy conservation engineers. Several spoke of the confidence they gained in Koch's classes (Morley 276–77). Eliza Bailey ("I used to be a slumchild, but now I am a poet") was inspired to enter the teaching profession, earning an education degree at the University of Colorado. She was teaching kindergarten upstate, reading poems from *Wishes* to her four-year-olds and using its simpler exercises (272–73).

Even though Koch said that the point of his classes "was never to train future poets any more than the point of gym class is to produce future Reggie Jacksons," some PS 61 graduates continued to write verse, despite the hardships they faced. Fontessa Moore, who read her poems on national television during the media blitz surrounding *Wishes*, was living in East New York, dealing with economic uncertainty but writing daily, claiming, "It's my peace of mind." Candy Dipini, who remained in the Lower East Side, had lost one of her children in an apartment fire. Although she composed sporadically, she had written collaboration poems with her boyfriend (these also perished in the fire) and hoped to begin writing more often. "I always used to like it when I was a little girl and we used to write poetry," she told Morley. "It pushed you to say your true feelings, your inside feelings. It might make you sad inside, but even that, once you feel it, feels good. It's sad but you feel calm." Dipini's ambitions are small, but for her the process of writing offers real rewards. Morley, the professional writer, comes to a similar recognition, recalling that when his fifth-grade poem, "The Dawn of Me," appeared in *Wishes*, he was embarrassed, thinking it was not of high literary quality. "But as I looked up my old classmates, I started liking 'The Dawn of Me' as much as I had the day I wrote it, maybe even more. Writing poetry was the dawn of all of us; I like to think we're still living in its light" (280).

To underscore the lasting value of Koch's educational experiments in Fun City, I will conclude with a poem that sounds as though it could have been written by one of the PS 61 kids, though it was actually written by Koch late in his life. "A Big Clown-Face-Shaped Cloud" shows an aging Doctor Fun looking up to the skies to enjoy the shifting designs of a comical universe. Searching these skies for ourselves, we see how Koch's teaching left him limber enough to adopt a child's view of the world:

You just went by
With no one to see you, practically.
You were in good shape, for a cloud,
With perhaps several minutes more to exist
You were speaking, or seemed to be,

Mouth open wide, talking, to a
Belted angel-shaped cloud that was riding ahead. (*CP* 708)

Sophisticated readers can get as highfalutin with these lines as they wish. Shakespeare scholars might make reference to Polonius's ridiculous discourse on clouds, and biographers might find in the precarious cloud formation commentary on Koch's fragile health. Based on my foregoing discussion, I prefer to picture Koch as an overgrown kid left slack-jawed by the mysteries all around him. Like the big clown-face-shaped cloud, his mouth is wide open, signaling his amazement, his appetite for imagery, and his readiness to speak or perhaps to laugh. The piled-up adjectives in the title are themselves indicative of Koch's irrepressible nature, his ongoing inquiries, his capacity for fun. Epistemology takes a backseat to the basic affections sustaining the poet day to day. Similarly, in the NEA film from 1970, Koch tells fifth-graders struggling to understand one of Morley's colorful lines, "You don't have to know what it means in order to like it. I don't know what *you* mean, but I like you" (*Wishes, Lies, and Dreams: Kenneth Koch*).

Encountering "A Big Clown-Face-Shaped Cloud," I am reminded of Roland Barthes, who said that the pleasure of reading a text derives not so much from the meaning one gleans from it, but from the pleasure the writer felt in composing it.[22] I am reminded also of the experimental sculptor in Koch's poem "The Artist," who after considering the uncertain legacy of his installation *Play* (described as "an open field with a few boards in it") decides to relax, placating himself with the following mantra: "I look up at the white clouds, I wonder what I shall do, and smile" (*CP* 113). What I recall most of all are the photographs in *Wishes* that show New York City children beaming with pride as they compose and read their own verse. They show that we begin life as happy creators, finding freedom and fun in situations others might consider grim. We may as well continue to live that way. Consciously avoiding stentorian, "child-is-father-to-the-man" philosophy, Koch suggests that experimenting with common objects and images—regardless of regulations or meanings—is one of best things humans learn to do. His late poem about an overcast sky may serve as his epitaph, but Doctor Fun prefers to engage in childlike behavior as long as he can. Despite all the clouds, his metropolitan forecast is as sunny as the grin he wore in dust jacket photographs. Like the young writers he met in a Lower East Side elementary school, he wants to tell readers what the clown-shaped cloud wants to tell the angel-shaped cloud, which is just how curious and joyous it is to be alive.

6 THE PLACE WHERE YOUR NATURE MEETS MINE
Diane di Prima in the West

IN HER MEMOIR of the Beat generation, Joyce Johnson describes a moment in 1947 when Jack Kerouac, languishing in his mother's apartment in Queens, began to dream of a life on the road:

> In the eternal, spotless order of his mother's kitchen, a long subway ride from the all-night haunts of Times Square, he spread maps out on the table after the dishes were cleared, and like a navigator plotted the route of his contemplated journey. The western place names were magic words of incantation. Cimarron, Council Bluffs, Platte, Cheyenne. Thoughts of Neal stirred in him, merged with romantic images of plainsmen and pioneers. Cassady loomed large in Jack's mind as archetypal, both his long-lost brother and the very spirit of the West in his rootlessness and energy. (23)

Because Johnson was only twelve years old in 1947 and would not meet Kerouac for another ten years, she is clearly imagining this scene. Still, I wonder how far she would have been able to move beyond the "spotless order" of Gabrielle Kerouac's kitchen had she been present on this occasion. Women like Johnson may have defied their middle-class parents with their bohemian lifestyle, but few experienced the thrill Kerouac must have received when he spread out the map and imagined a "rootless" mobility. Nor did they have at their disposal a stable of friends like Neal Cassady, ready to drop everything and hit the road at a moment's notice. For nearly all of these women, far-flung pastoral sites would remain mysterious, since domestic responsibilities kept them anchored in place. Meanwhile, freewheeling men continued to roam.[1]

According to Maria Damon, the "foregrounding of homosocial and mobile masculinity" in the writings of Kerouac and his peers "obscured both the actual domestic arrangements many Beats made and the artistic achievements of their female counterparts and partners." Meanwhile, Beat women "hung out, married, cohabited, eloped, drank, drugged and held it together. In short, they did everything the men did in addition to child-bearing and domestic 'duties' which, in accord with the tribal ideology of the movement, took on a positive aura" (145, 146). Those who ventured into the literary sphere discovered it was rife with patriarchal mythology and misogynistic attitudes (Davidson 175–77). As a result, many decided to stay home. Women of the Beat generation may have been "feminists before the term was coined," Brenda Knight asserts (6), but for the most part theirs was a life spent "off the road." Diane di Prima offers a wry description of the claustrophobia they suffered when she defines homesickness as a longing "not for where you have been but for where you will never go" (*Dinners* 153).

Along with LeRoi Jones and Anne Waldman, di Prima is a second-generation Beat writer tangentially connected to the New York School, thanks in part to the strong friendship she forged with Frank O'Hara in the downtown arts scene. In histories of the Beat movement, di Prima is depicted as the leotard-clad icon staring back at the camera in defiance. She is remembered as a "ferocious individualist" (Pinchbeck 387) who knew the ways of the streets, and celebrated as an iconoclastic revolutionary who devoted herself to the "bloody process" of self-marginalization (Libby 47). An "archetypal Beat woman" (Watson, *Birth* 270), she made serious headway in a male-dominant subculture, publishing verse in alternative magazines, coordinating performances at the Poets Theatre, putting out well-received books, and coediting an influential journal, *The Floating Bear*, with LeRoi Jones. At the same time, she was the doyenne of Beat domesticity, part of a retinue of women whose humanity and largesse made the gritty downtown scene more comfortable for their male counterparts. As George Butterick says, di Prima "reminds us that the [Beat] generation spent as much time in urban 'pads' as it did 'on the road', and that one can travel as far by human relationships as by the thumb" (149). Blossom Kirschenbaum offers a more flexible analysis, praising di Prima's ability to "flaunt defiance of family even while enlarging the circle of quasi-family, which comes to include other poets, those who share the pads, those with whom one breaks bread—one's true com-panions—and those with whom one maintains en-during relationships" (57).

Unfortunately, most critics tend to pit ("ferocious") individualism against ("enduring") domestic relationships, resistance against peaceful accommodation, movement against stasis. By doing so, they reinforce binary structures, obscuring viable options like communal identity and mobile domesticity. They overlook the fact that, as di Prima left New York to travel (and eventually settle) in the West, she fundamentally altered the Beat lifestyle, opening up a constellation of possibilities for the women suffering silently in bohemia's urban fiefdoms. Di Prima also pointed the way west for second-generation New York School writers, who by the end of the 1960s were gravitating to places like Bolinas, California, and Boulder, Colorado (home of the Naropa Institute, where Waldman taught). Simply put, she helped redraw the map of New York's countercultural poetry scene.

My consideration of di Prima's life in and out of New York City is influenced by theories of cultural geography. I have been inspired by several critics, including Caren Kaplan, who explains that "questions of travel" break down binary structures that naturalize arbitrary oppositions and suppress hidden terms, part of her effort to "signify the possibilities of multiple figures and tropes of displacement that might lead us to more complex and accurate maps of cultural production" (9); Mary Louise Pratt, for whom "contact zones" mark a "space in which peoples geographically and historically separated come into contact with each other and establish ongoing relations" (6–7); James Clifford, an anthropologist who reads "home" as a "series of locations and encounters" ("Notes" 128) and "fieldwork" as an exercise in autobiography (*Routes* 85–91); and Gilles Deleuze and Felix Guattari, who argue that one's "unknown homeland" or "natal" space is never fixed, conditioned as it is by a rhythmic and relentlessly directional drive toward the ecstasy in "melodic landscapes" (312–15, 318–23). Like these thinkers, Di Prima shows us that heuristic binaries such as domesticity/mobility, homeland/foreign territory, East/West, and city/country are always undergoing reconfiguration. Yet for her, boundary crossing has always been a practical concern, the personal stakes of which are easy to underestimate when we feather our intellectual nests with too many layers of abstract philosophy. Hence the attention I pay to daily details filling di Prima's poetry: the way she fed and clothed her family, the music and memories that served as the background for her sojourns, the challenges of setting up a household (or moving away from one), the qualities of light that filled the landscapes she traversed, the style and grace with which she moved through space.

AT AGE FOURTEEN, when she told her Brooklyn family she had decided to become a poet, di Prima knew that stepping over the line could bring dire consequences. "I cried," she told me, recalling her disclosure. "It was a sad day for me, because I knew I was saying goodbye to people and family and a basic everyday way of life" (Conversation). By the time she dropped out of Swarthmore College and dropped in on the bohemian scene in lower Manhattan, she was on her way to becoming a Beat icon. She was hip and well read. She dressed in black clothing, wore her hair long, and took many lovers. When Bob Kaufman spoke of "Mulberry-eyed girls in black stockings / Smelling vaguely of mint jelly and last night's bongo drummer," in his poem "Bagel Shop Jazz" (107), he was referring to fashion statements di Prima made popular. Meanwhile, her streetwise attitude surprised men on the scene. "I've actually had the balls to enjoy myself," she told Waldman. "Although my parents were sort of on the lower edge of the middle class, I'm definitely a street person. All my first writing was completely predicated on getting the slang of N.Y. in the period of the early '50's down on paper somehow or another" ("Interview" 45).

Di Prima's New York moxie is on display in "More or Less Love Poems," short lyrics that combine the compact wisdom of Buddhist aphorisms with the kind of backhanded compliments traded in barroom conversations. The result is a somewhat skittish acceptance of what love offered women of the Beat Generation. "In case you put me down I got it figured / how there are better mouths than yours / more swinging bodies / wilder scenes than this," she says in one poem. "In case you put me down it won't help much" (*Pieces* 9). Another poem, its laconic phrasing stripped to the bone, is even more piercing:

> In your arms baby
> I don't feel no
> spring in winter
> but I guess I can do
> without
> galoshes.
>
> In your arms baby
> I don't hear no
> angels sing

but maybe I forget
to turn on
the phonograph. (9)

Wary self-protection and deflective humor are the dominant keys here. For all her toughness, the poet seems to be holding something back. In *Memoirs of a Beatnik*, an erotic portrait of her salad days in the New York underground, di Prima speaks of an "eternal tiresome rule of Cool" that forbade emotional attachment (94). She admits she subscribed to a "philosophy of resigned desperation," the goal of which was to look "a little beat, a little down" (17). But di Prima's cool attitude could not fully suppress her restless longing for "wilder scenes than this": geographical sites where the glory of an early spring is an unmistakable event, not a futile hope; places where angelic songs pour down from the heavens. To find them, she needed to draw her own cognitive map, a daunting task for women in the 1950s and early 1960s, when few blueprints existed.[2]

Throughout the 1960s—that decade of long, strange trips—this New York native wended her way westward, part of her ongoing effort to establish new alliances and locate basic personal freedoms. For di Prima, "the West" was a series of encounters in places as diverse as California, Wyoming, New Mexico, and upstate New York (one of America's first frontiers). Her gradual assimilation in these regions had a profound effect not only on her psyche but also on her poetry, which discarded the harsher style of the New York Beats and edged closer to the ecological and mystical poetics favored by San Francisco Renaissance writers. She also adopted new modes of domesticity in the West's open-air settings. Above all, she proved that the on-the-road genre belongs to women as well as men. Di Prima's sojourn in the West is an intimate narrative, yet it is full of social significance. It is as fluid and honest a story as I have read.

DI PRIMA MADE HER first trip west in 1961, accompanied by her young daughter Jeanne. She went to San Francisco to visit Michael and Joanna McClure, who enjoyed one of the few equitable partnerships among Beat couples (Knight 217). From them, she learned about the natural cycles lending the region and its people their character. In "The Colors of Brick" (*Selected Poems* 57), di Prima thanks Michael McClure for showing her that poetry is a "process" in tune with the slipperiness of organic life. Accordingly, in "After McClure," she speaks of abandoning bop prosody for more natural rhythms, of "letting [her poetry] come & go like rain / like sunlight" (83). Crossing into Marin County, di Prima continued to witness the tranquility Californians enjoyed. "I cut a swath with my New York energy," she recalls, "but watched them all the same. To see: how they did it, this intricate dance. To keep the creative, but without so sharp an edge" (*Recollections* 265).

She elaborated on this point in our conversation: "The West really opened up stuff for me. I no longer felt bound by the exigencies of space and economics. There was free food to be gathered in the hills, you could dig clams on the beach, and pot was $85 for a big bale. I saw lots of single moms with kids, living by whatever came their way. I think my experience out there showed me new possibilities. It gave me permission, when I went back to New York, to have a second kid, this time with LeRoi Jones." The following year, di Prima returned to California, settling for a time at Stinson Beach, where she could "hear the sea / Right out the bedroom window" (*Selected Poems* 128). Her marriage to Alan Marlowe, a gay fashion model, was officiated in San Francisco by Shunryu Suzuki, a Zen priest from Japan, accentuating the Pacific Rim vibe. Di Prima calls the meeting with Suzuki pivotal. "It was the first time in my twenty-eight years that I had encountered another human being and felt trust. It blew my tough, sophisticated young artist's mind" ("Diane" 56–57).

Returning to New York in 1963, di Prima and Marlowe dedicated themselves to their "little arts empire," establishing the Poets Press and the Poets Theatre, important outlets for avant-garde writers, including charter members of the New York School. Yet it was a turbulent time for the city's bohemian community. The old networks di Prima relied upon had begun to splinter. Dancer Freddie Herko, a close friend, committed suicide in 1964. LeRoi Jones left his family, moved uptown to Harlem, and changed his name to Amiri Baraka, cutting off contact with white friends. In 1966, Frank O'Hara died, leaving a huge void and concluding the New York School's initial phase. Other artists and writers married, had kids, and moved away from the downtown scene. This sense of an ending made its way into di Prima's verse, which was becoming less urban and more ecological in temperament. In "Good Friday, 1965" di Prima flees to her building's rooftop and memorializes the closing of the stripped down ("defoliated") Poets Theatre on Easter weekend (*Selected Poems* 139). In a sequence reminiscent of West Coast meditations by Gary Snyder and Phil Whalen, she looks down from her high perch, mourning what has passed and taking note of what has endured, in spite of it all, in her home city:

> All things on earth have slipped away from me
> the gulf between this year & the one before

the last time I came to this roof to read Milarepa
the children were made of flesh & blood, I was certain
that there were duties that I had to do.
that there was work for Alan and for me.
that there were friends who loved us.

Now I sit alone in the sun on some kind of peak
the waters do not reach . . .

All things on earth are remembering what they were.
Roofs rise like rocks, the traffic sounds of the sea.
Women flock to the laundromat on their way
to the river, with their sheets, they have that look
The shapes are eternal, our vision
had grown obscure. (141–42)

The Lower East Side location is familiar, but di Prima's diction and tone have veered away from hipster irony to accommodate a more natural and compassionate perspective. Her mention of Milarepa is particularly telling, since the Tibetan Buddhist witnessed the destruction of his native land and the disappearance of his family on a fateful trip home, subsequently renouncing the fleeting *samsara* world to sit in mountaintop meditation (Evans-Wentz 175–82). A kindred spirit, di Prima exposes the "new vision" of the Beat Generation as illusory, but suffers for her bravery. Contemplating the void from her rooftop, she finds herself ostracized by a surprisingly closed-minded community of urban bohemians. "The people are good," she admits, "but there is no magic in them / So I am 'a guru'—I am not, as I was, among friends. / There has this change occurred" (*Selected Poems* 143). Apparently, her immersion in West Coast culture, including Pacific Rim religions, has caused her New York self to melt away:

This is not my house anymore: I have no house
I live in it like one who passes through
They are not my children: Mini may go to Roi
Jeanne may leave for the west, and Alexander
might go to the monastery when he is twelve,
And Alan must set out on a terrible journey
I pray will bring him closer to his peace.
Defoliating. I am becoming light.
My bones shine thru my flesh. It falls away. (142)

The "terrible journey" refers to Marlowe's long-standing plan to visit India, but di Prima's own travels sound just as sublime. The self-portrait she sketches includes a bleached skeleton in a defoliated landscape, the kind one might find in a Georgia O'Keeffe painting, though the image is also reminiscent of Sylvia Plath burning away her domestic self in the early morning hours, or of a Buddhist monk performing self-immolation. In any case, di Prima's city skin falls away as she becomes infused with the light of wide-open spaces. A similar situation exists in "Theatre Poems" when di Prima equates a New York hipster's smile with the grandeur of Zion National Park and claims that theater workers wielding staple guns and "dancing under the lights on St. Marks Place" remind her of Comanches on the warpath (130). It is as though New York City could no longer speak to a native daughter on its own terms. The West was already in her bones.

When their landlord sold their residence at 35 Cooper Square, di Prima and Marlowe decided to leave the city for the Catskills, moving to a Hindu ashram in Monroe, New York, before finding a house to rent in nearby Kerhonkson. The woman who had spent nearly all her life in the city was suddenly cut loose. No one visited for months. In "The Bus Ride," di Prima describes herself as a passive victim who has been spirited away to a chilly isolation "in these northern mountains . . . at the edge of the world" like a southern European taken hostage by a Nordic plunderer (*Pieces* 55). The experience was unnerving, yet there she was, braving the wilds, heating the house with firewood, gathering wild herbs and rhubarb for the supper table (honing her foraging skills, she recalled watching Italian-American women in the Bronx gather dandelion greens in vacant lots). A snapshot from the summer of 1966 (used as the frontispiece in *Kerhonkson Journal*) shows family members taking up their roles as hearty pioneers. Di Prima wears a long dress and a bonnet. In what is perhaps an ironic salute to the Statue of Liberty, she cradles a large book or tablet with her left forearm. Marlowe, shirtless and unshaven, towers above her. He holds the shoulder of Dominique, whose makeshift tiara is perched precariously on the springy hair she inherited from her biological father, LeRoi Jones. Young Alexander, by contrast, is the spitting image of Marlowe and is totally nude. With its hasty posing and prideful smirks, the frontispiece presents a slightly campy version of hippie pastoral, even as it suggests sincere acceptance of the open-air domesticity di Prima glimpsed in Marin County three years earlier. It has the antique quality of a daguerreotype unearthed on the prairie despite the fact that its portrayal of gay and interracial family members heralds a newer and more controversial social frontier.[3]

Poems written during this time emphasize the charadelike character of the family's rustic life. "Oh it is very like being a pioneer," di Prima declares in "Song for the Spring Equinox," before admitting that it is "slightly boring, / it tastes a lot of the times crossword poem / and ordering things thru the mail, which never come / or turn out wrong, or come the wrong color (wisteria)" (*Selected Poems* 152). Like Caroline Kirkland, a nineteenth-century New Yorker who tried her hand at frontier living in Michigan, di Prima registers her initial disappointment with rural life in offhanded language. "I want to see Shanghai Express at the Museum / of Modern Art, meet Frank [O'Hara] for a drink, or a bacon and egg sandwich / somehow involve myself in the national culture," she complains in "I'll Always Remember the Maltese Falcon." "[I]nstead I sit here, discussing acreage / not that we have any yet, discussing horses / and planning to grow buckwheat and make miso / have an apple orchard—all on our point 87th of an acre" (161).

In "First Snow, Kerhonkson," a poem addressed to Marlowe, di Prima continues to dispel the pretensions of their makeshift utopia:

This, then, is the gift the world has given me
(you have given me)
softly the snow
cupped in hollows
lying on the surface of the pond
matching my long white candles
which stand at the window
which will burn at dusk while the snow
fills up our valley
this hollow
no friend will wander down
no one arriving brown from Mexico
from the sunfields of California, bearing pot
they are scattered now, dead or silent
or blasted to madness
by the howling brightness of our once common vision
and this gift of yours—
white silence filling the contours of my life. (*Pieces* 54)

The poet seems magical, posing as a conjurer of spirits in front of a candlelit shrine, but she acknowledges her powerlessness in the face of rural America's crushing isolation. With her city friends out of the picture, she must find a way to make the white silence of upstate New York a part of her own being.

Surprising as it may be, di Prima's first step toward salvation involved sorting through the pastoral subtext of her New York years, gauging the extent to which nature affects the most inveterate of city dwellers. In *Memoirs of a Beatnik* she talks about the "blooming pads" of the Lower East Side as though she were describing lily pads (65) and calls 14th Street "the northern limit of our country," as though she were scouting uncharted territory (104). She also speaks of "woodshedding," which sounds natural enough but is actually a jazz term signifying "what you do when you hole up and practice your art . . . to the exclusion of all else" (97). A hilarious example of her faux-naturalism arrives in a prose piece entitled "What Do Frogs Say?" In a crowded pad, Freddie Herko works fruitlessly on a painting while di Prima puts tomato sauce on a low simmer and tries to steal a few minutes of quality time with her daughter: "Jeanne has this picture book. She doesn't really know what it's all about, but you point to things, and make noises, and she digs it. Gets you in trouble, though. Like with butterflies. What the hell do butterflies say? Nothing. So I moved my hands around like flying and she was happy. . . . I turned the page and there were these frogs. I pointed to them. Jeanne waited. I've never seen a frog. Never. Very peculiar life I've had. Seen an albino roach once. But no frogs. I said to Freddie What do frogs say" (*Dinners* 148).

Di Prima may have seen an albino roach and stalked its insect brothers as though she were hunting big game (*Dinners* 104), but she lagged behind her Kerhonkson neighbors in her knowledge of natural phenomena. In "Biology Lesson," she portrays herself as a hapless and somewhat fearful city slicker finding her way amid other signs of life. Biotic organisms permeate her domestic interior, much as they "crawl" across her indented poetic lines:

> the whole place practically crawls
>   the green moist chilly warmth yin air
>   busy as hell, the whole thing coming together
> all over the place
>
> they were dead wrong about no spontaneous
> generation. (*Pieces* 61)

In *Wickerby: An Urban Pastoral*, Brooklyn writer Charles Siebert tells of being unable to fall asleep in the countryside of Quebec because of all the noise. I myself know of New Yorkers who grow jumpy when visiting the country, waking up to the chirping of crickets or the rustling of an animal in the bush. In happier moments they mistake wind rustling through the trees for the whoosh of traffic on the Brooklyn-Queens Expressway. Di Prima was not so different during her time in Kerhonkson, and yet for a woman who once considered anything outside of New York City to be "the country" (*Memoirs* 65), she had already come a long way. She even switched to a macrobiotic diet. The coffee and speed she had ingested trying to keep up with the pace of New York City had given her a stomach condition. A natural diet soothed her ailments and helped her get in touch with her surroundings. "This may sound funny," she told me, "but you eat seasonally the wild food that grows locally, so you get in tune with the land" (Conversation).

Di Prima's connection with the land grew stronger when she hopped in a Volkswagen bus and embarked on one of the era's great road adventures: a twenty-thousand-mile reading tour across America. While editing the *Floating Bear*, di Prima established a network of friends in "funny little places" across the country (Di Prima and Jones vii).[4] Through her contacts she set up a schedule of readings, though in the spirit of the age she reserved time for exploration on days between stations. Marlowe handled the driving chores. Five-year-old Dominique and four-year-old Alexander came along for the ride, as did a pair of puppies and an ex-Marine from Louisiana named "Zen," who provided child-care support. Even in 1967, this unorthodox domestic unit must have elicited strange looks, especially in Middle America. But as Kirschenbaum says, di Prima decided "to live as though the revolution had already been accomplished—to separate sex from marriage and marriage from childrearing, and to improvise a quasi-familial supportive network" (64).

Zigzagging her way across the country, di Prima read at an array of venues, ranging from a discotheque in Buffalo, New York, to a Black Arts gallery in Pittsburgh, Pennsylvania, to a professor's house in Seattle, Washington, to various storefronts. Members of the hippie caravan were supported by funds collected from the readings, and from the LSD Timothy Leary supplied in lieu of a bankroll when they departed his estate in Millbrook, New York, earlier that year. Di Prima and company cooked and camped out of the bus, on roadsides and in fields, in all kinds of weather, making do with whatever their gypsy life offered and establishing a closer contact with the land and its people than Kerouac, for all his talk about becoming an "American careener" (*Portable* 111), established on his dashes across the continent. Di Prima remembers riding a "wave of excitement" as they encountered the country's diverse splendor. "As you moved west, you moved from the staid gray of the East, the academics and the teenybop-pers, to revolution and the whole music scene in Detroit, and the scene just got more crazy as you got further westward," she told me. "It was about to be the Summer of Love, you know. I remember these kids from White Horse, pilgrims from the hinterlands, came down to Vancouver when we were there and they all had tie-dye shirts on. Many of the profs were dropped out by that time and you did readings at their house rather than the university" (Conversation).

But life on the road also brought difficulties. In "Poem in Praise of My Husband (Taos)," di Prima and Marlowe are depicted as clueless explorers "blundering thru from one wrong place to the next / . . . look[ing] at the stars, about which they know nothing, to find out / where they are going" (*Pieces* 63). Especially vexing was di Prima's demand for a space of writing outside a prescribed set of domestic duties, which to her chagrin accom-panied her on the road. Viewed in this light, her "praise" for Marlowe is rather damning:

> I suppose it hasn't been easy living with me either,
> with my piques, and ups and downs, my need for privacy
> leo pride and weeping in bed when you're trying to sleep
> and you, interrupting me in the middle of a thousand poems
> did I call the insurance people? the time you stopped a poem
> in the middle of our drive over the nebraska hills and
> into colorado, odetta singing, the whole world singing in me
> the triumph of our revolution in the air
> me about to get that down, and you
> you saying something about the carburetor
> so that it all went away. (63)

Larry McMurtry has said that "interrupted domesticity is the dirty little secret of travel writing" (41). Yet di Prima has brought an extended family with her, enjoying few interruptions from a domestic routine that was itself a sequence of interruptions. It would seem considerably more difficult to strike the pose of a swashbuckling travel writer when one has kids and a husband tugging on both sides of one's dress, but then again, this is a hurdle many women have had to overcome as they moved into uncharted territories, as favorite songs (their own, those of folk singers, and those of the land) got interrupted by the mundane music of family life.[5]

Her tour of America complete, di Prima gave Marlowe her credit cards, in an effort to dispatch him to India, and took stock of her situation. Again, she found herself living in New York City but longing for western lands she had left behind. In "Stone Take 1/12/68," she tests her ability to make the city vanish or "go poof" (*Selected Poems* 184), much as she had done in "Good Friday, 1965." Similarly, in "City Winter," she registers her disgust with the "grey world" of New York: "Even the snow does not 'stick'/ doesn't whiten the ground" (192). "New Mexico Poem" is even more effective in tracking the geographic shift di Prima was working through on aesthetic and personal levels. In the first section, the poet reveals that the stunning sunsets she saw in New Mexico led her to believe she was standing on native ground, confirming the beliefs of other female travelers to the Southwest, including Mabel Dodge Luhan, Mary Austin, and Willa Cather.[6] She says she occasionally longed for New York on her reading tour, though in retrospect she recalls having been lured by a mirage, a "glimmering" but rather "brittle" city, "made of porcelain," where recently deceased friends like O'Hara and Herko lingered as ghosts. Later in the poem, she mentions bleached bones in the desert, a fit reminder of the mortality visited upon her New York comrades and another afterimage from "Good Friday, 1965." In the final section, di Prima measures New Mexico's vast beauty ("O wondrous wide open spaces!") against New York's cramped thoroughfares ("a dark tunnel you Indians wouldn't believe"), offering her hope that the violence visited upon Native Americans in their ancestral homelands will be reversed by African Americans rioting across the Hudson River in Newark, New Jersey. Di Prima ended up aiding Newark's insurgents, shipping them supplies via back roads after the National Guard blocked major highways. Yet she knew she would have to rekindle her own mission in the West, as her apostrophe to New Mexico's Indians makes clear:

> Where you are, it is two hours earlier
> the breeze is cold, the sun is very hot
> the horses are standing around, wishing for trees
> It is possible I shall see you dance again
> on your hill, in your beads, if the gods are very kind. (173)

The gods must have been kind, for during the tumultuous summer of 1968 di Prima pulled up stakes and moved west for good, finding an apartment in San Francisco large enough to house her entire tribe, including four kids, two of Marlowe's former lovers, and various artists enamored of communal living. Desperate for money, she began to write *Memoirs of a Beatnik*, acceding to the publisher's request that she include as many sex scenes as possible. The result was a titillating but rather skewed appraisal of a life she was trying to put behind her. Evaluating *Memoirs of a Beatnik* in an afterword to the 1988 edition, di Prima says, "I am really glad I wrote it when I did, before the West completely took me" (137). According to plan, she would work on the book only in the morning. "By noon or one I would have had enough for the day, and close up shop, and wander off to Japantown for raw fish and sake, which I had discovered was the only way to acclimate to the rain and mist and seawind that were a constant in the panhandle." Once immersed in San Francisco's Pacific Rim spirit, she felt ready to begin her "real writing" (138).

This real writing includes several poems about hippie men—"November," "Zero," "Chronology," "Aries, Again," "Deborah," and "Seattle Song" (dedicated to Peter Coyote)—most of which impugn their tendency to "split" when relationships grow difficult. In "A Spell for Felicia, That She Come Away" and "Dee's Song," di Prima considers hippie women, whom she portrays as defeated domestics mired in filth and encumbered by drug problems and dashed dreams. Di Prima occupied a position somewhere between these poles. She did her best to take care of the extended family under her roof, but she also demanded the freedom and mobility hippie men enjoyed. In the aptly titled "Poem of the Refusals" (*Pieces* 132), she gives conventional domesticity the heave-ho: "No checkerboard / linoleum. No. / No dishwasher; washing machine / unlikely." Yet as a loving mother she honors the natural resolve of her children: "like grass / on the hills—they hang / in there." In "These Days" (131), di Prima speaks of being "Permanently / removed from concern abt my / kitchen," but finds that the open-air setting of her new house in Marshall, California, made home life enjoyable. She takes her young son Rudi for a nature walk through a meadow, puts Alex's favorite record on the turntable when he gets up, and makes plans to take her children down a dirt road to visit neighbors that afternoon, summoning an "undisguisedly mirthful" form of country living.

On Tomales Bay, near the Marshall Tavern, the family caught fish in a net they draped over a pier. At night they slept on Japanese-style tatami mats, drifting off to the rhythm of waves lapping underneath the floorboard extensions of their bedroom.[7] Though peaceful, the situation resembled the "distinctly domestic disorder" described in Marilynne Robinson's *Housekeeping* (113). "I've never met anyone poorer than we were," Tara Marlowe tells Daniel Pinchbeck. "When I was a kid, my mother once told us that she was going on strike—she wasn't going to be the mother and cook for us anymore." Pressed by Pinchbeck to describe how her mother's lifestyle affected her, Tara replies, "It meant that no one ever taught me table manners, or how to dress or that I should clean myself, so I walked around like a filthy ragamuffin with matted hair" (387–88).

Di Prima had lived in voluntary poverty for years, but in the West she got more involved in Asian religions forbidding material attachment, visiting the Zen Center and East-West House in San Francisco and the new Buddhist monastery at Tassajara Springs. Nestled deep in the mountains, at the end of a fifteen-mile dirt road, Tassajara was originally settled by the Esselen people, who praised the healing properties of its water as well as its natural beauty. Nonnatives agreed. "It's great! Like China!" Shunryu Suzuki exclaimed after the Zen Center, with funds collected from Bay Area "zenefits," purchased the land in 1966 (Chadwick xi, 266, 278). In "Tassajara, 1969," di Prima offers her own encomium, in Asian-inflected rhythms:

> Even Buddha is lost in this land
> the immensity
> takes us all with it, pulverizes, & takes us in
>
> Bodhidharma came from the west.
> Coyote met him. (*Pieces* 86)

We see here mobile figures from different hemispheres confronting one another. Bodhidharma was the fifth-century monk who brought Buddhism from India to China, beginning its eastward transmission to Korea and Japan. Shunryu Suzuki extended that route when he brought Zen practice from Japan to California in 1959. The writings of D. T. Suzuki had already made inroads with American intellectuals interested in Zen, and San Francisco Beats had been listening to Alan Watts speak about the subject on KPFA radio. Not until "the little Suzuki" (as the Roshi called himself) arrived on these shores, however, was a Zen master able to persuade Americans to make a practice of Buddhism. Although Japanese monks chastised Suzuki for watering down Buddhism to appeal to the "beginning mind" of Westerners, di Prima saw that his teachings were not diluted so much as they were given new dimension. In particular, it was the pulverizing power of the American West, a landscape filled with vast panoramas and roaming trickster figures like Coyote, which challenged Buddhism to address a more dangerous and freewheeling reality. Suzuki captured the integrative spirit of West Coast Buddhism when he used the spear of a yucca plant instead of a Japanese brush to complete the *sumi* painting on the cover of *Zen Mind, Beginner's Mind*.

Far from being a hindrance, the vastness of the West facilitated Buddhist precepts, as di Prima explained some years later:

> Whether we are aware of it or not, something of Buddhism pervades American consciousness. When Bodhidharma came from India to China with the Buddhism that was to become Ch'an and later Zen, his answer to the Chinese emperor's request for "the holy teachings" was "VASTNESS, NO HOLINESS!" This seems to me to be at the very core of who we are, what we are doing in the world at this time, as a nation and as a species, as we move out of time into space. ("Diane" 58)

The sublimity of the West emerges even more powerfully in "Letter to Jeanne (at Tassajara)," a poem di Prima addresses to her eldest daughter. This verse epistle closes with a blessing, a wish that Jeanne's mountain retreat will teach her to cherish the "various life" her mother could never appreciate growing up in New York City:

> O you have landscapes dramatic like mine
> never was, uncounted caves
> to mate in, my scorpio, bright love
> like fire light up your beauty years
> on these new, jagged hills. (*Pieces* 99)

In 1971, the National Endowment for the Arts (NEA) tapped di Prima for its poet-in-the-schools program in Wyoming, expanding her range of western experiences.[8] During her six-year tenure, di Prima ranged far afield, from reform schools in Minnesota to Bureau of Indian Affairs (BIA) schools in Arizona, bringing literature to those with little access to books, teaching a population others claimed could not be taught. In return, the counterculture poet received new knowledge from characters living in out-of-the-way places. The closeted gay man in Casper who routinely checked himself into the state asylum so he could have access to Valium; the woman from Sheridan forced to hide her watercolor paintings from a husband who would not abide such a "waste of time"; the Indian schoolteacher in Arminto, forbidden from teaching on the reservation, trying his best to assemble educational resources in a town that consisted of two houses, a hotel, and a bar; the girl in reform school who refused to write in her notebook because she did not have money to buy another: these were the people who touched di Prima's soul. In the end, she bought six notebooks for the girl and left behind a bilingual edition of Lorca's *Poet in New York*

DI PRIMA IN THE WEST | **167**

(an ironic choice) for appreciative migrant workers. She left countless others with the belief that someone from the outside world truly cared (Conversation). Looking back, she recalls "trying to stretch myself to understand the circumstance of people's lives so that I don't enter them as an outsider with a pre-formed judgment. . . . So it's not only the work—the readings and the workshops—but what spills over because if you're a visiting artist in these places, you're kind of the local healer, shaman, psychiatrist, friend—a friend who is going away tomorrow so can be told everything" (Waldman, "Interview" 43–44).

A legacy of despair and loneliness pervades the interior West, a longing to reach out across wide-open spaces to communicate or hear others communicate. The Wichita Lineman, chilled to the bone and in need of a vacation, taps into telephone wires so he can overhear two lovers having a conversation, in the old Jimmy Webb song Glen Campbell made popular. In *Close Range*, Annie Proulx surveys the spare psychological outcroppings of Wyoming, a harsh terrain upon which even the most fiercely independent folks admit "you can't have a fence with only one post" (71). All the same, visionary writers and artists have unearthed unexpected cultural convergences in this region. In Gary Snyder's *Myths & Texts*, Zen masters and Sioux prophets mingle freely on the plains, sharing ancient teachings and engaging in cogent ecological commentary. In "Wichita Vortex Sutra," Allen Ginsberg (CP 394–411) finds that reports about the Vietnam War on his car radio are thrown into relief by a random series of prairie signifiers: weather reports, Holy Roller gospel shouting, billboard messages, movie advertisements, and Indian chants. Jazz musicians Pat Metheny and Lyle Mays cover the same territory in "As Falls Wichita, So Falls Wichita Falls," an assemblage of Asian and American sounds they recorded, as a kind of musical riddle, in 1981.[9] In each case, the expansiveness of the West facilitates the circulation of culturally coded messages emanating from far-flung locations.

Di Prima is attuned to these frequencies. She is in touch with the region's loneliness but keeps her ear to the ground, honoring those who never truly disappeared. In "Sixth Notebook Meditation," the restless poet joins a long line of rebel angels, many of them Asian in origin or spirit, who make this hardscrabble region a welcoming place.

Ping-ponging back & forth across America
starting small grass fires where I land
in Minnesota jail, Wyoming
community college, high schools of South Tucson

> may I always remember the Bodhisattvas
> sitting down in BIA cafeteria, may I
> cut hamburger with the sword of Manjusri
> pluck lotuses on windy Nebraska hills
> set jewels of Lokeshvara round my neck
> after I brush my teeth in steam-heated
> dormitory bathroom.
> Pure light of ancient wisdom, stay w/ me
> like a follow spot, pierce my
>   armored heart, clean
> cobwebs of plastic food & deadened
>   eternal sorrow.
> "How do you like it here?" "I like it
> very much." (*Pieces* 103)[10]

Inclusive by nature, di Prima propels herself forward, employing rushed syntax (ampersands and shorthand spelling) and "ping-pong" indentations, reciting daily activities alongside religious petitions as she tallies the rewards of NEA work. The simultaneity with which she summons heavenly figures and real folks puts me in mind of Kathleen Norris, a poet who left New York in 1974 to live and teach on the Great Plains. As she offers a prayer and receives the blessing of a straightforward question, di Prima realizes that the key ingredients to her happiness are unrestricted movement across a vast landscape and close contact with its people. The NEA extended her grant because she was able to get along with the West's rough-hewn characters. Even the rednecks were willing to give her a fair shake. "They respected my honesty," she says. "I was able to stand up to them and look them in the eye, and they liked that" (Conversation).

Although di Prima embraced the people of the West, she could not help but recall the Sand Creek massacre and the legacy of frontier violence. She sometimes winced upon looking at the desolate land, with its "short spiny grass & dusty wind" and "beef too expensive to eat." And she bleakly noted that two-thirds of its citizens "voted for madman Nixon / were glad to bomb the 'gooks' in their steamy jungle." Even so, she displayed the wherewithal in "Brief Wyoming Meditation" to seek a separate peace:

> I seek
> the place where your nature meets mine,
>   the place where we touch

nothing lasts long
nothing
> *but earth*
& the mountains (Pieces 106)

In "Wyoming Series" (134–37), composed in the late 1970s and reissued by the poet's Eidolon Editions in 1988, di Prima strengthens her regional connection. Dedicated to Shunryu Suzuki ("who visited me in a dream and brought me this poem"), the limited edition of this "love poem to a harsh land" is enhanced by the poet's pen and ink drawings of basin and range. Di Prima's smooth, abstract lines, erotic in their curvature, suggest an intimate bond between the land and her own body, accommodating the sprightly angels who fill the air of Big Sky country and the bodhisattva giants in the canyons who "give an edge" to lovers' dreams. Throughout the poem, feminine metaphors of immersion and enfolding supplant long-standing paradigms of violent penetration and rape, summoning a more sensual way of moving through the postfrontier West.[11] "The landscape itself is unobtrusive," di Prima told students at Naropa Institute in 1975. "It enters you, you enter it, it's there." The result is an uncanny homecoming in a not-so-foreign location. "When you see that land, or you recognize that feeling, you say, yeah, wow, I remember this, I've been here before, even though you never have. The most surprising things are always familiar, immediately. That's been my experience" ("Light" 22).

Di Prima writes frequently about the free play of light in the West, employing alchemical traditions to heighten her connection to landscape. In "Studies in Light," the vicissitudes of light assume an abstract energy, like the kind Charles Olson ascribed to Mayan glyphs, a model for "open field" poetics (Belgrad 87–94). For her part, di Prima cherishes "light / as a glyph that writes itself / over & over, on the face / of water, inscrutable / perpetual motion" (*Pieces* 144). In "How to Become a Walking Alchemical Experiment," she uses studies in light and metallurgy to illuminate public concerns, including nuclear tests that wreak destruction on desert communities. Mimicking the do-it-yourself instructions found in "whole earth" catalogues and macrobiotic diet books, she shows how polluted the West has become: "eat *mercury* (in wheat & fish) / breathe *sulphur* fumes (everywhere) / take plenty of (macrobiotic) *salt* / & cook the mixture in the heat / of an atomic explosion" (82).

Always sensitive to restrictions on free expression and mobility, di Prima also casts a cold eye on the capsule summaries of Native American life housed in the West's museums. In "American Indian Art: Form and

Tradition" (*Pieces* 101), she takes the Walker Art Center in Minneapolis to task for its cold storage policies, its entombment of tribes who identified so closely with the earth. Unlike "Brief Wyoming Meditation," with its open-air rumination on frontier history, this poem takes aim at a thoroughly sanitized version of western exotica, a version blindly accepted by thousands of tourists each year.[12] At issue is whether the white counterculture can speak on behalf of native peoples. Di Prima even goes so far as to ventriloquize the voice of Indian lament, repeating the line "Were we not fine?" as she passes by the empty shirts, labeled baskets, and disassembled pipes hanging in the museum's glass cases. As Philip Deloria argues, the Native American has routinely functioned for white audiences as an "open and unfixed" signifier of pleasure and rebelliousness, even if the "Indianness" conjured up in these instances is "the sign of something unchanging, a first principle" (167). So it was that San Francisco hippies painting their faces and adorning themselves with feathers announced their revolution with a little help from somebody else's traditions. This trend would seem to account for the "we" in "American Indian Art: Form and Tradition." Having said this, I believe di Prima offers a heartfelt lament for a culture that has been incarcerated, eviscerated, and put on display. As one who extended the realm through which counterculture women felt free to travel, she sympathizes with the Indian ghosts trapped in the museum. It would be foolish to call her a witness to the legacy of abuse Native Americans have suffered or a spokesperson for their rights, but it would be just as foolish to reject out of hand what she has to say about the effect of enclosed spaces on aesthetics and culture.[13]

DURING HER NEA YEARS, di Prima was assuming another identity without hesitation: that of Loba, the wolf-goddess who became the subject of a book-length poem. In *Loba*, di Prima assumes the mantle handed down by one of her favorite poets, H. D., whose *Trilogy* is the only long poem written by a modernist woman to be mentioned in the same breath as "The Waste Land," *The Cantos*, or *The Bridge*. It was not until the late 1970s, Lynn Keller reminds us, that a substantial number of American women, emboldened by "second wave" feminism, claimed the long poem as their métier. *Loba* seems to prepare the way for feminist "forms of expansion," which with their "openness to sociological, anthropological, and historical material [have been] particularly useful for poets eager to explore women's roles in history and in the formation of culture" (Keller, *Forms* 15). As Adrienne Rich says in a blurb for the 1998 edition, *Loba* is "a great geography of the female imagination."

Di Prima says that the vision of *Loba* came to her while she was working in a Wyoming reform school, where she met "people living in total
pain." Troubled by her surroundings, she had a dream. "It had to do with
being in an outcast or vagabond situation with my two children," she told
students at Naropa, emphasizing the nontraditional domesticity she favors.
Rich people living upstairs send a wolf to "hunt down" the poet and her
brood who, having caught wind of this macabre "entertainment," are already making their escape. According to di Prima, "this wolf digs what's
happening, and falls in behind us and starts walking with us. Keeping pace.
And at some point, I turned around and looked this creature in the eye,
and I recognized . . . this as a goddess that I'd known in Europe a long long
time ago" ("Light" 34–35). Throughout *Loba*, di Prima focuses not only on
the wolf but also on the animistic spirit running through the land, keeping
it alive. As her Naropa statement implies, her sequence combines goddess
legends from around the world with tales of the American West, seeking
balance between inner and outer wilderness. Emphasizing carnal connections between women and landscape (see Smith and Allen 181), di Prima
explains that she is trying to represent "feralness at the core of woman"
("Tapestry" 22).

Like other long feminist poems, *Loba* tells its story within a hypotactic
structure, with "elements from one lyric section [enhancing] an understanding of the lyrics that follow" (Keller, *Forms* 5). Di Prima's wolf goddess
takes on various useful disguises: sister, mother, lover, muse, witch, hunt-
ress, whore, junkie, bag lady, friend, maid, and hag. Only gradually, after a
series of manifestations and adventures, does a full portrait emerge. Like
the poet herself, the Loba moves in a wide arc, sniffing out freedom, roaming toward whoever might benefit from her influence. Early on, she appears
among urban bohemians, "lost moon sisters" wandering from Avenue A in
New York to Fillmore Street in San Francisco, symbolizing their solidarity
and resilient spirit (*Loba* 3). Before long, the Loba is taking her occasion
everywhere: "Her bower / lurks in the unseen muddy places / of yr soul, she
waits under the steps / of yr tenement" (43). At one point, the Loba enters
a redneck bar, and does her best to fit in:

> she strides in blue jeans to the corner
> bar; she dances
> w/ the old women, the men
> light up, they order wine,
> sawdust is flying under her feet
> her sneakers, thudding soft

her wispy hair falls sometimes
into her face

were it not for the ring of fur
            around her ankles
just over her bobby socks
            there's no one
wd ever guess her name (28)

A companion piece of sorts to Snyder's "I Went into the Maverick Bar"
(*Turtle* 9), this passage shows the extent to which a bohemian woman immersed herself in new surroundings. So strong is di Prima's attachment to
the wily wolf goddess that a reader labors to distinguish between the two.
"I am you / and I must become you," she tells the Loba at the outset of the
volume (*Loba* 6), and by the time we get to this poem—so full of womanly
swagger and the creaturely joy of striding, dancing, and drinking—we believe her. Fur around the ankles might give away the identity of the dancer
in the bar, but it is hard to say whether the Loba is masquerading as di
Prima, or whether di Prima has become the wolf. Whatever her identity,
there is a "feral core" that gives this woman the courage to forge new relationships in contact zones of the West. In such instances, di Prima locates
the uncanny space she calls "a surround," a special realm of being, an "outer
place more intimate than your blood" (281).

Di Prima anticipates an uneasy reception of her female epic in "The
Critic Reviews Loba," imagining a rational reviewer lambasting her for her
wild images and loosely structured historiography (*Loba* 138). Academics
might not understand her purpose, di Prima tells Waldman, but western
audiences accepted *Loba* instinctively: "I read one time up in a small college in northern California and all these folks came out from the surrounding communities, and communes, and towns, and a lot of women with
babies arrived and the reading seemed to reach everyone," di Prima recalls.
"Everyone was moved and it was a magical event and no explanation of
all these so-called eclectic references were [*sic*] needed. . . . Whereas I find
that reading *Loba* to an intellectual audience up at one of the universities in
Massachusetts or something endlessly requires explanations" (Waldman,
"Interview" 43). Presumably, there is a pulse in the West that exists beneath
the level of abstract intellect. The poet regards *Loba* as a lodestone drawing
those who love the West into its sphere of influence, its natural circulation
of energies, whether or not they understand what it is that draws them
there.

Later sections of *Loba* show di Prima coming to terms with her advancing age. "There is no myth / for this older, ample woman," she says in "Point of Ripening: Lughnasa" (*Loba* 305). "The harvest / is not for yourself // You no longer need to claim it" (307). Di Prima revisits this bittersweet theme in "Decline of the West," an uncollected poem from 1996, looking back at the broken dreams and personal losses that are part of any older person's vita:

> I guess I'll never buy a San Francisco mansion
> or one on the Big Sur coast & fill it w/ my friends
> artists in every room writing painting composing
> a big dance studio w/ barres & steamy windows
> wisteria tumbling over the porch & view of the
>   ocean on three sides
>
> most of the friends I mean to fill it with
> are dead by now & my knees are getting stiff
> for so many stairs & who wd do the cooking?

A life in the West has not provided the poet an easy solution to life's ills or an answer to its mysteries: "No comfortable spiritual armchair, either, alas, no practice / I know I can do just right & will do forever." Somewhat wistfully, di Prima admits that the "insane permission and vastness" she felt upon her initial encounters with the West have given way to little victories in smaller spaces:

>   I
> guess I'm just out there
> in my cluttered apartment in the Western Addition
> one well-strung mala, one well-knotted cord
> from a distant lama
>   the limits of elegance
> in my unkempt life. ("Decline")

Her San Francisco appartment is hardly a mansion. Still, her dreams of tumbling wisteria and expansive ocean views suggest the possibilities of unrestricted motion. The "well-strung mala" points toward the spiritual realm of the Pacific Rim, the region to which the West is unmistakably linked. Di Prima probably uses the Tibetan prayer beads for counting mantras. But I get the feeling the mala symbolizes the episodes and people filling her life, the "well-knotted cord" that becomes more visible as she ages. However "unkempt" her domestic situation, she finds serenity whenever she looks down the Dharma path to see how far she has traveled.

There are "two kinds of motion," di Prima once heard an astrologer say, "the kind that does / and the kind that does not displace the center of being" (*Selected Poems* 227). The fact that she now feels more at home in the West than she ever did in New York suggests that she edged closer to her true center during the 1960s, when she ceased to be the leotard-wearing icon featured in Beat history books. During this time she showed a new breed of New York poets that spiritual impulses need not surrender to sappiness, but that they could align instead with edgy avant-garde attitudes. Di Prima gave others what she gave herself: room to roam. She might have been describing her own aesthetic trajectory when she recited lines from H. D. during a 1987 lecture. Kerouac's example also lingers, for I can imagine di Prima unfurling the map of America and following her heart straight out of town, all the while proclaiming, "I go to the things I love / with no thought of duty or pity; / I go where I belong, inexorably" (*Mysteries* 24).

7 A WORLD WITHOUT GRAVITY
Jim Carroll and Kathleen Norris in the Warhol Underground

IN HIS 1956 poem "America" (*CP* 146–48), Allen Ginsberg directs a series of questions to his nation, including a spiritual petition: "America, when will you become angelic?" With this remark, Ginsberg joined a host of madcap characters (Neal Cassady, Jack Kerouac, Gregory Corso) who expressed heavenly convictions without feeling burdened by moral rectitude. By telling America, "You made me want to be a saint," Ginsberg is situating himself in the camp of Jean Genet, Sartre's existentialist hero, not in a canon of sanctified Christians. Although some continue to regard his "mystical visions and cosmic vibrations" as dilettantish, Ginsberg paved the way for a new generation of rebel intellectuals whose search for spiritual salvation has been fortified by equal measures of purity and danger.

A decade after Ginsberg issued his beatific challenge, around the time Frank O'Hara died, a scruffy collection of writers, artists, and musicians in New York City's East Village sought their own version of angelic selfhood, advocating the simplicity found in pastoral idylls while searching for the purity religious institutions promised, but often failed to deliver. Curiously, those who have written about the East Village have not paid this trend much notice. Rock journalist Robert Christgau refers to the music that came out of this neighborhood as "noisy," "brutal," and "crude," albeit strangely "sophisticated" (189–90, 200), overlooking the wistful lyrics that lurk beneath dissonant layers of sound. Literary critics like Daniel Kane advance a bit closer. But by focusing on the collaborative energies and angst-ridden edginess of East Village writers, they fail to address the spiritual aspirations of bohemians who read their poems at St. Mark's Church in the Bowery and published their work in *Angel Hair* magazine.

These New Yorkers were street-smart and cocksure about their contributions to avant-garde art, yet they possessed a surprising capacity for piety and an incessant hunger for transcendent experiences. In 1969, on their eponymous third album, musicians in the Velvet Underground, undisputed exemplars of downtown cool, claimed they were "set free" and "beginning to see the light," with Lou Reed piling on layers of irony so heavily they ultimately canceled each other out. The result was a particularly hip way of pursuing beauty and truth. In an era when "Jesus freaks" inspired Broadway musicals such as *Godspell* and *Jesus Christ Superstar*—not to mention radio favorites like Norman Greenbaum's "Spirit in the Sky" and Elton John's "Tiny Dancer"—New York's avant-garde writers offered a more penetrating analysis of religious experience within bohemian culture.[1] Like their bankrupt city, New York's rebel angels fell upon hard times in the 1970s, but some were resourceful enough to take flight from urban frustrations while searching for what Jim Carroll, in one of his best songs, called "a world without gravity."

Researching the spiritual sensibilities of second-generation New York School poets has led me to pair Kathleen Norris, author of inspirational books about contemporary Christianity, with Carroll, a former heroin addict whose reputation rests mainly upon the bad-boy antics contained in his colorful memoir, *The Basketball Diaries*. This pairing may strike many as odd. Forty years ago, however, these writers forged an intimate friendship as they circulated in Andy Warhol's orbit at Max's Kansas City (a legendary downtown bar) and participated in the St. Mark's Poetry Project. Eventually, this milieu of sex, drugs, and rock 'n' roll took on a darker cast, prompting each writer to flee the scene. Their escape routes are visible in their first volumes of verse, Norris's *Falling Off* (1971) and Carroll's *Living at the Movies* (1973).[2]

For Norris, surreal visions of farm silos and angels dotting the Manhattan skyline become harbingers of a pilgrimage spiriting her away to her family's South Dakota homestead. Norris remembers her decision to leave New York as "agonizing," but her move to the Great Plains was long-standing. Carroll's disaffection with the New York demimonde was registered covertly in meditations he composed in urban pastoral borderlands like Coney Island and Jones Beach. On such occasions, a vaguely defined spiritual undercurrent guides him through junk-saturated dreams of exaltation. In 1973, Carroll left his native city for the slower pace of California, where he was able to kick his heroin habit and move "closer to [his] heart" (*Forced*

179). Unlike Norris, though, he felt a "magnetic impulse to return to New York" (149), and today his name is synonymous with the city's punk rock and spoken word scenes. During their period of transition, each writer mixed natural imagery with the language of religious salvation, thereby manifesting two overlapping aspects of the pastoral mode: the need to leave the city for rural havens and the need for spiritual guidance.

To literary audiences, pastoral usually signifies a tradition of nature writing handed down by Theocritus, Virgil, the Wordsworths, Clare, and Frost, among others. On the other hand, many of my City University students are blue-collar Catholics for whom the term retains a strictly religious (and religiously strict) connotation. Knowing little of the spiritual entreaties embedded in works by Petrarch, Mantuan, Spenser, and Milton, they tell me pastoral signifies a congregational paternalism characteristic of priests and local parish leaders, a form of guidance they sometimes resist but acknowledge as part of their identity. For them, the idea of pastoral as rustic refuge is less important. In less guarded moments, they express a longing for tranquility in rural locations: the Poconos or some place upstate. Usually, though, they regard trips into the countryside as boring, preferring to take nature where they can get it quickly and conveniently, in city parks and beaches. This explains their preference for Carroll, whose unorthodox quests for idyllic repose within the metropolis mesh subtly with the lurid episodes filling his books and albums, over Norris, whose dowdy depictions of church suppers in South Dakota towns and "cloister walks" in Minnesota abbeys are too far removed from their own experiences. They take to Norris's early poetry more readily, however, for amid its surreal imagery they perceive the brash attitude that is the city dweller's governing code. Although her stories of heartland spirituality can seem cloying and passive-aggressive in their proselytizing, the poems in *Falling Off* remain relevant to young New Yorkers, whose dreams of pastoral utopia tend to be more circumscribed than those in traditional genre exercises, though no less powerful when they come true.

Like my students, for whom independence and consistency are crucial to street credibility, I am drawn to writers who pursue salvation on their own terms. I admire Norris and Carroll because they refused to betray their core system of values, regardless of whether those values were learned in church, picked up on the street, steadfastly defended at raucous all-night parties, or meditated upon in peaceful spots removed from the city's merry-go-round. Their separate accounts of time spent in Warhol's entourage prove particularly telling. Like Carroll, Warhol was born into a Catholic family, and, like Norris, he became a devoted churchgoer once he hit middle age. Warhol's Upper East Side townhouse was filled with religious paintings and statuary, and featured a shrine in the basement (Rayns 84; Watson, *Factory* 378). Many of the artist's assistants (Gerard Malanga, Paul Morrissey, and Billy Name) and "superstars" (Ondine, Viva, and Ultra Violet, the first a former altar boy, the latter two convent educated) were also raised Catholic. On their 1968 track "Temptation Inside Your Heart," the Velvets sang of a "pope in a silver castle" (*VU*), presumably referring to Warhol's role in the Silver Factory on East Forty-seventh Street. Similarly, Carroll referred to the Union Square Factory as a "medieval abbey," with Warhol as the "pope in exile," Morrissey the protective "abbot" doubling as "Grand Inquisitor," and himself the lowly "monk" or "novitiate" (*Forced* 44–46). Art critics also mentioned the beatific presence of "Saint Andy," with Jack Kroll emphasizing the pop artist's role as sacred thief (reminiscent of Genet), David Bourdon and Philip Leider likening him to a pastoral shepherd for New York's "black sheep," and Barbara Rose elevating him to "lacerated hero" status following Valerie Solanas's 1968 assassination attempt.[3]

There is a will-o'-the-wisp quality to "Saint" Andy's religiosity. After all, he rarely emphasized spirituality in his work, save perhaps when he was contemplating the death of "beautiful" people. Even in these circumstances, irony trumped sincere expressions of faith. "The Factory was a church," artist Gary Indiana surmised, but one in which "the sanctity of the institution and its rituals is what's important, not personal salvation" (Shaviro 91). Instead of prayer and contemplation, Warhol emphasized the maneuverability of salable images. In such an environment, Carroll explains, "a soup can on canvas is not so very different from a reliquary of precious stones stripped down by the dealers in a marketplace" (*Forced* 44). In the public realm of celebrity, his natural habitat, Warhol regarded religion as just another production and ritual as just another happening. Whatever petitions he made at St. Mary's Catholic Church of the Byzantine Rite were kept separate from the freewheeling world of the Factory, where campy commercialism and insouciant cynicism distorted most religious representations.[4]

Norris and Carroll, by contrast, latched on to the sacred aura of urban bohemia, even while playing witness to its depravity. Amid the Factory's weightlessness, they maintained their sense of grounding, thereby avoiding the fate of Freddie Herko and Andrea Feldman, would-be superstars whose suicidal leaps from apartment windows proved that laws of gravity still governed in this dizzy environment. Although Norris and Carroll joined Warhol's acolytes in seeking an unbearable lightness of being, epitomized by the pop artist's 1965 launch of helium balloons he called *Silver Clouds*, they perceived the dangers of substituting an ironic version of transcendence for their own core beliefs. Fleeing a postmodern worldview that spelled the death of commitment, these writers located beauty where others found none, learning to appreciate purity in all its forms. With a quirky but solid reliance on Christian faith, and with a longing for *loci amoeni* described in traditional pastoral texts, Norris and Carroll emerged in the 1970s as unlikely spiritual guides, announcing natural locations as the best refuge for urban angels weary of New York's hothouse atmosphere.

IN *THE BASKETBALL DIARIES,* Carroll chronicles his rambunctious youth in such colorful terms as to make narcotics abuse and petty crime seem attractive. "It's New York picaresque—Oliver Twist with a habit," Alex Williams wrote in 1995, as New Line Cinema was readying the film version for release (64). Back in the 1960s, few of Carroll's peers knew he was recording his experiences. "There was no one who wrote in my family before me," Carroll reports in *Gang of Souls*, a documentary film of the East Village poetry scene. "I came from three generations of bartenders." Carroll's working-class parents were not thrilled to learn about his adventures in literature, but he was confident enough to put pen to paper. By age eighteen, this multitalented schoolboy was not only earning All-City honors for his basketball skills but also publishing his work in *Poetry* and the *Paris Review*. His writing attracted the notice of Jack Kerouac, who sent an adulatory letter shortly before his death in 1969. "He thought I was carrying a torch," Carroll recalled, "and in a spiritual sense, I was" (Gladysz). To hear Carroll tell it, he owed his success to his urban muse, "the greatest hero a writer needs, this crazy fucking New York" (*Basketball* 159). But he felt New York owed him, too. "I've given so much of myself to feed its insatiable, tick-ridden underbelly," he wrote in his diary, "and I expect the use of its character, without threats or intimidation, in return" (*Forced* 2).

Like Arthur Rimbaud, to whom he is often compared, young Jim believed a derangement of the senses represented the writer's first step toward a visionary literature.[5] Drugs aided the boy as he searched nefarious facets of inner-city life for something "pure." The cornucopia of mind-altering agents he ingested and injected—including the "pure, pure white" of heroin (*Catholic*)—helped him gauge the bizarre beauty of New York with heightened clarity. Carroll's early work contains a pharmacological tour of urban attractions. We find young Jim dropping LSD on St. Mark's Place (*Basketball* 133), smoking marijuana in Inwood Hill Park (41), shooting heroin outside the Cloisters (210), enjoying hashish in Sutton Place (139), ingesting peyote in Central Park (197), sniffing Carbona cleaning fluid aboard the Staten Island Ferry (4), and drinking codeine cough syrup on the subway (*Forced* 189), foreshadowing the "white punks on dope" motif popularized by bands like the Ramones.

For a time, drugs accommodate a purity Carroll associates with an otherwise irretrievable childhood, even if that means curling up in the fetal position while nodding out (*Basketball* 210). Catholic symbolism begins to infuse Carroll's drug references around the time Franky Pinewater, a fellow addict, admits that the votive candles he glimpsed in a side altar during Mass reminded him of cooking smack, defeating his religious "cure" (*Basketball* 203). Shortly thereafter, Ju-Ju, an adult friend, explains that the "junk halo" Carroll has worn since age thirteen actually signifies the loss of innocence (206). Inspired perhaps by Ju-Ju's choice of words, Carroll describes his road to redemption as a twisted passion play. "My dreams, my unconscious, that is, my inner registry, was made up of Catholicism, for good or bad," Carroll explains in *Gang of Souls*, a documentary film about New York's downtown poetry scene. "That was the myth that was thrust into me, and which, you know, made sense intellectually in a certain way . . . as well as in a heart sense. So I kind of came to terms. I threw away my anger and looked at the ritual and mythology of it." Kerouac once said that his philosophy was "Catholicism mixed with gin."[6] A generation later, Carroll followed with a philosophy of his own: Catholicism mixed with heroin.

The dual grip of drugs and religion is apparent throughout *Forced Entries*, "downtown diaries" that recollect Carroll's life between 1971 and 1973, but were written ("forced" out of him) years later to fulfill a publishing agreement (Gladysz). Carroll's status as a lapsed Catholic is the basis for much ironic laughter, such as when the poet recalls scoring dope outside St. Agnes Church at the hour of High Mass, or posing naked with Gerard Malanga on the altar of St. Mark's Church at the urging of Gloria Excelsior, another Catholic "superstar" (*Forced* 12, 29). Carroll's religious connections grow dark when he bites his lip during a drug-fueled dream about being chased by a priest, and darker still when a girlfriend informs him about his sleeping habits. Carroll is under the impression that he remains perfectly still during his drug sleeps, with his legs together and his arms folded diagonally across his chest, "exactly like those tombs of the crusaders that I've seen at the Cloisters in New York" (132). But his clairvoyant girlfriend (named Cassandra, aptly enough) reveals that he constantly caresses the deep needle tracks in his arm, as though he is partaking in "some religious ritual" (133).

Inquisitive by nature, Carroll is inspired to investigate the authenticity of her bizarre analogy, which in hindsight appears to have been prophetic. "She made it sound like I was sanctifying this oozing pit, this cavern created by the abusive entrance of syringe points and the narco-garbage within them. . . . Though it's only, in fact, about a quarter-inch in diameter, in my mind that hole is sometimes large enough to insert my own head, my whole body. I could climb in and see my past transgressions among the slime, or, if I have been doing this routine Cassandra describes, perhaps I can put my lips to it and drink from it like a chalice. But will this act purify, or just further the decay?" (*Forced* 133–34). Carroll's linkage of needle tracks with stigmata seems blasphemous, even if it signals his search for redemption. Clearly, he does not feel like a role model. "Susan Sontag once told me that a junkie has a unique chance to rise up and start life over," Carroll told *Newsweek* in 1980. "But I want kids to know it's not hip to indulge yourself at the bottom unless you're planning one hell of a resurrection" (Graustark 80). As in the closing lines of *The Basketball Diaries*—where the drug-addled youth utters his famous confession, "I just want to be pure" (210)—we must sort through a host of contradictions before deciding whether this renegade Catholic speaks sincerely about salvation.

Carroll's search for purity ultimately leads him to pastoral locations around New York City. Bucolic corners of the metropolis not only provide safe haven for illicit drug use but also the opportunity to ruminate on existential mysteries. Consider the following passage from *The Basketball Diaries*, composed shortly after the thirteen-year-old boy moves from the rambunctious East Twenties to the relatively isolated and leafy neighborhood of Inwood, situated high above Harlem on the northern tip of Manhattan:

The only good thing about this new neighborhood up here in Inwood is the giant park and the woods. . . . Way up top is a meadow, and past that a cliff overlooking the Hudson. I come up myself and smoke reefer when I have some (can't get it up in this lame place so I get a little off Bunky on 29th when I go down the old neighborhood once in a while) and watch the boats going up along the Palisades. Today I smoked with Willie, the only guy from the school that smokes too, and we watched two jets moving across the sky like it was flat and they were racing in one long strip. I just want to be high and live in these woods. (41)

Carroll's shift from rebelliousness to sensitivity seems amazingly abrupt, but this is precisely the message he wants to convey, namely that he can be tough and tender by turns. A small patch of urban forest allows him to make this transition easily. One moment he is a juvenile delinquent, scoring dope in the old neighborhood and hauling it uptown. The next he is a nature boy, sharing his stash with a schoolmate, recording the comings and goings of sea and air traffic near Inwood Hill Park's high meadow, and using this site as a launching pad for his own journeys.

Carroll has from the beginning of his career attempted to transcend everyday life in New York through cosmic release, a phenomenon that for him is associated with sex as well as drugs. For the most part, Carroll's "I shit you not" brand of realism draws upon the same emotionally detached lexicon Diane di Prima used, especially when sex is involved. "Finally I realize that I got to meet some friends uptown soon," Carroll explains after a fortuitous tryst with a rich girl in her Sutton Place penthouse, "so I split about midnight after checking out what pills I can rob out of her old man's medicine cabinet. I got about eight ups and a lot of downers. I give Heidi the big kiss, munch on a pear and cut out" (*Basketball* 139). But sometimes his pursuit of sex heralds a higher calling. When the teenage firebrand speaks of heading up to his apartment roof in pursuit of onanistic pleasures, he brings to mind Whitman's unembarrassed worship of the human body. Carroll's virile frame is taut with excitement, intimately connected with the starry spheres above his head and the soft tar below his feet:

> "Up" is my roof, and what I do is simply take off all my clothes, stand around awhile, a totally naked young boy, stare into the star machine and jerk myself off. . . . I love it this way. My feet bare against the tar which is soft from the summer heat, the slight breeze that runs across your entire body . . . the breezes always seem to hit strongest against my crotch, and you feel an incredible power being naked under a dome of stars while a giant city is dressed and dodging cars around you five flights down. (42)[7]

Elsewhere in *The Basketball Diaries*, Carroll seeks galactic communion during an acid trip. Informed about an imminent lunar eclipse, the inquisitive man-child scampers up to a brownstone roof to catch sight of this "cosmic bonus" and finds "a night up there as clear as windy music." A gifted but restless scholarship student at Trinity High School, Jim prefers to receive his education out-of-doors. "I had always thought the sky was flat," he admits while on the rooftop, revising his reefer-induced meditation on airplane trails above Inwood Hill Park, "but now I realized it was a friendly dome, watching secret U.F.O.s zipping over the horizon. And the eclipse was fantastic. I watched it in slow motion and understood it" (134).

In his poetry, too, Carroll refers to revelations under the night sky's "friendly dome" (*Fear* 12), though he appears self-conscious about distancing himself, Peter Pan–style, from his buddies on the street. "It's sad this vision required / such height," he writes in one poem. "I'd have preferred to be down / With the others / in the stadium." Ultimately, he is influenced by his "urgency to deliver light, at least / a fragment, as if it // Were news from the far galaxies" (225). Similar thinking colors "Fragment: Little N.Y. Ode," a sidereal drug poem drawing together earthly city and heavenly cosmos. "I sleep on a tar roof / scream my songs / into lazy floods of stars," the chemically induced lyricist writes. "A white powder paddles through blood and heart / and / the sounds return / pure and easy . . . / this city is on my side" (30). In "Love Rockets," he offers another encomium for the city sky, defending it not just against its detractors but also its would-be saviors. His street corner wisdom flecked with surrealistic flourishes, Carroll models his poem on O'Hara's urban meditations:

> Wet leaves along the threshold of the mid-day
> and I'm off to rescue the sky from its assassins
> jogging and screaming and launching my clean mortars
>
> into the March obscene air . . . the enemy.
>
> I suppose I'd rather be sitting in Samoa now
> sipping a quart of Orange Julius and being fanned
> by Joey Heatherton in black tights and white glossy lipstick.
> but I'm not. I'm here. and I have something to say,
>
> as well as something to take care of.
>
> And that something is probably more important than
> you realize. I like the sky (don't you) its warmth, its friendliness,
> I'm not going to let all this fucking soot taint that terrific blue.
>
> battle the filthy airs with your mortars and your prayers.
>
> you'll soon be overcome with lovely sensations of the sky.
> you'll be thinking of me as this happens. (18)

Adopting what he calls his "street rap" voice (Gladysz), Carroll depicts himself as a reluctant hero whose dream date with a starlet and a novelty beverage in an exotic location fails to materialize. Like other bored teenagers, he must make do with a deteriorating environment. Turning serious, he makes it his business to recast the sooty sky of New York City as an object of wonder. With adolescent bravado, Carroll assumes that we will end up thanking him, much as we thank the great nature poets, once we follow his lead and look deeper into the life of things.

"Love Rockets" was included in *4 Ups and 1 Down*, a chapbook published by Anne Waldman and Lewis Warsh for Angel Hair Books in 1970. Befitting the author's preoccupation with "cosmic bonuses," the cover shows the rangy Carroll, his shoulder-length mane and bell-bottom trousers swinging freely, striding confidently beneath moon and stars (Waldman and Warsh 615). But outer space was not the only realm drawing Carroll's attention. Three of the chapbook's poems discuss the sea, the surface of which hides watery depths and mirrors the limitless sky. "Blue Poles," "Styro," and "To a Poetess" are love poems addressed to unnamed women accompanying the streetwise poet to seashore retreats. In "Styro," Carroll and his lover ("a girl from kansas") appear in an erotic embrace, their "youth clung tightly / in white dunes." Here, as in the other two poems, the emphasis is less on adolescent sex than it is on the oceanic horizon, the sublimity of which puts human relationships into perspective. "There is no other place that allows us / to understand so little, you see," Carroll is forced to confess (*Fear* 9).

In "Blue Poles" (*Fear* 3), Carroll invokes the spirit of Jackson Pollock, hampered in his later years by alcohol addiction and prone to melancholy seaside meditations prophetic of his death. Many critics consider *Blue Poles*, completed on Long Island in 1952, to be the painter's last great work before he was overtaken by drink and a car crash. In 1945, Pollock's move from Manhattan to Springs provided necessary refuge from overbearing art world types, and for a time it put a halt to the destructive tendencies that trailed him into the Cedar Tavern and other urban watering holes. The move also put the Wyoming native back in touch with the sublimity of wide-open spaces. As he explained in 1944, "I have a definite feeling for the West: the vast horizontality of the land for instance; here [in New York] only the Atlantic Ocean gives you that" ("Jackson" 15).[8] Oceanic influence was recognizable not only in the titles of Pollock's works (usually supplied by friends or collectors) but also in the fluid painting techniques he was adopting. *Full Fathom Five* and *Sea Change*, created shortly after Pollock's move to Long Island, mark the juncture at which the artist began to pour paint directly onto the canvas. *Blue Poles* was the last painting in which Pollock employed such methods, leading Kirk Varnedoe to call it "an orgiastic wake for the idea of poured abstraction" (49, 65). As in other works Pollock completed in Springs, the viscosity of poured paint suggests a roiling sea surface, one that incites viewers to plumb the mysteries lying underneath.

The effect is not unlike that in Carroll's verse, which for all its surface energy harbors deeper truths. Just as the painter claimed to be "in" his canvases during their spontaneous composition ("My Painting" 548) and inseparable from the natural phenomena he depicted—"I *am* nature!" he crowed to Hans Hofmann (Glaser 28)—Carroll inhabits the turbulent natural spaces he describes, seeking transcendence through immersion. Having a pastoral guide proves useful in such instances. In "A Short Reminder," Carroll seems to invoke Pollock as mentor, revealing his belief that "when space comes into the formula the only thing / you concede is that you're 'in it' / guided by another like you" (*Fear* 44).[9]

Growing up in New York, Carroll had little knowledge of the western landscapes Pollock encountered. He only knew the urban seascapes that functioned as their equivalent. As rock-and-roll sociologist Donna Gaines explains, the stretch of beach from Coney Island to Far Rockaway, initially demarcated as a getaway for middle-class families, had become by the 1960s a hangout for "marginal young people adrift on an anomic sea" ("Ascension" 14).[10] Carroll was among their number, though like Gaines he was intellectual enough to submit his hormone-driven escapades to critical judgment and allegorical enhancement. He could be brutal toward those who did not share his urban pastoral vision. In "To a Poetess," he chides a private-school girl for not understanding the sea and its mysteries. "You sit to have waves rush to your open hands / and you're surprised as cities grow there," the poet snarls; "the horizon goes limp / and finally / you're not so beautiful afterall" (*Fear* 47). Conversely, in the poem whose title he borrows from Pollock, Carroll meets a woman who is on his wavelength, so to speak. "Blue poles" appear on an urban beach "in a snowless winter," prompting in Carroll a round of existential musing and occasioning the apparition of "lovely Mary kneeling along the quick tide." Although Mary might be the name of the lover with whom Carroll "grinds in the sand," he might also be referring to the Blessed Virgin, the "Star of the Sea" (*Stella Maris*) in Catholic tradition. The poet keeps the sexual-spiritual interplay ambiguous, perhaps in an attempt to mimic the "lovely confusion" represented by ever-present seagulls (3).

Still, Mary's apparition seems important. Associated in various legends with the stars, the moon, and the tidal currents under their control, Mary guides voyagers who travel on storm-tossed seas, providing direction for people who suffer emotional turbulence and saving those who might otherwise feel abandoned (Warner 257–64). As Norris reminds us, the Virgin Mother ("mysterious, and therefore for Catholics," she believed during her Protestant girlhood) has been for poor and oppressed people around the world "a catalyst for boundary-breaking experiences, contradiction, and paradox" (*Amazing* 116, 120). That the Virgin should visit a melancholy teenage junkie on a desolate New York beach is not all that surprising, given her track record of being sighted by humble folks in out-of-the-way locations such as Tepayac, Lourdes, and Fatima.[11] Whatever her true identity, the "lovely Mary" appearing in "Blue Poles" helps Carroll overcome various barriers blocking his route to transcendence.[12]

Unfortunately, the transcendent path Carroll espies from urban beaches contains its share of dangers. In an untitled poem dedicated to O'Hara, Carroll looks off toward the vast stretch of blue ocean and laments the fate of his literary hero, who felt hemmed in by the metropolis he so famously celebrated:

> My footsteps in the shallow
> Ocean pools, the poisoned lips
> Of the anemones set loose my eyes
> To fly to the horizon, time's own memory
>
> I see a single ship passing,
> Shadowless, that one which never
> Arrived, as you stood, years before,
> Waiting in the harbor, dressed for love,
> Your loose breasts throbbing as if beneath
> Their surface small fish were feeding on your heart. (*Fear* 197)

Although the poem's beginning is reminiscent of "Eternity," Rimbaud's brilliant meditation on oceanic horizons, the primary allusion in the second verse paragraph is to O'Hara's great poem about sexual longing, "To the Harbormaster," the first of his works Carroll remembers reading (Gladysz). "I wanted to be sure to reach you," O'Hara declares (*CP* 217), only to admit that tangled moorings and ocean waves have frustrated his quest for human connection. Recognizing O'Hara's emotional predicament while tapping Rimbaud's aesthetics and Heidegger's philosophy, Carroll suggests that the horizon is the constantly receding source of our temporal existence as well as "time's own memory" of itself. As Hans-Jost Frey and Wallace Fowlie assert in separate readings of "Eternity," Rimbaud's oceanic vanishing point ("the whirling light / Of sun become sea") represents the confluence of spiritual and natural forces ("The sky has an angel's face. / Air and water are one and the same," Rimbaud declares in "Banners of May," a poem from the same sequence) (Frey 38; Fowlie 58–59).[13] Yet for city dwellers this utopia is difficult to reach. How unapproachable the far horizon seems in Carroll's poem, how very different from the saltwater shallows, where meddlesome creatures sting the poet's feet with poisonous lips. Substitute "art world socialites" or "Warholian acolytes" for "anemones" and "small fish," and this poem becomes an allegory for the public pressures preventing two generations of New York School poets from enjoying proper refuge. In the end, Carroll's little poem serves as both elegy and warning, since he appears to regard O'Hara the same way O'Hara regarded James Dean, lamenting the fact that death alone held the power to deliver his hero to a place of peace.

Carroll's affection for "deep" thinkers like O'Hara and Pollock is clarified in a diary entry entitled "The Art of Using." Recounting the times Warhol and Gloria Excelsior taped his amphetamine-fueled phone conversations, Carroll expresses his discomfort with "Saint" Andy's manipulative methods, preferring private revelation over public display, a key aspect not only of traditional pastoral but its urban variant as well.[14] He associates the work of O'Hara and Pollock with the "blue clarity" he enjoys while journeying alone, or with a lover, on New York beaches:

> I'm not coming down on [phone taping]; the premise is really not that different, in an abstract way, from that used by two of my artistic heroes, Jackson Pollock and Frank O'Hara, the former with his drip canvases, the latter with his book of lunch poems. That is, the act of creating the piece and the finished work become one and the same . . . the subject and object meet, as the sky and the sea meet to form the line of horizon, the point of reflection. I used to go to the beach and stare at that line all day, in the blue clarity of winter. Winter defines the passage of the earth and its forms better than any other season, as if the cold froze each frame of moving film. I can stare at Pollock or read Frank's poems all day. But I can't stand another moment of listening to these fucking tapes Gloria is always playing me when I show up at her room and all I want is to rattle speed into my shaft.
>
> The distinction is simple. With Pollock or Frank, it was the private struggle from within which created that incredible tension, the drama of their human voices overlapping, the forces of their wills

conflicting . . . with grace or complete vulgarity. With phone taping the "art" is dictated totally by the merits of the conversation. Sure, it can be funny or interesting for a while, but eventually it's always going to be boring. That's because it is, by the nature of the medium, bereft of the privacy which is essential for that conflict, that struggle of forces to ignite into something beyond itself. It's all on the surface, like Gloria's other art form, the Polaroid picture, another obsession of Warhol's. . . . I can remember when you had to wait an entire sixty seconds before the Polaroid ejaculated the print . . . then it was thirty . . . then it was ten. Now it's fucking instantaneous. I mean, talk about premature art. (*Forced* 31–32)

For Warhol, Tony Rayns says, "the *avoidance* of personal involvement and the *embrace* of neutral, non-judgmental recording technology generated exactly the kick that a shy and repressed Catholic boy needed" (87). Missing in Warhol's hasty productions, however, is the stamp of authenticity that Carroll—an unrepressed Catholic boy—finds in O'Hara, Pollock, or Rimbaud, artists whose inner torment fueled intellectual conjectures about modern selfhood. Warhol had become famous for recording everything in sight, ultimately refusing to probe the meaning of his subjects. To the extent that the pop artist admired someone like Pollock, it was "because he was so prolific" (Bourdon 205).[15] "Nothing is hidden in Andy's church, and nothing is transcendent," Steven Shaviro contends. "What you see is what you get" (91).

Carroll asked more of his own art. "Nobody is going to ruin me / If I have to I will ruin myself," he tells an inconstant lover in a later poem (*Void* 112). Carroll may as well be alluding to his experience at the Union Square Factory, where the enterprising Warhol, increasingly withdrawn since the attempt on his life, nonetheless continued with a maddening cycle in which he located interesting people, made them subjects of pop iconography, then promptly forgot about them. Any self-respecting artist interested in more than fifteen minutes of fame would want to avoid such a scenario. "I've spent too much time / Expended angelic energy / On my own disintegration to hand the contract over / To another now / As if it were / A finished painting / Needing only a signature," Carroll declares, having been granted clear perspective in middle age (112). The abundant talents he chose to share were destined for greater powers: God, winter horizons, heroin, or whatever else qualified at that moment as "pure." Succumbing to Warhol's star-maker machinery, by contrast, would have brought early artistic death.

But steering clear of death was not so easy in the Warhol underground. "Saint" Andy was obsessed with fatality, especially after beginning a series of "disaster paintings" in 1962. Yet there is little evidence to suggest he ever grieved for the young people who died in his midst. Addicted to the ambiguity of sensational "events," Warhol endeavored instead to turn youthful tragedy into grist for his production mill, albeit with a religious twist. "In the 1960s' narcissistic worship of youth, in its supposed liberation of energy, in those disastrously simple resolutions of ethical dilemmas that only innocence—call it ignorance—can propose, Warhol discovered his ethical world," Stephen Koch explains in *Stargazer*. "Possessing the smoky mirror of a Catholic sense of damnation, he reflected these values in ways that sometimes touched the profound, where innocence and viciousness, energy and enervation, life forces and their opposites, became indistinguishable" (12).

The spectacular suicides of Freddie Herko and Andrea Feldman loom large here. Herko, a dancer and choreographer involved with the Judson Dance Theater, appeared in two of Warhol's early productions, *Haircut* (1963) and *Thirteen Most Beautiful Boys* (1964), the first a "film portrait," the second a "screen test." The intense visual focus on human subjects in these cinematic portraits, while ostensibly flattering, actually highlighted their imperfections and insecurities, gradually tearing them apart. In a certain sense, these films represented an audition nobody could ever pass. Not that Warhol cared much about the effect on fragile souls like Herko. "The people I loved were the ones like Freddie, the leftovers of show business, turned down at auditions all over town," Warhol effused. "They couldn't do something more than once, but their one time was better than anyone else's. They had star quality, but no star ego" (Watson, *Factory* 171).

It was shortly after Warhol's first films were shot, during the autumn of 1964, that the increasingly desperate Herko, suffering from ankle injuries, an addiction to amphetamines, and the recent dissolution of the Judson, took his own life, in dramatic fashion. Stepping naked from a perfumed bath in Johnny Dodd's Greenwich Village pad, Herko danced to the strains of Mozart's *Coronation Mass* wafting from Dodd's hi-fi while gazing at a baroque scene of heaven painted on the apartment ceiling. "As the orchestra began to play the 'Sanctus,'" Steven Watson reports, playing up the religious irony of the event, "Herko made a grand leap out the [open] window, missing the frame and, for a moment, seeming to go straight up. And a few seconds later Herko landed five flights down on the far side of Cornelia Street" (*Factory* 172). Many memorials were held for the young man *Film Culture* dubbed "The Incandescent Innocent" (McDonagh), with Diane di Prima staging a forty-nine-day service from the *Tibetan Book of the Dead* and composing an elegiac series she called *Freddie Poems*. Meanwhile, Warhol simply expressed his wish that he could have been present to film Herko's fatal leap. Even friends regarded Warhol's remark as callous. Undeterred, the artist spent the following year making a film entitled *Suicide* (having already completed a "disaster" silkscreen with this title). Eventually, he dedicated one of his *Flowers* paintings to Herko's memory, briefly invoking a tradition from pastoral elegy, only to reveal his newest desire, which was to record Edie Sedgwick's suicide, should she ever decide on that particular option (Watson, *Factory* 173: Bourdon 200, 216; Wolf 75).

Eight years after Herko's suicide, history seemed to repeat itself, for Warhol almost farcically so. During the summer (or autumn) of 1972, Andrea Feldman, after having composed a searing suicide note (or a fawning love letter), leapt to her death from the fourteenth (or seventeenth or eighteenth) floor of an apartment building on Park Avenue South (or lower Fifth Avenue), carrying a can of soda and a rosary (or a Bible). Although accounts obviously vary (see Bourdon 321; Koch, *Stargazer* 121; Colacello 126–28, 187–88), most writers agree that, by the time of her leap, Feldman had been circulating in Warhol's orbit for five years. She attracted the artist's attention at Max's Kansas City, where she did Ethel Merman impersonations in the nude while squatting obscenely on an upright Coke bottle. A born exhibitionist, she briefly basked in the counterculture limelight, accompanying Warhol to parties and premieres, and appearing in three of his films, including *Imitation of Christ*, the title of which possessed an ironic sheen. Denied entry to a party celebrating the Broadway premiere of *Jesus Christ Superstar*, Feldman raised a ruckus, shouting, "I'm Andy Warhol's biggest Superstar." By this point, though, she had fallen from Warhol's favor, and she suspected religion was to blame. "She was obsessed with Catholicism, thinking that Andy had rejected her because she was Jewish," Bob Colacello says. Characteristically, Feldman made a performance of her passion, starving herself down to eighty-five pounds and sitting for a photograph wearing a crown of thorns, her stigmata clearly visible on palms she wearily raised toward the camera (Colacello 126–27).

When it came time for her dramatic death leap, Feldman was just as symbolic, and no less calculating. According to Carroll, she invited several ex-boyfriends to meet her outside her apartment at eight o'clock one evening to "see something special" (*Forced* 52). As it happened, eight o'clock was the hour one of New York's most interesting art installations, Frosty Myers's red laser beam, was automatically switched on. Watson remembers that "the laser was beamed across the deserted night street and bounced off a mirror that sent it down Park Avenue, off another mirror, and through the plate-glass window of Max's Kansas City, where it beamed in over the heads of the customers in the bar and all the way to the backroom wall," leading habitués to think they had followed a star, or some other beacon, to their downtown destination (*Factory* 316). "Like those libraries in medieval cloistered abbeys," Robert Smithson teasingly warned Carroll over a drink at Max's, the laser beam "is a labyrinth which is not supposed to be penetrated" (*Forced* 42–43). But Carroll was too curious not to investigate the beam's Christian symbolism. The night before Feldman's suicide, under the influence of heroin during a visit to Max's, the poet recalls "holding my hand up to the laser beam, letting the light pass through and considering the possibility that I had, perhaps, missed the vein on the last shot, and thus the rush was just coming on, slowly and with a vengeance. Lost in this rumination, hand still poised in the beam passing red through my palm and onto the white wall, where it simply hung like a stigmata, Andrea comes up to me and leans into my ear, 'Wouldn't it be nice if we could pass through the light, instead of the opposite, such as you are now experiencing?'" (51).

Carroll proceeds to tell Feldman that the speed of light is actually not approachable, since it is relativity itself. She in turn divulges her belief in a faster speed: the "speed of death." More specifically, she explains that people who have been revived after being pronounced clinically dead "always describe the same sensation . . . of entering a long tunnel and passing into the purest light . . . and just then they're brought back . . . but they *did* really pass through that light, and would have become the light itself if the doctor didn't fuck things up" (Carroll, *Forced* 52). It is not known whether Feldman heard firsthand testimony from Warhol, who was pronounced dead for ninety seconds following Solanas's assassination attempt, but she speaks confidently about such matters, inviting Carroll to her apartment to learn more about "relativity."[16]

The following night, keeping his date with Feldman but remaining unaware of her date with death, Carroll follows the "menacing" laser down Park Avenue toward her apartment, only to realize that he has arrived moments too late. Feldman's body lies splattered on the pavement, her blood staining a nearby string of rosary beads. Emilio, another boyfriend, had arrived early. He tells Carroll what he saw:

"It was like she was jumping onto the laser beam . . . as if she were trying to grab it . . . but with her mouth, not her hands. Like she wanted to swallow it."

"Or be swallowed by it," I mumbled, remembering her talk last night. . . .

"Yes . . . and, well, it was really very strange. . . . You see, it seemed from down here like some illusion of optics, yes? It seemed that for a moment, like a whole second of time, that she actually hung onto the beam from the laser as if it were a line for clothes. And the can of soda and the rosary? She was a Jew, no?" (*Forced* 54–55)

Approaching the "speed of death," Feldman seeks union with a line of light that, according to the Christian registry she purportedly shares with Carroll, represents both stigmata and salvation. Her leap is hardly death-defying, and yet for a moment she appears to defy gravity by "jumping onto" a laser beam suspended above street level. Like Herko, who reportedly ascended toward the heavens before falling to his death, Feldman imbues her desperate drop with a strangely buoyant form of religiosity.

Left behind to ponder the implications of Feldman's impulsive act were Warhol, who characteristically applauded her for "being really creative" and "deliberately [making] suicide a comedy" (Colacello 128), and Carroll, who dissimilarly discovered that forced laughter in the wake of this event made it hard for him to breathe.[17] Taking a long look in his mirror the night of Feldman's suicide, Carroll writes in his diary, "I see too much of myself there" (*Forced* 55). Taking a "there but for the grace of God go I" approach to the tragic occurrence on Park Avenue South, hoping to avoid the fate of fallen superstars, he began to remove himself from the downtown scene. "I've become so weary of New York's speed, the ever-accelerating and forced perversity and vacillation," he admits. "I'm sick of the need to take it all in . . . every part, every opening . . . constantly tearing my body, almost literally, in different directions. . . . There's no cool left in me. . . . I can't keep a steady style in my writing standing on these shifting platforms of artifice and quick change" (119–20).

The following year, after lighting a candle for St. Francis in the "long church" that had become his clandestine retreat, Carroll left New York for California, joining Bill Berkson, Lewis Warsh, and other East Village émigrés in Bolinas, a Marin County enclave Daniel Kane calls "an extension of the New York–based alternative poetic community" (*All Poets* 176). Times had changed. At the dawn of the counterculture movement, New Yorkers lagged behind their West Coast brethren when it came to communion with the land. During a 1966 tour of California, neither Warhol nor members of the Velvet Underground dared leave their limousine, choosing to gaze at the Pacific Ocean from behind car windows, which kept the sand from soiling their black clothing and the laid-back vibes from impinging on their nihilist chic (Watson, *Factory* 283–85).

A few years later, though, a number of New York bohemians, including Ginsberg, who bought a farm in 1968, were lighting out for rural spots.[18] "A lot of poet friends have abandoned the squalor of Alphabet City and the Lower East Side for the bovine whines of this little coastal town outside San Francisco," Carroll muses on the eve of his departure for California and its "cleaner angles" (*Forced* 116). "I can't throw up that hackneyed shit about 'getting back to the land,' because I've never been there in the first place," the streetwise New Yorker acknowledges, but once settled in Bolinas he sings a new tune: "the city . . . no longer owns me. I'm giving my time to the country life" (117, 130). In Bolinas, Carroll claimed he was able to "watch nature perform," whereas in New York he had simply "watched people react" (139). I regard his distinction somewhat warily, since his early writings uncover a pastoral beauty that exists bountifully in and around New York City. All the same, I recognize his need to flee a scene catering to his most destructive impulses. Carroll's relocation to California would be temporary, but the natural turn he made in the early 1970s was long-lasting. He could not have known at the time how inspiring his journey would be for another young poet yearning to escape New York.

ON THE SURFACE, Kathleen Norris appears to have little in common with Carroll. "A middle-westerner by heritage, and far-westerner by virtue of having spent [her] adolescence in Hawaii" (*Virgin* 1), she was born into a Protestant family. She remained chaste and drug-free during her teenage years. She graduated from an elite private college. Moving to New York after graduation, she flourished under the mentorship of Betty Kray, director of the Academy of American Poets, and gained entrée into "official verse culture," joining a network of established writers. Then, in 1974, to the surprise of her peers and herself, she left New York for her grandparents' homestead in Lemmon, South Dakota, where she has remained (splitting time with Hawaii) for more than three decades. From this outpost Norris has authored a series of books about contemporary Christianity, three of which were named "Notable Books" by the *New York Times*. She has lectured on theology at Notre Dame and Harvard, and has served as editor-at-large for *The Christian Century*. In sum, she has received a stamp of officialdom Carroll could never hope (or wish) to achieve.

In *Dakota* (1993), *The Cloister Walk* (1996), *Amazing Grace* (1998), and *Acedia & Me* (2008), Norris combines the historical objectivity required of religious scholars with the subjectivity found in literary memoir, depicting her move to South Dakota and her growing immersion in Catholic traditions as a modern-day pilgrimage (*Dakota* 93, *Cloister* ix). In *The Life You Save May Be Your Own*, his impressive study of twentieth-century Catholic writers, Paul Elie defines pilgrimage as "a journey taken in the light of a story," the primary purpose of which is to bear witness to miraculous events. "Pilgrims often make the journey in company," Elie argues, "but each must be changed individually; they must see for themselves, each with his or her own eyes. And as they return to ordinary life the pilgrims must tell others what they saw, recasting the story in their own terms" (x). Elie notes that the motivation for pilgrimage—"the impulse to find and inhabit an 'other' world over and against the present one"—usually occurs after the believer has succumbed to excessive sinfulness, though many confessions of waywardness, including those of Dorothy Day and Thomas Merton, are exaggerated for maximum effect (31–32, 96).

Norris's own pilgrimage evolved slowly and quietly. For years, she dwelled on her decision to light out for Dakota, and even edited a collection entitled *Leaving New York*, but disclosed little about the experiences giving rise to her move. Not until *The Virgin of Bennington* (2001) did readers learn about her wayward life in New York City. In this personal book, Norris flashes back thirty years to discuss her association with the Warhol crowd and the experimental poets holding court at St. Mark's Church. Of course, reading Norris on the topics of sex and drugs is quite different from hearing Carroll hold forth on such matters. Her sins pale in comparison. Both writers work in a confessional mode—indeed, each is fond of quoting St. Augustine—but Norris lacks the braggadocio style New Yorkers wear on their sleeves. "New York was an impossible place for me," she admits. "My shyness and trepidation put me at odds with Manhattan's brash atmosphere." Yet its allure was powerful for an ambitious young writer: "The daimon of the city, like the genius of poetry itself, could be both nurturing and destructive. It seemed all wrong, yet I chose to come to terms with my life and art there" (*Virgin* 68).

Looking back, Norris has referred to New York's "literary hothouse" as something she needed to escape if she hoped to find proper grounding (*Dakota* 19; *Cloister* 245, 350). "It wasn't until I had moved to the place of my childhood summers, my grandparents' house, where my mother grew up, that my voice as a writer emerged," she explains. "A friend, reading the new poems I began to write there, commented, 'When you moved to South Dakota, it's like you discovered gravity'" (*Cloister* 245–46). Regarding the title of her first poetry volume, *Falling Off*, Norris says she wanted "to capture my uneasiness in New York, my sense of the city as a place where one might indeed fall off the world and disappear" (*Virgin* 63). In the title poem, Norris complicates that old cartographic fear, explaining that the "vertical / And bottomless" corridors of Manhattan ("Where the worst things happen / And everything stays the same") tend to hide the far horizon, which stands as a marker of possibility as well as danger (*Falling* 39). Elsewhere, she implies that a world without gravity might not be so bad. In urban pastoral fashion, she must reconcile contradictory images while seeking the right path. Consider "At a Window, New York City," a poem in which Norris, her escapist reverie abetted by alcohol, allows her inner vision of rural landscapes to modify her view of city skyline:

> An exile from Afghanistan
> might find his mountains.
> I look for silos
> on the tops of buildings:
> penthouse treebelts,
> breaks of shadow.
>
> When I drink I live alone,
> a piece of skyline
> going out
> like ice and alcohol
> in the pattern of light. (*Journey* 25)

Even as she immersed herself in Warhol's freewheeling milieu, Norris pined for the simple places and honest people she encountered in her youth, realizing later on that "if it was the illusion of love that spurred my move to New York City after college, it was the real thing that gave me the courage to leave" (*Virgin* 159). Such an attitude colors "Kansas Anymore," a new poem from *Journey* that is actually a collection of fragments culled from *Falling Off*. Extending the motif introduced in "At a Window," Norris tries to fool the "soldiers" who roam Manhattan's streets and subways by becoming a "trick of light," one "so purely / and invisibly present / that they will not think to look at me / as I walk beside them, or appear as a window" (*Journey* 24). In "Bean Song," she already seems to have turned away from cosmopolitan artifice, imagining herself as an organic sprout rooted in the nourishing soil of the Midwest. "Bean Song" brings to mind William Stafford's great early poem, "Midwest." "Cocked in that land tactile as leaves, / wild things wait crouched in those valleys / west of your city outside your lives / in the ultimate wind, the whole land's wave," Stafford reminds the East Coast literati, closing his poem with a Whitmanian invitation: "Come west and see; touch these leaves" (60). Similarly, Norris speaks up for a bean flower whose modest beauty goes unnoticed by preoccupied New Yorkers. "No one hears it singing, / Only a few ever learn the song: // At night, when I sleep alone, / I sing it for you" (*Falling* 28).

While dreaming about an organic alternative to urban life, Norris was also visualizing her impending departure from New York as a flight into an angelic realm. She found what she was seeking on the Great Plains, depicted in her later books as a holy space where down-to-earth people are surprisingly ebullient in their expressions of spirituality. Prominent among this region's beatific population are a Benedictine monk who once laughingly "splashed [Norris's] face / with holy water . . . / flew down a banister, and / for one millisecond / was an angel—robed, / without feet— / all irrepressible joy / and good news" (*Journey* 76); an impoverished Hidatsu girl in Norris's poetry class who drew an Annunciation scene in which "Gabriel stands before Mary, his blue wings ablaze with stars" (*Dakota* 42); and a drunken cowboy in a Bismarck bar, who likened the poet to "an angel from outer space" before leaning in close with a whispered confession: "I believe in God" (*Journey* 35). Glad to be out of Warhol's orbit, Norris saw these folks as truly "countercultural" (*Cloister* 119; *Dakota* 3, 8). A monk taking vows and remaining celibate; a shy Indian girl impressing a writer-in-residence with heavenly visions put down on paper; a cowboy retracting his pick-up line with an unexpected display of piety; a poet deciding to leave a literary capital for a midwestern farm town: each has made an unconventional choice in this day and age.

In *Dakota*, Norris quotes St. Hilary, a fourth-century desert monk, explaining how the bleak landscape of the upper Midwest accommodates unusual displays of faith: "'Everything that seems empty is full of the angels of God.' The magnificent sky above the Plains sometimes seems to sing this truth; angels seem possible in the wind-filled expanse" (11). Closely tied to Hilary's belief is the epiphany Norris recounts in her wonderfully titled poem, "Why the Image of a Starry Womb Is Not Poetic Claptrap but Good Science." Here, she espies "the pregnant Virgin / contained in a rush / of seraphim wings, her blue mandorla / shot through / with starlight, shadow." She eventually learns from a quantum physicist that "each atom of your body / was once inside a star." Informed of scientific facts and inspired by her vision of a God "who labors to give us birth," Norris resembles di Prima during her first encounters in the West, asserting that "we come, / as all things come, / to light" (*Journey* 85). In Manhattan, nebulae and the spiritual messages they encode are usually washed out by artificial light.

Not so in Big Sky country, where miracles are abundant. As Norris points out, "the flow of the land, with its odd twists and buttes, is like the flow of [a] Gregorian chant that rises and falls beyond melody, beyond reason or human expectation, but perfectly. Maybe seeing the Plains is like seeing an icon; what seems stern and almost empty is merely open, a door into some simple and holy state" (*Dakota* 157). Taking inspiration from twentieth-century naturalists Loren Eiseley and Terry Tempest Williams, as well as from ancient monks, Norris explains that desert landscapes in the West, though harsh, are also unrestrictive, and thus conducive to surprising emanations of joy.[19]

I find it interesting that in "The Middle of the World" Norris calls the Plains an "inland sea" (*Journey* 37), and that elsewhere she refers to her relocation as a "sea change" (*Dakota* 145). Just as Carroll found enlightenment by staring at the "blue clarity" of the Atlantic horizon, Norris discovers on an oceanic expanse of prairie "that time and distance, those inconveniences that modern life with its increasingly sophisticated computer technologies seeks to erase, have a reality and a terrifying beauty all their own." She implies that the Midwest's desolate, landlocked "sea" is responsible for her religious *conversion*, "a word that at its root connotes not a change of essence but of perspective" (145). Literary possibilities exist there as well. "In all of these places that couldn't be more deprived by worldly standards I also find an expansiveness, a giddy openness that has allowed me to discover gifts in myself and others that most likely would have remained hidden in more busy, sophisticated, or luxuriant surroundings" (118).[20]

Norris was already searching for open spaces in New York, where the horizon was not so visible. In early lyrics, she calls upon angels to be her pastoral guides, adopting a slightly sardonic tone to describe urban spirituality at its most neurotic. As Paul Carroll (no relation to Jim) remarks in his foreword to *Falling Off*, "the more radiant and mysterious aspects of the angelism in some of [Norris's] best poems" are advantageously modified "when her angel refuses to conform to stereotype. Instead, the angel may hide its bejeweled wings under the bed, where they gather dust; or its visitation will leave sores on the inside of her mouth; or the angel will receive a lot of business calls. . . . Miss Norris is able to achieve a peculiar tension, beauty and strength by allowing disparate elements to exist within the same poem or within the same book" (5, 7). These tensions certainly influence "The Consuming Angel" and "The Most Secret Angel," poems placed side by side in Norris's debut volume. "The Consuming Angel" who visits the poet is "more a demon than anything else." Its primary message is to warn a New Yorker "tired of running / At one hundred miles an hour

/ (Such speed is possible, if the pain is great)" that the time has come for her to leave the urban "jungle" (59). "The Most Secret Angel" is calmer in its dispensation of knowledge but also more elusive, a best friend no one else can see. This angel is a powerful force heralding literary inspiration, the arrival and departure of which are hard to predict. "I always look where it's pointing, / But I've never been able to feel its shape," Norris admits after one chance meeting. "When it ventures out, / A feeling like the wind comes to claim its place; / Nothing fancy, just simple suspicion and fear" (60).

Similar frustrations fill "Tomorrow," as Norris claims that she—a subletter burdened with empty suitcases, piles of shoes, and a rental deadline—would like to travel as effortlessly as an angel once her lease is up, realizing this feat is impossible (*Falling* 34). In "Her Application to Elysium," Norris attempts once more to attain angelic status, answering a series of questions like those found in "applications to colleges such as Bennington, or Sarah Lawrence" with the hope of being admitted to heavenly paradise. Among the salutary achievements and influential contacts Norris provides are entries we would expect from a Warhol rebel. "French pornographic novels" are listed prominently in the booklist section, and "vibrators of various shapes and sizes" are mentioned alongside a "museum curator" and a "local Democratic assemblyman" in the "most meaningful relationships" column. This prospective angel is in no hurry to be pigeonholed. "In response to the first question, requesting name, address, and schools previously attended," the applicant adopts a sleight-of-hand approach useful to urban pastoral thinkers, confessing that "she had always kept a certain distance from her surroundings" (43).

In "Excerpts from the Angel Handbook," a poem begun at Bennington College, Norris confronts her initial fear of the big city. Years later, she would describe this poem as a "memo from heaven" for cherubim who feel out of place in the urban jungle (*Virgin* 47–48). The first excerpts contain street-smart advice for sensitive souls hoping to survive in a competitive metropolitan environment:

Be careful how you unfold your wings—
there are some in the world who are not content
unless their teeth are full of feathers. . . .

When you ride subways wear ornate silver shoes
and always stand near the door

When you cross at intersections look both ways, then up. . . .

It will often be expedient to remove your wings altogether
from your back, where people will first think to
            look for them,
and carry them around inside you—
at such times be careful that your hands do not forget
and begin to imitate their beating in your heart,
for if you begin to fly, the police will be called
and you will only confuse them (*Falling* 29)

The dicey situations facing Norris's urban angels resemble those in Charles Baudelaire's "The Albatross." In that poem, the majestic "monarch of the clouds / Familiar of storms, of stars, and of all high things," flounders pathetically on deck after being captured by mariners. "Exiled on earth amidst its hooting crowds, / He cannot walk, borne down by his giant wings" (Baudelaire 10). Innocent angels, out of their element in crowded New York streets and subways, withstand similar indignities. Norris's poem also reminds me of Sherwood Anderson's short story "Hands," in which Adolph Myers, a kindly Pennsylvania schoolteacher, runs seriously afoul of townsfolk after he is seen tousling the hair of his beloved students. Forced to flee to a distant town in Ohio, Myers changes his last name to Biddlebaum and eventually comes to be known as "Wing," his pseudonym a reminder of the birdlike motion his hands instinctively make whenever he tries to tell his torturous life story. Then again, Wing is an appropriate name for an angelic person whose compassionate gestures are misunderstood by an insular citizenry. Because people tend to avoid close contact with the angels in their midst, Norris treads lightly on the subject. Although ostensibly offering advice to urban angels, she appears to be talking to herself later in the "Handbook" when she says, "You will never tell a lie, / but you will have many secrets" (*Falling* 30).

Judging by her forlorn tone, it must have thrilled Norris to befriend Malanga and Carroll, New Yorkers also enraptured by angelic visions. Norris recalls that, "for all [their] bad-boy behavior," these two downtown poets "had consciences formed in the Catholic Church, and where aesthetic values were concerned, they cast their choices in moral terms" (*Virgin* 137). Malanga was "rich in ambiguities: a street-wise but essentially gentle person, soft-spoken with the trace of a Bronx accent, ambitious enough as an artist to be able to survive in New York, yet not terribly jealous of the success of others, particularly if he thought it well deserved. In those days he looked like an Adonis, but he didn't seem overly vain" (78). Like a pastoral shepherd, he steered the impressionable young woman away from danger in the Warhol underground, dispensing advice during late-night discussions in the back room of Max's, remembered "fondly" by Norris as "a state-of-the art den of iniquity that could be oddly beneficent in spirit."[21] Norris and Malanga reportedly enjoyed the "group therapy" the bar provided but kept some distance, warding off potential pitfalls by reciting inspirational passages from Bunyan's *Pilgrim's Progress*, with Norris taking up the example of Feeble-Mind, an archetypal character "who never thinks he has the fortitude to complete his pilgrimage, but keeps going nonetheless" (89).

By this point, Malanga had already taken control of his destiny, having left his post at Warhol's Factory to concentrate on his own work, which included a stunning collection of black-and-white photographs. Among his most poignant works is the portrait of Norris gracing the cover of *The Virgin of Bennington*. Shot on Christmas Day in 1971, following their blissful night of cohabitation, Malanga's photograph shows a raccoon-eyed Norris sitting demurely beneath the Angel of Waters fountain in Central Park's Bethesda Terrace, looking beaten down and beatific all at once. Long straight hair frames her face and falls down to her gloved hands, which rest together on her lap in a gesture suggestive of prayer. Norris sits as lightly on her low perch as the angels, positioned high in the fountain, do on theirs. In an epigraph to *Resistance to Memory*, a collection of Malanga's photographs, musician Thurston Moore praises America for "leaving angels / to their own device." After seeing his Christmas Day portrait of Norris, I want to congratulate Malanga for the very same reason.

Encouraged by Malanga, Norris discovered that beneath Carroll's rakish reputation there existed a sensitive soul appreciative of spiritual matters. One "wild night," Norris confesses, she and Carroll made love in Riverside Park (*Virgin* 135). Far more typical were quiet evenings spent in Norris's tiny apartment watching Knicks games on an old television set, with Carroll providing colorful commentary and regaling his host with episodes from his misspent youth. Carroll was as streetwise as Norris was innocent, yet he too was searching for inner peace, even if that meant leaving the city that made his name. Norris gladly nurtured him. "I had never known a heroin addict, but Jim had a sweetness about him that overcame my unease," she recalls. "He did not shoot up in front of me, and I came to suspect that he appreciated my apartment as a refuge from the frenetic druggie world he has described so vividly in *The Basketball Diaries* and . . . *Forced Entries*.

I had made a quiet place for myself, without a gang of people looking for the next party, the next fix" (136).

When Carroll departed for California, Norris was understandably upset, but she took instruction from his pilgrimage. "If a New York native like Jim could pick up and leave," she mused, "I might do it too" (*Virgin* 139). Called by Norris "an unwitting catalyst for my move west" (132), Carroll does not seem that different from the alluring cherub she addresses near the end of "Excerpts from the Angel's Handbook":

> You will meet some whose faces give a glow
> as if they once had halos:
> these are the lovers,
> you will make a lot of love . . .
>
> and your flights (even though you are careful
> to keep them invisible) will make those you love sad
> they will not understand that you never go
> > anyplace you're not meant to be. (*Falling* 32)

Years later, when she picked up the Jim Carroll Band's debut album, *Catholic Boy* (1980), and came across its searing opening number, "Wicked Gravity," Norris was reminded of the impetus leading both writers to search for purity and pastoral guidance beyond the downtown scene. Backed by a propulsive punk rock beat, Carroll uses a rapid-fire vocal delivery to register his angelic ambitions and earth-bound frustrations:

> I want to drift above the borders against my will
> I want to sleep where the angels don't pass
> But then my lips turn blue
> Gravity does it to you
> It's like they're pressed against a mirrored glass
>
> I want my will and capability to meet inside the region
> Where this gravity doesn't mean a thing
> It's where the angels break through
> It's where they bring it to you
> It's where silence, silence can teach me to sing
>
> A world without gravity
> That could be

Just what I need
I'd watch the stars move close
I'd watch the earth recede. (*Catholic*)

Reporting from her listening post on the Great Plains two decades after *Catholic Boy* was released, Norris makes Carroll's song part of her wistfully beautiful memoir:

> When I met Jim, we were both trying to escape the demands of gravity by living in our heads. With contempt for what we saw as the drag of ordinary life, we had indulged in the dangerous folly of thinking we had found a better way. I was absorbed in writing cerebral verse about angels, and Jim sought inspiration in drug-induced hallucinatory dreams and nods. But we both believed enough in what Jim has called "the poem within" to let it save us. And it led us back to the real world, where, as the poet Meredith Carson reminds us, "Gravity is undone / by spider web and wing of butterfly." (*Virgin* 141)

"Gravity was unsure of me from the start," Carroll brags in "Me, Myself, and I," an autobiographical prose poem he composed during his California interlude. "As I slipped from the womb I did not fall, but rose into the sky and over the cities. . . . Without trying, I have made an alliance with angels" (*Fear* 150).

A fellow survivor of the Factory scene, Norris knows how lucky Carroll has been. After all, Herko and Feldman, much like Warhol's *Silver Clouds*, appeared to rise "up to God" (Watson, *Factory* 245) as they took their respective leaps into the great unknown, only to fall violently to their deaths.[22] Carroll and Norris, by contrast, were buoyed by their faith in a spiritual realm, a place where traditional boundaries separating the surreal, the natural, and the miraculous magically dissolved. Disappointed by Warhol and other bohemian elders who should have had his best interests in mind, Carroll concludes one verse of "Wicked Gravity" with the following pronouncement: "My guardians quit before they started their search." Fortunately, at crucial moments in their lives, some other guiding force spirited Carroll and Norris away to remote locations where gravity was no longer a hindrance, beatitude no longer a fashion statement, and purity no longer an illusion.

"IT'S HARD to be a saint in the city," Bruce Springsteen sings on his debut album, released around the time Carroll and Norris left New York. The intersecting stories of these poets show Springsteen to be right, even if faith ultimately won out. Returning to New York after his initial trip West, Carroll settled in his old neighborhood of Inwood and seemed to welcome the isolation. "In particular, I have avoided like a leaky reactor my old haunts such as Max's Kansas City," he confesses near the end of *Forced Entries*. "There are too many white powdered memories which I've left spilled on the floors of those places, too many faces with too little in their eyes" (165). Happily concealed in the "wilds of upper, upper Manhattan," he strived instead to appreciate the "almost visual" silence of this and other working-class neighborhoods, the remote beauty of which is most apparent in the wee hours (165, 180). But old reputations are hard to kill. Although dedicating himself to a life "where wisdom is more involved than ecstasy" (*Gang of Souls*), Carroll admitted to being haunted by his youthful persona in restaurants, in the movies, or on the street (*Void* 85). Yet unlike his hero O'Hara, who failed to escape New York's pressures, Carroll managed—by means of an urban pastoral aesthetic he developed in parks, beaches, and on rooftops—to carve out a peaceful niche for himself within the city limits. At the time of his death in September 2009, Carroll was reportedly putting the finishing touches on a highly anticipated autobiographical novel.

Ensconced in the rural Midwest, Norris has had fewer opportunities to run into her younger self, but she remains a "city person" by South Dakota standards (*Cloister* 350). Like Carroll—or like di Prima and Barbara Guest, for that matter—she has achieved sanity and balance by juxtaposing her diverse life experiences. "I am conscious of carrying a Plains silence with me into cities," Norris says in *Dakota*, "and of carrying my city experiences back to the Plains so that they may be absorbed again back into silence" (15). Indeed, she admits to keeping a map of the New York City subway system on the wall of her South Dakota farmhouse "to tell me where I've been" (*Virgin* 243). As her pilgrimage evolved, Norris realized that New York was crucial to her development as a writer and a person. She seems genuinely inspired by the words of Basil the Great, a desert monk who left the city of Caesura in the fourth century: "I have abandoned my life in the town as the occasion of endless troubles, but I have not managed to get rid of myself" (*Cloister* 379). Her understanding of "spiritual geography," defined in *Dakota* as "the place where I've wrestled my story out of the circumstances of landscape and inheritance" (2), is certainly broad enough to encompass rural and urban situations, and flexible enough to admit profane elements alongside traditional notions of the sacred. Like Carroll, this angelic writer assumes that salvation lies in the daily pilgrimages we take, however reactionary they may seem to ironists like Warhol, and however unorthodox they may appear to more conventional believers. Expanding our appreciation of the pastoral mode, Norris resists stereotypical assessments of the "fallen city" while pointing out the literary possibilities that exist in out-of-the-way places. Like the other writers I have profiled in *Urban Pastoral*, she knows a "happy place" when she finds it.

NOTES

INTRODUCTION

1. Regarding gay migration to "tolerant cities" in postwar America, see Abraham.

2. Also notable, Deborah Laycock says (1, 15), is Gay's perambulatory sketch, "Of Walking the Streets by Night" (1716), which presents London as a "rural-urban conjunction," a place of "provocative heterogeneous yokings," the full power of which are realized through the "georgic" activity of walking.

3. For accounts of Cornell's "dime store alchemy," see Simic and Solomon. For pastoral themes in Burckhardt's *Under the Brooklyn Bridge* (1953), Mekas's *Walden* (1968), and Hutton's *New York Portrait* (1979–1990), see MacDonald, who notes a "city symphony" genre granting city dwellers "a reprieve from the usual near-hysteria of our lives" (232).

4. Regarding O'Hara's posthumous fame, see the eerily prophetic lines of "Oedipus Rex," a journal fragment from April 1966 discovered after his fatal accident: "He falls; but even in falling he is higher than those who fly into the ordinary sun" (Ferguson 142).

5. In 2008, William Logan picked up the term in his review of O'Hara's *Selected Poems*, emphasizing the insouciance of his milieu: "The poems describe an urban pastoral where no one has a real job, where martinis flow like nectar and where the days of Elysium are marked by the arrival of *New World Writing*. Whitman's search for the democracy of the American demotic—what he called slang—had a century later become the hilarious musings of a vain young man about town" (9).

6. Of New York School poets, only Ashbery and Anne Waldman (for her Naropa-based mythic poetics) receive mention in *This Compost*, Jed Rasula's far-ranging study of ecological imperatives in "open field" poetry.

1. SEMIOTIC SHEPHERD

1. Hazel Smith refers to the New York School as a "hyperscape" and its writing as a "hypertext," concentrating on "discontinuous texts [that] can be instantly juxtaposed,

forming links between very disparate materials and distant nodes" (12). Smith spends less time considering the human body roaming the hyperscape. When she does, she represents O'Hara as a well-adjusted flaneur (46), a strolling artist who, in Charles Baudelaire's words, "sets up house in the heart of the multitude, amid the ebb and flow of movement, in the midst of the fugitive and infinite (but is still a spectator hidden from the world)." Ignoring the emotional and physical costs exacted, she associates O'Hara's movements with "hypergrace," a beatific variety of homeostasis that "implies bodily and mental composure, mediation between emotional intensity and campy self-irony" (55).

2. O'Hara also lauds Goodman in "Song (I'm Going to New York!)" (*Selected Poems* 19).

3. For a classic account of Baudelaire's sensation-gathering in Paris, see Benjamin, 155–200. For O'Hara's role in this tradition, see chapters dedicated to his poetry in Rosenbaum and Gilbert.

4. David Lehman asserts that historians reading "The Day Lady Died" "a century hence could piece together the New York of that moment in the same way that archaeologists can reconstruct a whole extinct species of dinosaur from a single fossil bone" (202). Other critics dispute this assertion. According to Lytle Shaw, "As details and names accumulate, O'Hara's New York becomes, for later readers, an increasingly impossible act, one held in fictive unity only by its absent experiential center." For Shaw, the question becomes whether to imagine O'Hara as an "intimate interlocutor" we think we know or as a receding presence, signifying in death the metropolitan magic later generations can never hope to know (24). Citing Jean-Luc Nancy, Terence Diggory refers to O'Hara's milieu as an "inoperative community," one "founded on an encounter with death experienced as bliss." Gradually, this community "assumes the impossibility of its own immanence" ("Community" 24). Still, Diggory implies that O'Hara's physical absence is compensated by the immediacy of his verse, which urges readers to imagine themselves part of a milieu that no longer exists. Maggie Nelson likewise acknowledges the "moment of being" O'Hara conjures while decrying the "normalizing" approach of Lehman, who she says views O'Hara's poetry as a monument to a bygone era rather than as a living thing (80–81).

5. For discussion of James Merrill's "An Urban Convalescence" and James Schuyler's "Dining Out with Doug and Frank," two other New York poems that take commercial change in stride, see Nelson, 84–85.

6. Likewise, in Hartigan's painting *Oranges*, O'Hara seems to "stand at the crossroads of abstraction and representation" as a "recognizable figure half-submerged in a broad gestural field" (Ferguson 43). O'Hara's ambiguity led friends to make wildly different assessments. Schuyler praised his "elegant" bearing ("Poet" 82) and "feline grace" (*CP* 155), while Ashbery noted his pugilistic "punk-angel look" (*Selected Prose* 172). John Myers thought O'Hara looked like an "over-bred polo pony" ("Frank" 34). Peter Schjeldahl labeled his body type "classically bantam" ("Frank" 141), whereas Alice Neel, regarding her painting of O'Hara, said he looked like a falcon ("I Met Frank" 96).

7. In "To Frank O'Hara," Schuyler refers to his friend's rambunctious behavior in words that recall Button's painting: "And in the crash / of certain chewed-up words / I see you again dive / into breakers!" (*CP* 155).

8. In "Les Luths" (*CP* 343), O'Hara considers Gary Snyder, a San Francisco Renaissance poet who spent twelve years in Japan, free from unwanted social scrutiny (in O'Hara's poem he sits alone under a dwarf pine). As the sun tracks westward across the Pacific to shine mellower light on another American poet, we discover a contrast between Snyder's tranquil life in Kyoto and O'Hara's frenetic life in New York.

9. Analyzing Alice Notley's verse, Nelson rightly asserts that the "I" avant-garde poets inhabit "cannot be properly understood [either] as a consolidated lyric speaker or as a fragmented linguistic predicament." Assaying the limits of semiotics, Nelson notes that "for Barthes, the enigma that muddles up the neatness of the poststructuralist platitude is the body" (249n). My reading of "In Memory of My Feelings" follows a similar trajectory, arguing that O'Hara's role as semiotic signifier did not erase the personal and physical costs he felt at the level of the "I."

10. Dan Chiasson contends that O'Hara's poems are "best seen as displacements of the personal onto sturdier, more objective sites" (135). A similar argument is offered by Rosenbaum (167–68). Both read O'Hara's bodily conflation with cityscape more affirmatively than I do.

11. In "US," a lithograph in their *Stones* series, Rivers and O'Hara reproduce the sort of postcard Dean might have sent back to Indiana upon his arrival in Hollywood: "It's swell out here" (Ferguson 53). O'Hara felt that way about New York, but like Dean he may have felt a veil lift once he became mired in its celebrity culture.

12. Lehman, who argues vehemently against any suicide thesis, Gooch's especially, provides an encapsulation of the debate in *The Last Avant-Garde* (170–73). Looming large in Lehman's discussion is Perloff's speculation that if O'Hara "had wanted to commit suicide, if he had 'courted death' as the myth has it, there would have been a much surer way of doing it" than by being hit by a dune buggy going twenty miles per hour (171). Ward (194–95) agrees with Lehman and Perloff, whereas Watkin surmises that O'Hara's death "was a statement totally in keeping with his aesthetic process" (127). Like Lehman, I would counsel against a rush to judgment in the case of O'Hara's death. But like Watkin I would also have us see that his verse—composed of "two parts melancholy, three parts joy," to use Lehman's language—is haunted by death, and furthermore, that the seascapes toward which O'Hara gravitated held for him the promise of easy repose and anonymity, qualities that Romantic poets have traditionally linked with our final rest. As O'Hara baldly put it, "There's nothing more beautiful / than knowing something is going / to be over" (*Poems Retrieved* 190).

13. Citing several critics, Perloff likens Leslie's *The Killing of Frank O'Hara* (1975) to Renaissance paintings of Christ on the cross (*Frank* 1–2).

14. The term "fire-escape" can be found in "Second Avenue" and "In Memory of My Feelings," joining the surreal cityscape portrayed in those poems, and additionally in "For a Dolphin" (*CP* 407), a beachside poem closer in theme to "Dear Jap" (and written around the same time). Cambridge friend Bunny Lang, who once said that

"New York has brutalized Frank," had her play *Fire Exit* produced in New York in 1954, with disastrous results (Gooch 270). Additionally, Gooch reports that O'Hara escaped with valuable paintings when MoMA was ravaged by fire in 1958, suggesting a fire escape of a different kind (304). Most ironic of all is the fact that Johns's Edisto beach house was consumed by fire in November 1966, just months after O'Hara's death. Johns escaped.

2. LOCUS SODUS

1. For an underhanded review of Pollock's greatness, see the 1949 *Life* feature by Seiberling. For the ambivalent acclaim Ashbery received after winning major literary awards, see Kostelanetz, Richman, and McDowell. "Difficulty," mentioned by David Shapiro in his 1979 study, forms the basis for many interview questions posed to Ashbery.

2. Drawing upon a distinction put forth by Friedrich Schiller, Paul Alpers labels Theocritus a "naïve" realist and Virgil a "sentimental" escapist. His reasoning is that the former poet's idylls, composed before the advent of civilization, simply and realistically recorded the peaceful state of nature that actually existed in Arcadia. Virgil, by contrast, wrote during the turbulent decline of the Roman Empire. Traumatic events prompted him to take a sentimental journey into the past, toward a faraway place that existed before civilization, a fantasyland upon which he might project his sentimental longings for warmth and tenderness (Alpers, *What* 29–37).

3. A charged issue in Ashbery criticism is whether keeping one's sex life "general" means keeping it secret. In the 1990s, John Shoptaw and Catherine Imbriglio stepped away from canonical literary influence, emphasized by Harold Bloom ("Charity") and Helen Vendler (*Music* 224–41; *Soul* 130–40), to consider "the rhetoric of the closet," or "the relationships between homoeroticism and Ashbery's celebrated disjunctive language strategies" (Imbriglio 249). For Shoptaw, the evidence of things *not* said in Ashbery's work is the key to his "misrepresentative poetics," a semiotic language characterized by "crypt words," those "displaced" but "still recoverable" phrases that to him "suggest both a puzzle, something encoded, and a burial plot, something hidden, forgotten, or simply covered up" (6). The split in scholarly perspectives emerges as we contrast the approach adopted by Aidan Wasley, who aligns Ashbery's "love poetry" with Auden's "civic tradition," with that taken by Marjorie Perloff, who in a 1998 *Jacket* piece joins "queer" critics Michael Moon and Thomas Yingling in railing against "normalizing" discourse. Altieri, Herd, Hollander, and Mohanty and Monroe support Wasley by emphasizing Ashbery's "civic" strain, whereas Bergman, Edelman, Imbriglio, McCorkle, Shoptaw, Vincent, Moon, and Yingling foreground his homoeroticism. According to Bergman, Ashbery joins Whitman in his "rejection of the heterosexual male ego" (391), adopting a homoerotic voice that is less unitary than the romantic pastoralists' yet less impersonal than the high modernists'. Ashbery, meanwhile, shows little patience with criticism that participates in outing. Imbriglio reveals that his work has never appeared in any anthology of homosexual literature (254–55).

4. As a City University student reading Ashbery's poetry once told me, "It seems like all the lines are made up of the last parts of sentences." Professional critics concur. Kinzie calls Ashbery's poetry "irreferential." Shoptaw calls it "misrepresentative." Lehman, trying to counter Shoptaw's homoerotic readings, prefers "antiprogrammatic." Dana Gioia may have said it best: "Ideas in Ashbery are like the melodies in some jazz improvisation where the musicians have left out the original tune to avoid paying royalties" (166).

5. For similar reasons, Ashbery loves reading Proust: "I don't know why it is so gripping, but it seizes the way life sometimes seems to have of droning on in a sort of dream-like space" (Stitt, "Art" 42).

6. In "Nothing Is True," a song from *Catholic Boy*, Jim Carroll summons the licentiousness of New York bohemia by repeating a refrain made popular in Andy Warhol's circle: "Nothing is true; everything is permitted."

7. "All my stuff is romantic poetry," Ashbery once told the *New York Quarterly* ("Craft" 129).

8. Herd notes that Ashbery came across Parmigianino's *Self-Portrait in a Convex Mirror* in 1950, the same year he composed "Picture of Little J. A.," but that he did not sit down to write the poem based on this painting until 1973, when he stumbled upon a book on Parmigianino in a Provincetown bookshop (*John Ashbery* 161).

9. Ashbery's second-person addresses are intimate but teasing. "This poem is concerned with language on a very plain level," he muses in "Paradoxes and Oxymorons." "Look at it talking to you . . . / I think you exist only / To tease me into doing it, on your level, and then you aren't there / Or have adopted a different attitude. And the poem / Has set me softly down beside you. The poem is you" (*CP* 698).

10. During the 1960s, James Schuyler continued to call Ashbery "Little J. A." in letters to friends (*Just* 208, 241).

11. Ashbery encounters a similar crisis in *The Double Dream of Spring*, predicting that "The pretensions of a past will some day / Make it over into progress, a growing up. . . . // And the purpose of the many stops and starts will be made clear: / Backing into the old affair of not wanting to grow / Into the night, which becomes a house, a parting of the ways / Taking us far into sleep. A dumb love" (*CP* 195). In such moments, he sacrifices the virile passion of his youth, settling for "states of creation," which, although they represent "progress," produce little more than a "dumb harvest" or a "dumb love."

12. Ashbery often refers to the "polyphonic" quality of his work, citing "floating pronouns" as the cause (Stitt, "Art" 50; Koethe 184; Munn 61). "Personal pronouns in my work very often seem like variables in an equation," he says. "'You' can be myself or it can be another person, someone whom I'm addressing, and so can 'he' and 'she' for that matter and 'we'; sometimes one has to deduce from the rest of the sentence what is being meant and my point is also that it doesn't really matter very much, that we are somehow all aspects of a consciousness giving rise to the poem" ("Craft" 123). Unlike O'Hara's use of proper names, Herd notes, Ashbery's use of pronouns holds an allure for readers stationed outside the New York School's cliquish circle (*John*

Ashbery 67). Indeed, Ashbery's invitation for others to participate in his fantasies is almost always there. In "The Problem of Anxiety" he asks, "Suppose this poem were about you—would *you* / put in the things I've carefully left out: / descriptions of pain, and sex, and how shiftily / people behave toward each other?" (*Notes* 121). Yet he also winks knowingly at the protective cover pronouns provide, as in "The Laughter of Dead Men": "You could have told me all about that / but of course preferred not to, / so fearful of the first-person singular / and all the singular adventures it implies" (*Wakefulness* 39).

13. Ashbery tells MacArthur (153) that his mother discovered he was gay "by accident" in 1945, and that afterward "she sort of repressed it. And I never discussed it with my father, who never brought it up with me."

14. Shoptaw declines to supply a gay context for "Soonest Mended," identifying the "Barely tolerated" people "living on the margin" as "poets and other no-accounts," including protestors against the Vietnam War (106). His reticence is peculiar since the poem's final clause ("that day so long ago") bears such a close resemblance to "that horrible, blatant day / To be avoided at all costs because already known" (*CP* 239), mentioned in "Fragment" and identified by Shoptaw as the day Ashbery's homosexual affair was leaked to neighbors, before the case was "officially closed" (118). Ashbery's fear of detection arises decades later in "The Fortune Cookie Crumbles," a poem that uses FBI-style interrogation to explore Little J. A.'s pastoral identity: "You were a tulip / in some past life, it says here" (*Your Name* 44).

15. As Herd notes, a "decoy" is a "risky means of distracting attention from something more important; the risk being that, if decoded as such, the effect of a decoy is to heighten suspicion" (*John Ashbery* 116). The same dynamic exists when Ashbery's critics strain to locate gay subtexts. In such instances, Herd explains, the "willful infelicity" of Ashbery's "knowingly maladroit poetry" (117) incites readers to decipher missing textual evidence.

16. "The radical repetition of one moment in the next is the source of our life in nature," Angus Fletcher argues in an essay on Ashbery, "but we are born to accept an indistinct, imprecise, wary existence. As we intently look back into our past, we meet ourselves as if not detached from the imperious present that provides the temporal grounding of retrospection" (78).

17. For discussion of the Virgin of Walsingham ballad and its permutations in seventeenth-century England, see Empson, 68–69. For discussion of Protestant revivalism in the "Holy Land" of western New York in the nineteenth century, see Paul Johnson.

18. Although ravines are plentiful in western New York, Ashbery implies that their topographical features are transposable to urban environments. In some poems, ravines and streets flow into one another. Consider this passage from *Flow Chart*: "I have found my home in a narrow cleft / stained with Indian paintbrush and boar's blood, from which an avenue eventually leads / to the flatter, more civilized places I have no quarrel with either" (110).

19. In "Steps," Frank O'Hara sets up a similar scenario, mentioning an apartment "vacated by a gay couple / who moved to the country for fun," only to reveal that they

have "moved a day too soon," missing out on possibilities available only in New York (*CP* 371). Joe LeSueur, O'Hara's longtime apartment-mate, recalls that Tennessee Williams retained a West Side apartment primarily for erotic rendezvous (187–88).

20. In "For John Clare," a prose poem, Ashbery summons the spirit of the troubled Romantic poet while reflecting on the missed opportunities for natural communion haunting contemporary city dwellers: "There ought to be room for more things, for a spreading out, like. Being immersed in the details of rock and field and slope— letting them come to you for once, and then meeting them halfway would be so much easier—if they took an ingenious pride in being in one's blood. Alas, we perceive them if at all as those things that were meant to be put aside—costumes of the supporting actors or voice trilling at the end of a narrow enclosed street" (*CP* 198).

21. Richard Davalos, the actor who played Aron Trask in the film, bore a striking resemblance to the young Ashbery.

22. Note the images Ashbery uses: "As one tendril / after another unclasps" (*Flow Chart* 50); "Talk it over with your gardener, see / the bright shoots" (55); "You were afraid of setting out shoots" (65); "shoots keep popping up" (82). Even before he invokes *East of Eden*, Ashbery taps the world of 1950s Hollywood to comment on the irrepressible nature of human sexuality and organic growth. When he talks about the "beautiful girls wearing peasant aprons" who thoughtfully "chewed on a spear of hay" (94–95), he summons the provocative film still of "full-figured gal" Jane Russell (lying supine in a hayloft) used to sell bras in 1970s television commercials. At the same time, he liberates the image of a closeted adolescent, "a block of hay from which no strand is permitted to extrude" (67), doing away with a bale that, like Russell's bra, was meant to confine natural protrusions.

23. Fairfield Porter's estimation of Ashbery as "lazy and quick" (Lehman 111) reminds me of the catlike creatures the poet presents in *Flow Chart* and in "At North Farm."

3. FICTIONS DRESSED LIKE WATER

1. In 1998, Koch looked back guiltily on his appraisal of the School, saying, "I had a very narrow view of it back then" (Kane, *All Poets* 101). According to Schuyler, Koch upbraided Padgett and Shapiro for not including Guest in their collection (*Just* 341). In the 1980s, Schuyler sought to include Guest in an anthology of young poets, even if she was "old as the hills" (190, 413, 419).

2. Lundquist takes the title of her essay from Schuyler's May 1971 letter to Guest, which laments their exclusion from New York School discussions: "They do not realize that the Founders of the NY School . . . are not a trefoil, but a star, a five-pointed star at the very least" ("Fifth Point" 11). This letter is missing from William Corbett's selection of Schuyler's correspondence, *Just the Thing*.

3. In 1969, Myers remarked upon Guest's airy poetics, arguing that "the very rhythm of her lines implies a quicker breathing" (*Poets* 25). In 1960, Ashbery told Guest he had located in her verse "quite a few currents of air which are very refreshing to breathe. Which is so rare in poetry now—being able to breathe I mean. I love the

spaces between the things in your poems." He hoped Guest would visit him in France, "especially in the south of it where the air is so wonderful it makes breathing a pleasure, as in your poems, rather than a duty" (Lundquist, "Fifth Point" 17).

4. Hadley Guest, Barbara's daughter, supplied biographical details in April 2005 correspondence.

5. In a photograph from her 2005 album *Nolita*, Zeidel waves languidly from behind the Café Gitane's plate glass window, which sparkles with raindrops, reflecting lights from the street. Situated alongside her pensive musical tales (several awash in rain), Keren Ann's gentle salutation proves inviting to urbanites who grow ruminative on rainy days.

6. Ashbery praised Cezanne for twisting nature out of shape, thereby satisfying our collective urge to see nature for something other than it is (*Selected Prose* 213). In *Seeking Air*, Guest's 1978 novel, the claustrophobic Morgan Flew also gravitates toward Cezanne, realizing that he too "must continue to seek 'a harmony parallel to nature'" (137).

7. Vickery reveals that Guest composed "The Screen of Distance" during psychotherapy sessions, the narrative arc of which failed to affect her as much as did the scenery (sidewalks, parks) outside her therapist's windows (257).

8. "I don't think I'm literal," Guest told Hillringhouse. "I think I try to be sometimes. I become too abstract in my thinking and then I try to give my poems a literal ending because I've gotten too abstract" (28).

9. Citing Charles Segal's assertion that an "atmosphere of suspension amid contraries, of rest amid disturbance, sets the tone for the *Eclogues*," Alpers explains that the avoidance of resolution in classical pastoral texts, far from being a sign of inefficiency, "reflects the protagonist's strength relative to his world" (*What* 68). Virgil had the ability to "suspend" post-Theocritean pastoral's sentimental crises, emphasizing rather than sublimating the tensions of belatedness, committing himself to the present even as he addressed the past. For Alpers, Virgilian suspension "suggests a poised, even secure contemplation of things disparate or ironically related, and yet at the same time does not imply that disparities or conflicts are fully resolved" (68).

10. At other times Guest uttered these terms quite earnestly, as when she referred to O'Hara as "my dear" in "White Cloud Poem," a touching update of a Chinese friendship poem, included in *Homage to Frank O'Hara*.

11. Renowned for her seascapes, H. D. capitalized on the same biological ambiguity. "The whole notion of reality disturbed her," Guest has said of H. D. "She couldn't pinpoint it" (Hillringhouse 29). This "union of self and nature," Louis Martz argues in his introduction to H. D.'s *Collected Poems*, allowed the Imagist poet "to live constantly at the juncture of such forces, inner and outer, to inhabit constantly the borderline." Ultimately, this "enabled her to control the surges that arose from the depths of her violently responsive nature" (xiv, xiii).

12. Comparing three poems published in different decades—"Sante Fe Trail" (1962), "Nebraska" (1973), and "Borderlands" (1993)—shows how Guest's journeys

were increasingly shaped by abstract language, the opaque materiality of which complicates intention and meaning (CP 41–42, 101–2, 288–89).

13. Keller connects the ornamental flamingos with "Dido's defiance of convention through imaginative excess, figured within the mode of bourgeois consumerism," contrasting the birds with the "stately realm of urns and fountains" ("Becoming" 219–20). For me, these items smack of nouveau riche pretension.

14. Guest occasionally imagined what would happen if she reduced the risk in her work. Tellingly, these poems are set indoors. In "Safe Flights," the sobering decision "to no longer like the taste of whisky" initiates a series of retreats and retractions, showing a daredevil "aerialist" what her life might look like "under a tent where promises perform" (CP 17). No big top excitement there. Similarly, in "A Way of Being," Guest admonishes "excursionists" who travel in cars rather than sandals with the hope of avoiding "another mishap of nature" (81–82). In "The Blue Stairs," she arranges her typography selectively, her right-hand column approximating the landings one would find after successive flights of stairs. Again she confounds expectations, assigning to the landings, places of safety and rest, her most suspenseful language: "balancing," "floating," "kicking the ladder away," "republic of space," "secret platforms," "eternal banishment." Guest explains that "There is no fear / in taking the first step / or the second / or the third" up the flights of stairs, but she excoriates those who ostentatiously celebrate their ascents, reserving particular disdain for those who are "Spatially selective / using this counterfeit / of height // To substantiate / a method of progress // Reading stairs / as interpolation / in the problem of gradualness / with a heavy and pure logic" (61–63). Guest briefly revisits this argument in later poems, referring to a "stair swindle" in "Shifting the Iris" (136) and enigmatically claiming that "The reason for caterwauling / on the stair was simple" in part four of Biography (185).

15. Regarding Stevens's imaginative voyages in landscapes of his own making, Guest says in her interview with Hillringhouse that "tension" is "something that's missing from Wallace Stevens" (28).

16. In Seeking Air (23), Morgan Flew receives a gift book entitled The Care of Books in a Tropical Climate, another sly reference on the part of Guest to Prospero's role in The Tempest.

17. Kenward Elmslie's 1975 volume, Tropicalism, and Patsy Southgate's equation of summertime in the Hamptons with the tropics (119) are possible exceptions, but it is clear that neither New York School member matched Guest's knowledge of subtropical climates. In the 1970s, Victor Hernandez Cruz and the Nuyorican poets summoned their own tropical energies.

18. O'Hara's "Oranges: 12 Pastorals" (CP 5–9) was printed as a limited edition by Tibor de Nagy in 1953. The cover featured a brilliant painting of oranges by Hartigan, but as O'Hara brags in "Why I Am Not a Painter" (261–62), he lasts the whole poetic sequence without ever mentioning orange, either as color or fruit.

19. Even Guest found it difficult to minimize her "footprint" on the earth. In "Fan Poems," she "who walks softly" through a garden "causes mutiny among the lilies,"

which in turn causes blossoms to fall. Nevertheless, the "unique flower beds . . . / . . . hasten to lift themselves to a cautious heel print," suggesting that this garden takes human activity in stride, making it a part of its ongoing narrative (*CP* 79–80).

20. "Special azure was once our way," Guest says in "Even Ovid" (*CP* 104), offering a characteristically cryptic allusion to phrases and images used in earlier poems.

21. In "A Reason," another poem from *The Blue Stairs*, Guest again heads out for the "wild wild whatever / in wild more silent blue," though whether she is speaking about the sky or the ocean is less clear on this occasion (*CP* 74). For Hillman, Guest's focus on wildness "predicts a kind of disintegration of the speaking presence that never happens" (219). In the ocean or in the air, her personae are on the verge of faltering, but they always manage to keep their cool.

22. It should be noted that Ashbery praised O'Hara for not taking an overt stance on Vietnam or other political topics (*Selected Prose* 81), setting off heated exchanges among American poets determining their place in contemporary political debates. In *The Seventies Now*, Stephen Paul Miller supports Ashbery, arguing that the poet's deconstruction of macrolevel systems—though admittedly abstract and difficult to fathom—helped him unravel the ideological apparatuses of Vietnam-era politicians without resorting to sloganeering.

23. Ever ironic, the Clash used this phrase as a song title on their anti-imperialist masterpiece, *Sandinista!*

24. The Helen Frankenthaler painting on the cover of *The Blue Stairs* is an abstract illustration of a blue oval abutting a vertical line. Given the themes of Guest's poetry, one can view this picture as a ladder reaching into the heavens or as a diving board above a body of water. The line can suggest a way into, or a way out of, the blue elements piquing our desires. In 1975, Guest praised Frankenthaler's "manner of flaunting space," claiming that this landscape artist, so dependent on "color structure," rightly "forces nature to copy art" ("Helen" 58, 59).

25. Du Plessis has expertly analyzed gendered aspects of *le marveilleux* in Guest's verse ("Gendered"), while Schuyler cites the "marvelous" qualities cherished by New York School poets in letters to Koch and Joe Brainard (*Just* 240, 249). J. J. Mitchell (144) and Bill Berkson ("Frank" 164) likewise speak of the "marvelous" aura O'Hara cast over the New York arts scene.

26. Contrarian by nature, Morgan favors the cargo-laden East River over the poetic Hudson (*Seeking* 123), exhibiting the resourcefulness shown by Guest's Countess in her Minneapolis nocturne. Prompted by Miriam to find a quiet corner of New York—"somewhere hidden, the noise perhaps muffled by trees, [where] there would be a nook, a variant on seclusion"—Morgan considers how peaceful his Upper East Side neighborhood has been all along: "I don't think you know, I said to myself, how attached you are to your neighborhood. Remember when the hoots and cries were the noise of the river? Remember when a freighter narrowly missed the bridge and the scrape of that? Remember the narrows? Remember the silence as the river gathers its sand to enlarge the islet that each year grows before you?" (50). Rather wistfully, this

devotee of urban pastoral admits that "the sweet rhythm of a boat filled with garbage or worse . . . added a little tempo to my day" (101).

4. NEW WINDOWS ON NEW YORK

1. Freilicher also said that visiting the Southampton house "was really like stepping into a nineteenth century novel." Porter nurtured this atmosphere by buying old hanging lamps at a junkshop and by putting up patterned wallpapers so that his rooms would resemble interiors depicted in the Bonnard and Vuillard paintings he so admired (Spring 171–72).

2. Porter is rumored to have joked that Schuyler's poems were more visual than his own paintings (Ward 2).

3. Diary entries reveal that Schuyler read Andrew Young's portrait of nature poets, *The Poet in the Landscape* (1962), and the Northumberland memoir of Thomas Bewick, who likened sheepfold hedgerows to city avenues (*Diary* 57n, 83–84). Schuyler likely introduced Ashbery to the poetry of John Clare (MacArthur 181), and he was inspired late in life by Gilbert White, reciting a poem based upon the British naturalist's journal during a radio interview (Savage).

4. Schuyler was just as likely to find traces of the city in the countryside. Consider his art catalog note "Appearance and Reality" (*Selected Art* 52–53). On an isolated Long Island beach, Fairfield Porter wanders off to "make a sketch: just of nature" while Schuyler stays behind to write up his notes on a New York art show. In a scenario reminiscent of Coleridge's "This Lime Tree Bower My Prison," the sedentary Schuyler partakes of his own natural flights of fancy and finds that he is aided as much by the artworks he is reviewing as by the tranquil setting he presently inhabits. Of particular relevance on this day is John Button's painting *Fire Escape*, which Schuyler calls an "urban echo to [the] elms, privet, orchards, [and] grasses" of his Long Island surroundings. A similar urban pastoral interchange emerged when Schuyler visited the Porters in Amherst, Massachusetts. At that time he likened 5:15 A.M. rooster crows to "trucks in stalled traffic" (*Diary* 78). Detailing Schuyler's writing routine in Southampton, Porter told O'Hara, "Sometimes I hear him typing and often I hear a woodpecker and think it is he" (*Material* 132–33).

5. So it was that Porter praised Vuillard for making an art that is "concrete in detail and abstract as a whole." His art "seems to be ordinary," Porter explains, "but the extraordinary is everywhere" (Spring 121, 122).

6. Other O'Hara poems about Freilicher include "A Sonnet for Jane Freilicher" (*CP* 61), "A Terrestrial Cuckoo" (62–63), "Jane Awake" (72–73), "Jane at Twelve" (88–89), "Jane Bathing" (89–90), "To Jane: And in Imitation of Coleridge" (182–85), and "To Jane, Some Air" (192).

7. For more on these controversial landscaping projects, see Iver Peterson ("Hamptons") and Steven Gaines (*Philistines*). Late in his life, Schuyler wrote a scathing poem, "Horse-Chestnut Trees and Roses" (*CP* 383–85), decrying changes made to Porter's Southampton property after the painter's death.

8. Klaus Kertess maintains that skewed angles in Freilicher's paintings derive from her reliance on observation and memory instead of photographs ("Art" 44).

9. Picking up on this dynamic, Porter saw that Freilicher used her apartment's wainscotting as an "interior horizon" ("Jane" 66). William Corbett calls these her "inner-outer paintings" (96).

10. The exception to agrarian eradication in 1950s New York was Staten Island, where farms existed until the opening of the Verrazano Narrows Bridge in 1964. Catholic reformer Dorothy Day established an "agronomic university" on Staten Island in 1935, but it had closed by the 1960s (Jamison and Eyerman 196).

11. At Harvard, Porter learned from Alfred North Whitehead that "the artist doesn't know what he knows in general; he only knows what he knows specifically. And what he knows in general or what can be known in general becomes apparent later on by what he has had to put down. And that to me is the most interesting art form.... In other words, you are not in control of nature quite, you are part of nature. ... The whole question of art is to be wide awake, to be as attentive as possible" (Spring 38).

12. In 1966, Freilicher told Schuyler, "I'm interested in landscape, but there's a paradox: it's depressing to get that realistic look, 'Why, that's just how it looks!' or, 'I know that time of day.' At the same time, I don't really want to lose the place" (*Selected Art* 33). Four decades later, she told Klaus Kertess, "I don't render objects faithfully; I like to balance the subject and the painting. It's the tension between them that interests me" ("Art" 43).

13. Ron Padgett may have had this poem in mind when he composed his Shelleyan spoof, "To a Schuyler," in which the elder poet, the "blithe spirit" of the New York School, offers offhand aphorisms during a 1967 trip to Vermont. In one, a blustery Schuyler shouts, "You can *have* New York City!" ("To a Schuyler" 10). This phrase reappears, modified and free-floating, in one of Schuyler's own poems, "Now and Then" (*CP* 38).

14. Bruce Cormin, who was Schuyler's next-door neighbor at the Chelsea and later used 625 as his painting studio, told me the room was more messy than beautiful.

15. Schuyler's appreciation of Victorian floral ironwork was sparked by Park, who lived near him in Chelsea and, like Porter, invited him to stay at his house on Long Island (in Bridgehampton). In a review of Park's 1988 show at Tibor de Nagy, Schuyler singled out for praise a painting called *The Plane Tree*, which he described as "a transparent maze of cast iron Chelsea railings seen at various angles and recessions and in counter-play to plane tree branches, swooping and leaf-laden, before the rose window of a rose-red church" (*Selected Art* 59). In 1985, Schuyler and Park composed a collaborative journal, with the poet supplying words and the artist graphite drawings. Tibor de Nagy published *Two Journals* in 1995. On the cover is a sketch Park drew of Schuyler's Chelsea balustrade, with a watering can in the foreground, as though the railing's metal chrysanthemums required constant nourishment. In another picture Park depicts Schuyler's bedroom mirror, recognizable by the leaf pinned alongside a haphazard row of photographs, a souvenir the poet had taken from Willem de Kooning's Southamp-

ton residence. Park was thus well aware of the urban pastoral synthesis affecting Schuyler and tended to feature it in his own work. In fact, Gerrit Henry has called Park's *View of Chelsea* (1988) "probably the first pastorale of New York City" (77).

16. Williams would have been familiar with natural "dependence," since as a child he collected rainwater dripping down from a roof (Felstiner 11).

5. FUN CITY

1. Besides Brown's "Santa Claus, Go Straight to the Ghetto," Mayfield's "Little Child Runnin' Wild," The Spinners' "Ghetto Child," and Presley's "In the Ghetto," consider The Supremes' "Love Child" and Marvin Gaye's "Inner City Blues (Make Me Wanna Holler)." Regarding the creation of *Sesame Street* and other educational television programs for children, see Morrow.

2. Lopate's *Journal of a Living Experiment* chronicles progressive arts education in New York City from the mid-1960s to the mid-1970s, including the poets-in-the-schools and artists-in-the-schools programs.

3. For perceptive accounts of New York's decade-long decline, see Cannato and Mahler.

4. Aware of how his temperament differed from Koch's, James Schuyler dubbed himself "Doctor Fuss" (*Just* 373).

5. In *New Art City*, Jed Perl describes the metropolitan meanderings of de Kooning, Burckhardt, and Cornell, whose gathering of random images and discarded objects revealed "the paradoxical nature of the modern dialectic" (84). Emphasizing the plurality and messiness of city streets, these artists sought to replace the clean latticework and grid patterns favored by Piet Mondrian. "De Kooning's nitty-gritty New York," Perl notes, "was all knock-you-in-your-teeth actualities, all surprising particulars: the dramatically contracted sizes of adjacent buildings, the abandoned lots and demolition sites, the oil stains and graffiti on the pavements, the reflections of neon signs on wet streets" (95). Various works (collages, films, photographs, poems) by Burckhardt, Cornell, and mutual friend Edwin Denby followed in this vein, as did *Violet Hour*, a 1943 canvas by Loren MacIver, which "imagined Manhattan as a series of hieroglyphic images—pedestrians, seagulls, fire escapes, chimneys, street" (168). MacIver's rendering of urban dusk anticipates Jane Freilicher's paintings, yet her imagery is more blurred and funky, like graffiti art on sooty facades. Encouraged by visiting artists, New York schoolchildren tried similar experiments in the 1970s, composing works in which the city's grid was not only softened by shadowy imagery but also, according to filmmaker Theresa Mack, "haunted by it" (218–19, 223).

6. About Jarry, Guillaume Apollinaire said, "His smallest action, his pranks, everything was literature" (Shaw 51).

7. "Yet always beneath the rainway unsyntactical / Beauty might leap up!" Koch declares in "The Great Atlantic Rainway," a vertiginous poem drawing on a conversation with Freilicher (*CP* 73).

8. Especially popular in this outpouring of books was the "teacher's journal," a di-

ary detailing the harsh introduction to city life an instructor received upon his arrival and the trials endured during the academic year. Some narratives deserve acclaim, but others contain troubling moments, as when James Herndon, author of *The Way It Spozed to Be*, calibrates the attractiveness of black students by referring to the Caucasian features they possess (13).

9. In comparison, *Sesame Street* appeared outdated, relying as it did on children's passive responses to spoken language rather than their active engagement with their environment. Critiquing *Sesame Street* in *The Atlantic*, John Holt asked the show to concentrate less on helping children "get better at the task of pleasing their first-grade teachers" and more on "the vastly more interesting and important task—which they are already good at—of learning from the world and people around them" (Morrow 146).

10. According to Koch, poems in elementary school textbooks "characteristically dealt with one small topic in an isolated way—clouds, teddybears, frogs, or a time of year. Nothing was compared to any serious emotion or to any complex way of looking at things. Everything was reassuring and simplified" (*Rose* 6). Herbert Kohl, who ended up ditching assigned textbooks in his Harlem classroom, voiced similar concerns: "The curriculum and textbooks as they now exist do not present life as the children know it. The books are full of bland creatures without personalities who don't know conflict, confusion, pain or love" (Lopate, "Interview with Herbert Kohl" 31). When contemplating poetry as a profession, Ron Padgett says he "had always been afraid that people would think I was a creep, because only a creep would write the stuff they put in the high school textbooks we had growing up" ("Nine Years" 285).

11. Reporting on his work with "culturally deprived" children in deaf schools, Henderson says, "We have found that lifting the correction ax from over the child spurs him on to a fuller expression in writing" (80). In this era, Ravitch reports, black educators began linking "cultural deficiencies" and "cultural disadvantage" to misguided curricula, which tended to separate inner-city children from their own cultural heritage (*Troubled Crusade* 268).

12. A photograph in *Wishes* (34) shows the street housing PS 61. There are no trees or any other sign of greenery. Upon reaching the corner of Avenue B and 12th Street, Padgett said he "felt silly carrying a book instead of a gun" ("Nine Years" 283). "You could not have found a less pastoral place," Padgett told me. "It was pretty barren, not the Alphabet City we have come to know today. The main landmarks you could see from the top floors of the school building were the Consolidated Edison smokestacks" (Conversation).

13. Assigning Robert Herrick's "Delight in Disorder," Koch counters the logic of the grid, asking students, "Do you like anything that seems sloppy or messy or disorganized, such as a room with books and cushions all around, or an unmowed lawn with tall and short grass and weeds and dandelions, or a sky full of straggly-looking clouds, or a painting full of bog splashes and gobs of different colored paint, or a person with fluffy hair and shirttails out and different colored casual clothes? Write a

poem saying what you like about something like that and why you like it more than something absolutely orderly and neat" (*Rose* 233).

14. De Certeau says that "the childhood experience that determines spatial practices later develops its effects, proliferates, floods private and public spaces, undoes their readable surfaces, and creates within the planned city a 'metaphorical' or mobile city, like the one Kandinsky dreamed of: 'a great city built according to all the rules of architecture and then suddenly shaken by a force that defies all calculation'" (110).

15. Elsewhere, Koch attributes Housman's line to her reading of John Donne (*Rose* 12), but think of O'Hara's great image, "The stars blink like a hairnet" (*CP* 216), with its suggestion that nature is best understood in combination with artificiality. Koch encouraged PS 61 students to write about "'crazy things'—a pineapple dog, a radio strawberry, flowers kissing New York" (*Rose* 68)—images that would be at home in one of his own poems. He referred to his university teaching as generative, admitting that he tapped certain students at the New School and Columbia as heirs apparent of first-generation New York School writers (Kane, *All Poets* 258n). Lopate complains that this generative approach filtered down to (and adversely affected) Koch's elementary school exchanges, asserting that his "emphasis on pleasure and on color, and on linguistic surface where two words chemically bounce off each other" (as when kids write about "the raspberry coming out of the trees" and "purple monkeys") not only "overstressed empowerment and hedonism" in the elementary classroom but also turned students into clones of New York School poets. Koch counters by saying that his avant-garde techniques helped children articulate their own surrealist dreams (Lopate, "Interview with Kenneth Koch" 278, 280). Koch's reasoning is echoed by other artists-in-the-schools, including Barbara Siegel, who reports that her students in Fort Greene possessed an "organic" aesthetic vision and an appreciation of the city's "endless absurdities," but needed experimental art to help them express those thoughts (244–45).

16. In *Left Back*, Ravitch outlines the "home geography" curriculum designed by New Deal progressives. Instruction was centered on "socially real situations" and "the major activities of childlife." Elementary students were gradually introduced to larger spheres of influence, with separate units on home and family, neighborhood, and municipal community (256). Koch went further, urging children to color "socially real situations" in their home geography with overlays of imaginative discourse.

17. For illustrations of city rubbish done up colorfully in pastel hues, see *I Stink!* by Kate and Jim McMullan, a children's book that follows a garbage truck on its nightly rounds.

18. Klinkenborg, a member of the *Times* editorial board who spends half his time at his upstate farm, writes the popular "Rural Life" column, but his city writings are usually just as pastoral. The *Times* has highlighted a number of debris artists over the years, among them Leonardo Drew, a Brooklyn-based sculptor who uses a shopping cart to gather abandoned objects polluting city streets (Dobrzynski).

19. Bernadette Mayer, Koch's pupil at the New School, issues similar advice when

teaching sonnets, asking students to walk fourteen city blocks, writing one line for each block. "You can do it easily in a city," she explains, "because there are so many words around" (Kane, *What Is Poetry* 122). O'Hara practiced this art better than anybody. Known for composing poems during lunchtime walks, O'Hara "succeeds in conveying the city's atmosphere not by writing directly about it but by writing about his emotions, all of them somehow filtered through its paint supply stores and its aspiring April smog," Koch wrote in 1961 (Perloff, *Frank* 69). O'Hara was likened to Apollinaire by his New York School peers, including Ashbery (*Selected Prose* 128) and Philip Guston (Gooch 11).

20. Allan Jacobs and Donald Appleyard explain that the "townscape movement," to which Jane Jacobs belonged, found "the sights, sounds, feels, and smells of the city, its materials and textures, floor surfaces, facades, style, signs, lights, seating, trees, sun, and shade all potential amenities for the attentive observer and user" (167). Poetry by Apollinaire, O'Hara, Koch, and New York schoolchildren followed suit, asking urbanites to get a palpable sense of themselves in relation to their environment, even if that means gravitating toward zones where common beliefs and identities are suspended. Today, the townscape Jane Jacobs fought to preserve is threatened by the homogenization of city neighborhoods (Disney in Times Square, a Starbucks on every corner) and by rigidly supervised opportunities for childhood play (travel teams with expensive equipment, ballet classes with waiting lists).

21. Koch's "right amounts" reappear in "To the City," a late poem: "West Tenth Street / Was right. Charles / Street and Greenwich / Avenue were right. Cold-water / Living rooms and soot / Floating through bright / Hard-to-push-up windows / On Third Avenue / Were right" (*CP* 604).

22. Regarding Barthesian pleasure in Koch's poetry, see Pelton.

6. THE PLACE WHERE YOUR NATURE MEETS MINE

1. "I have begun a huge study of the face of America itself, acquiring maps (road-maps) of every state in the USA," Kerouac exclaims in an early letter, "and before long not a river or mountain peak or bay or town or city will escape my attention" (*Selected Letters* 107). Dean Moriarty, Cassady's alter ego, tells Sal Paradise that the road promises a "whole life of non-interference" (*On the Road* 251). Kerouac said as much in a 1958 essay: "If there is any quality that I have noticed more strongly than anything else in this generation, it is the spirit of non-interference with the lives of others" (*Portable* 564). Beat women, by contrast, met interference at every turn.

2. Joanne Kyger and Anne Waldman also bucked the trend. Kyger went to Japan in 1960, marrying Gary Snyder in Kyoto and traveling with him to India (*Japan*). Waldman took to the road in 1965 after hearing a rumor about a big poetry conference in Berkeley (Tonkinson 349–50). She admits she faced fewer travel restrictions as a second-generation Beat, since certain gender taboos no longer existed (Knight 289).

3. Asked by Waldman what it was like to raise children by different men in unconventional surroundings, di Prima says, "I realize now I've probably from the

beginning had the sense to avoid strong father figures, to avoid the patriarch." About her marriage to Marlowe, she says, "The relationship was more or less matter of fact, almost a contractual relationship, and a warm friendship. He's a very erratic man, but basically a warm person. And we'd made a whole lot of things happen that we really wanted to. . . . If I had had at that point no children I probably would have gone off to a Zen monastery or something and a viable solution was this marriage with a gay man, where the sexuality was very seldom, and was intense when it happened, but in between I led a celibate writing life, which is exactly what I wanted and I got a lot done in the arts I really cared about" (Waldman, "Interview" 38).

4. Regarding isolated pockets of avant-garde community, Snyder once said, "In the spiritual and political loneliness of America in the fifties you'd hitch a thousand miles to see a friend" ("North" 45). Di Prima estimated that "there was a only small handful of us—perhaps forty or fifty in the city—who knew what we knew: who raced about in Levis and work shirts, made art, smoked dope, dug the new jazz, and spoke a bastardization of the black argot. We surmised that there might be another fifty living in San Francisco, and perhaps a hundred more scattered across the country: Chicago, New Orleans, etc." (*Memoirs* 126). Updating the *Bear's* mailing list, she realized that bohemians resided in all corners of the nation, including remote rural outposts.

5. Di Prima says the folk songs (like Odetta's) she heard in Washington Square Park "gave to city-bound creatures like myself their first taste of the West, of what those spaces might be like, the flavor of life and death under those stars" (*Recollections* 112–13).

6. For homecoming experiences of women writers in the desert, see articles by Rudnik and Fryer. For an ironic update on this theme, see Jill Sobule's "Palm Springs" (*California Years*).

7. Gauging the effect of open-air domesticity on counterculture lifestyle, di Prima explained that her California friend Louise Herms found it difficult to raise kids when she moved to New York, since "she had never had to raise her babies in an inside where there was no real outside in which to turn them loose, and there are no special techniques for that" (*Recollections* 383). Ironically, di Prima asked Andy Warhol for funds to help the Herms family move east in 1964 (Wolf 166n).

8. For a discussion about the establishment of the National Endowments for the Arts and Humanities in the 1960s and funding to state arts councils in the 1970s, see Cummings.

9. This title track, featuring an Asian-inflected guitar played by Metheny and a synthesizer played by Mays, is by turns evanescent and foreboding, not unlike the region's weather. Stirring the confusion are the sounds of bombs, which enter just after the din of male voices ringing low in an enclosed space (a prison? an army processing center?) and just before the uplifting sound of children playing and laughing in an open-air setting. The album cover shows a hand holding up a lineman's test phone to a vast prairie sky, which although it is ablaze at sunset is almost entirely subsumed by encroaching darkness and crisscrossed by telephone poles and wires. Because the test phone picks up waves of communication in an "empty" landscape, the cover may

be a tribute to the Wichita Lineman, though I cannot help thinking the threatening sky signals doom and that these musicians are eavesdropping on a more significant political drama.

10. Di Prima presents a more bemused view of her NEA travels in "Ramada Inn, Denver" (*Pieces* 109–10), dodging pickup lines while sitting on a barstool between a rancher and a narcotics agent. In "Visit to Katagiri Roshi" ("Diane" 61), she recounts the difficulty of attempting to sit *zazen* (Buddhist meditation) in noisy motel rooms.

11. For a classic account of gendered violence in America's frontier paradigm, see Kolodny. Sadly, revisionist scholars of the "New West" have ignored di Prima, so strong is the academic bias against the counterculture. In one off-putting invitation, Krista Comer maintains that "the dominant western geocultural field—given its cultural identity as the nation's dreamscape and its emplotment with radical individualism and shadowy notions of native-inspired mysticism—is 'ready' for or receptive to those very kinds of individualistic, inchoate, or politically 'immature' impulses that are conventionally associated with countercultural politics." But, Comer hastens to add, "to date we do not have a series of memoirs by countercultural participants that are somehow comparable to those of radical northeast feminists, memoirs wherein, say, cultural feminists map out their evolving political identities in western or ecofeminist or some other terms" (52). Certainly, I believe di Prima fills the void Comer announces, neither "inchoately" nor "immaturely."

12. Contrast di Prima's analysis of the Walker exhibit with Timothy Egan's experience of viewing petroglyphs of Kokopelli, the indigenous humpbacked flute player, in open-air settings: "There are no handy written summaries in five languages next to velvet rope, no self-serving notes from patrons corporate or Medici, no artists' explanations of any kind. No signatures or authorial symbols, even. It is first-hand information, without spin, revision, or self-confident ego. And it reveals itself in a gallery of oversized geographic wonders, mounted on walls of stone where it can look grand or goofy, pedestrian or brilliant depending on the light, the weather, the mood of the sky" (77).

13. Because more museums are consulting with Native Americans in an effort to reform curatorial practices, tribes are able to show museum-goers that their culture still thrives (Clifford, *Routes* 107–46, 188–219).

7. A WORLD WITHOUT GRAVITY

1. Consider also Led Zeppelin's "Stairway to Heaven" (*Led Zeppelin IV*), a neo-pagan updating of Jacob's theophany, his dream of angels climbing a stairway toward God.

2. Since poems from *Falling Off* are sometimes modified or combined in *Journey*, I cite both volumes in this chapter. *Living at the Movies* is reprinted in full in *Fear of Dreaming*, from which all citations of Carroll's early verse are taken.

3. Warhol bared his abdominal scars for Richard Avedon and Alice Neel portraits following the shooting, as though flaunting his "stigmata" (Bourdon 290).

4. Examples abound when describing what Christopher Hitchens calls Warhol's

"cultish Catholicism, with its hints of camp and guilt" (8). In *The Chelsea Girls*, Warhol's best-known film, Ondine is cast as the "pope" of the famous hotel. "I just want to be true to my flock, whoever they may be," this unorthodox pastor announces after advising a confessor, Ingrid Superstar, to dose her mother with LSD. "My flock consists of homosexuals, perverts of any kind, queens, thieves, criminals of any sort, the rejected by society." Though his improvised performance is over-the-top ("I'm not a real priest; this is not a real church," he tells Ingrid), Ondine bristles with rage when Rona Page, unaccustomed to the rituals of Warhol's inner circle, regards his "popage" too ironically. "I'm a *phony*? Well, so are you," Ondine shouts, before throwing a glass of soda in Page's face and violently slapping her. Reportedly, this was Warhol's favorite scene (Bourdon 243, 247; Koch, *Stargazer* 94–97; Watson, *Factory* 291–92). In *Nude Restaurant*, filmed the following year, Viva launches into a long monologue on her Catholic upbringing, regaling the audience with tales of lesbian nuns and lascivious priests. "Since I left the convent, all I've met are a bunch of faggots," she complains. "At least in the church you were sure of a good lay." At one juncture, however, she asks that the camera be turned off. Evidently, some confessions were too private to share with the masses (Bourdon 261; Koch, *Stargazer* 103). In each case, deep-seated Catholic guilt threatens the improvised cinematic narrative. "Andy surrounded himself with people who knew how to strike a choirboy's innocent look while being caught in a 'naughty' act," David Bourdon writes. "At heart, they remained aware that they might someday be penalized for their breaches of conduct" (391). Catholicity for Warhol meant leaving nothing out, judging nothing while reserving plenty of room for ironic reversals. As Ralph Rugoff says, it seems appropriate that the memorial service for Warhol in St. Patrick's Cathedral was held on April Fool's Day (104).

5. Carroll included a sequence entitled "Rimbaud Scenes" (*Fear* 136–41) in *The Book of Nods*, but he was not the only musician channeling the rebellious French poet. In *The Time of the Assassins*, a study of Rimbaud that led Carroll to try his hand at rock music (Flippo 32), Henry Miller claims that "the authors of *Really the Blues*, or a man like Lord Buckley, are closer to Rimbaud, though they may not be aware of it, than the poets who have worshipped and imitated him" (vi). Patti Smith, Carroll's former girlfriend, says her decision to leave factory work in New Jersey for the artist's life in New York was inspired by her reading of Rimbaud's *Illuminations* during a lunch break. According to a friend, Smith made it her mission to "look like Keith Richards, smoke like Jeanne Moreau, walk like Bob Dylan, and write like Arthur Rimbaud" (McNeil and McCain 101, 108). Dylan himself referred to Rimbaud in songs, and as Smith told an interviewer, the folk rocker's resemblance to the French poet on his mid-1960s album covers "was the big thing for me" (Delano 56). In 1994, Wallace Fowlie, translator of a 1966 edition of Rimbaud's work featuring Pablo Picasso's tousle-haired portrait of France's enfant terrible on its cover, caused a stir when he published *Rimbaud and Jim Morrison: The Rebel as Poet*, which links the Doors singer with the previous century's "god of adolescence" (an epithet assigned by Andre Breton). As Fowlie explains, rockers were known to wear "Go, Rimbaud" T-shirts festooned with Picasso's portrait of the poet (9, 14).

6. Reminded of his statement during an interview with Ben Hecht, Kerouac quickly retracted it.

7. Carroll's passage recalls lines by Rimbaud scrawled in Paris's Père-Lachaise cemetery: "I piss toward the dark skies, very high and very far, / With the consent of the large heliotropes" (Fowlie 17–18).

8. In "Digression on *Number 1, 1948*," a poem about a Pollock painting set on a winter shoreline, Frank O'Hara, suffering himself from Manhattan claustrophobia, remarked, "They'll / never fence the silver range" (*CP* 260).

9. In "Order in Pollock's Chaos," Richard P. Taylor supports Pollock's boastful claims about inhabiting nature. Using computer analysis, he shows that Pollock's drip canvases adhere to "fractal patterns" in the natural world, including windstorms in deserts, seaweed deposits on coastlines, and cloud movements in the sky.

10. Elsewhere, Gaines describes the Irish Catholic kids she met in Belle Harbor, Queens, as "rock & roll in the flesh, standing before me, bad boys bopping around, blowing spit like James Dean (or at least Jim Carroll)" (*Misfit's* 53).

11. As Sally Cunneen says, Marian symbolism represents a "creative theology of those who feel marginalized" (xvii). Highlighting the Virgin's proletarian appeal, Cunneen cites Clarissa Pinkola Estes, who insists that if she were alive today, "Mary would be a teenage gang leader" (13). As Norris says, "there's a lot of *room* in Mary" (*Amazing* 123).

12. As Paul Elie notes, Thomas Merton believed Mary's intercession was instrumental in "preparing the seas" as he departed England for America, leaving behind his mistress and child to devote himself to God alone (42).

13. Citations of "Eternity" and "Banners of May" are taken from Rimbaud's *Complete Works*, translated by Paul Schmidt. As Fowlie mentions, Rimbaud's "Eternity" was inspirational for experimental filmmakers, its final stanza appearing in Jean-Luc Godard's *Pierrot le fou*, when Pierrot is fleeing, and in Federico Fellini's *Satiricon*, when Encolpio flees the city for the seashore.

14. Along with Ondine, Ingrid Superstar, and Brigid Polk (speed freaks all), Carroll was one of Warhol's "talkers." As Norris notes, Warhol would hang up if he discovered Carroll was sober (*Virgin* 137).

15. Rosalind Krauss and Yve-Alain Bois maintain that Warhol's "oxidation paintings," which he composed by urinating onto a metallic paint ground, honor the "abject" legacy of Pollock's drip canvases, but I find Warhol more ironic than adulatory, even if his emphasis on "lower body functions" sought to make Pollock relevant again in the age of AIDS (Varnedoe 54–55).

16. In *The Philosophy*, Warhol appears not to have learned much from his brief "death" in 1968: "I don't believe in [death] because you're not around to know that it's happened. I can't say anything about it because I'm not prepared for it" (123).

17. Recollecting a stroll he took on the Bowery shortly after someone made a suicidal leap, Warhol writes, "a bum staggered over and said, 'Did you see the comedy across the street?'" One wonders whether Warhol had this episode in mind when he spoke about Feldman's death. "I'm not saying you should be happy when a person

dies," Warhol inveighs, "but just that it's curious to see cases that prove you don't have to be sad about it, depending on what you think it means, and what you think about what you think it means" (112). Despite recovering from his own "death," Warhol must have known that suicide was a performance Herko and Feldman "couldn't do more than once."

18. Regarding the role Ginsberg's Cherry Valley retreat played in helping addicted urban artists kick their chemical dependencies, see Miles (411–35) and Carroll (*Forced* 108).

19. "If the desert is holy," Williams maintains in *Refuge*, "it is because it is a forgotten place that allows us to remember the sacred. Perhaps that is why every pilgrimage to the desert is a pilgrimage to the self. There is no place to hide, and so we are found" (148).

20. An anecdote in *Amazing Grace* proves one does not have to be a poet to pick up on this landscape's possibilities. A farmer woman shows Norris a paper placemat she has kept from a church bazaar. On this modest relic there is a picture of a wheat field and a quote from Martin Luther: "If you could understand a single grain of wheat you would die of wonder" (245).

21. In "Fragment from a Death Festival," Norris casts aspersions on Warhol's favorite watering hole. "You have to watch your laughter around here," she reports from this trendy (and catty) environment. "It's likely to spill over everything / And ruin someone's silk and suede burnoose // Here they come," she says of Warhol's fading superstars, "looking like refugees from a mercy killing. . . . // They sit around and discuss their histories, which they've filled with enough mythology to sustain them / They like the tiny replicas of themselves that shine in each other's eyes" (*Falling* 42). Carroll, too, describes how Max's patrons tried to create a lasting impression, to the exclusion of all else, including people's feelings: "The real world is hard on the ego and the back room of Max's is out of the question altogether" (*Forced* 51).

22. In "Evaporation Poems," Norris refers to a "religious aunt," another suicide, who "flew out a window into the Ideal" after warning her niece that "even transformation has its price" (*Falling* 47).

WORKS CITED

Abraham, Julie. *Metropolitan Lovers: The Homosexuality of Cities.* Minneapolis: U of Minnesota P, 2009.

Allen, Donald, ed. *The New American Poetry 1945–1960.* 1960. Berkeley: U of California P, 1999.

Alpers, Paul. "Pastoral and the Domain of Lyric in *The Shephearde's Calendar.*" *Representations* 12 (1985): 83–100.

———. *What Is Pastoral?* Chicago: U of Chicago P, 1996.

Altieri, Charles. "Ashbery as Love Poet." Schultz, ed. 26–37.

Apocalypse Now. Dir. Francis Ford Coppola. United Artists Films, 1979.

Ashbery, John. *And the Stars Were Shining.* New York: Farrar, Straus, Giroux, 1994.

———. *Can You Hear, Bird?* New York: Farrar, Straus, Giroux, 1995.

———. *Collected Poems 1956–1987.* Ed. Mark Ford. New York: Library of America, 2008.

———. "Craft Interview with John Ashbery." *The Craft of Poetry: Interviews from "The New York Quarterly."* Ed. William Packard. Garden City, NY: Doubleday, 1974.

———. *Flow Chart.* 1991. New York: Noonday, 1998.

———. "Introduction." Freilicher, *Jane Freilicher.* N.p.

———. "Introduction." O'Hara, *Collected Poems,* vii–xi.

———. *Notes from the Air: Selected Later Poems.* New York: Ecco/HarperCollins, 2007.

———. *Other Traditions.* 2000. Cambridge, MA: Harvard UP, 2001.

———. *Reported Sightings: Art Chronicles 1957–1987.* 1989. Cambridge, MA: Harvard UP, 1991.

———. *Selected Prose.* Ann Arbor: U of Michigan P, 2004.

———. *Wakefulness.* New York: Farrar, Straus, Giroux, 1998.

———. "Works and Days." Kertess, ed. 9–10.

———. *Your Name Here.* New York: Farrar, Straus, Giroux, 2000.

———, ed. *Fairfield Porter: Realist Painter in the Age of Abstraction.* Boston: Museum of Fine Arts, 1986.

Ashton, Sally. "Poetry: In the Manner of David Lehman." *Writer's Chronicle* 38, no. 4 (February 2006): 4–11.

Barthes, Roland. "Semiology and Urbanism." *The Semiotic Challenge*. New York: Hill and Wang, 1988. 191–201.

Baudelaire, Charles. *The Flowers of Evil*. Rev. ed. Ed. Marthiel and Jackson Mathews. New York: New Directions, 1963.

Belgrad, Daniel. *The Culture of Spontaneity: Improvisation and the Arts in Postwar America*. Chicago: U of Chicago P, 1998.

Benjamin, Walter. *Illuminations: Essays and Reflections*. Ed. Hannah Arendt. Trans. Harry Zohn. New York: Schocken, 1968.

Bennett, Robert. "'Literature as the Destruction of Space': The Precarious Architecture of Barbara Guest's Spatial Imagination." *Women's Studies* 30, no. 1 (March 2001): 43–55.

Bergman, David. "Choosing Our Fathers: Gender and Identity in Whitman, Ashbery, and Richard Howard." *Gaiety Transfigured: Gay Self-Representation in American Literature*. Madison: U of Wisconsin P, 1991.

Berkson, Bill. "Art Chronicle." *Kulchur* 2 (Autumn 1962): 30–40.

———. "Frank O'Hara and His Poems." Berkson and LeSueur, eds. 161–65.

Berkson, Bill, and Joe LeSueur, eds. *Homage to Frank O'Hara*. Bolinas, CA: Big Sky, 1978.

Bernstein, Charles. "Introducing Barbara Guest." *Jacket* 10 (October 1999). http://jacketmagazine.com.

Bernstein, Roberta. *Jasper Johns' Paintings and Sculptures 1954–1974: "The Changing Focus of the Eye."* Ann Arbor, MI: UMI Research, 1985.

Berrigan, Ted. "Frank O'Hara." Berkson and LeSueur, eds. 11.

Bloom, Harold. "The Charity of Hard Moments." Bloom, ed. 49–79.

———. "Introduction." Bloom, ed. 1–16.

———, ed. *John Ashbery: Modern Critical Views*. New York: Chelsea House, 1985.

Bourdon, David. *Warhol*. New York: Abradale/Abrams, 1991.

Brainard, Joe. *I Remember*. 1975. New York: Penguin, 1995.

Bryant, William Cullen. "The Prairies." *The Columbia Anthology of American Poetry*. Ed. Jay Parini. New York: Columbia UP, 1995. 81–84.

Buell, Lawrence. *The Future of Environmental Criticism: Environmental Crisis and Literary Imagination*. Malden, MA: Blackwell, 2005.

Butterick, George F. "Diane di Prima." *The Beats: Literary Bohemians in Postwar America*. Ed. Ann Charters. *Dictionary of Literary Biography*. vol. 16. Detroit: Gale Research, 1983. 149–60.

Button, John. "Frank's Grace." Berkson and LeSueur, eds. 41–43.

Campbell, Glen. *Wichita Lineman*. Capitol-Nashville Records, 1968.

Cannato, Vincent J. *The Ungovernable City: John Lindsay and His Struggle to Save New York*. New York: Basic Books, 2001.

Carroll, Jim. *The Basketball Diaries*. 1978. New York: Penguin, 1995.

———. *Catholic Boy*. Atco Records, 1980.

————. *Fear of Dreaming: The Selected Poems of Jim Carroll*. New York: Penguin, 1993.

————. *Forced Entries: The Downtown Diaries 1971–1973*. New York: Penguin, 1987.

————. *4 Ups and 1 Down*. New York: Angel Hair Books, 1970.

————. *Void of Course: Poems 1994–1997*. New York: Penguin, 1998.

Chadwick, David. *Crooked Cucumber: The Life and Zen Teaching of Shunryu Suzuki*. New York: Broadway Books, 1999.

Chiasson, Dan. *One Kind of Everything: Poem and Person in Contemporary America*. Chicago: U of Chicago P, 2007.

Christgau, Robert. *Grown Up All Wrong: 75 Great Rock and Pop Artists from Vaudeville to Techno*. 1998. Cambridge, MA: Harvard UP, 2000.

Clark, Tom. "Schuyler's Idylls: Notes and Reflections on the *Collected Poems*." *American Poetry Review*, May/June 1994, 7–13.

The Clash. *Sandinista!* Epic Records, 1980.

Clemons, Walter. "New York Pastoral." Elledge, ed. 29–30.

Clifford, James. "Notes on Theory and Travel." *Inscriptions* 5 (1989): 177–88.

————. *Routes: Travel and Translation in the Late Twentieth Century*. Cambridge, MA: Harvard UP, 1997.

Clune, Michael. "'Everything We Want': Frank O'Hara and the Aesthetics of Free Choice." *PMLA* 120, no. 1 (January 2005): 181–96.

Colacello, Bob. *Holy Terror: Andy Warhol Close Up*. New York: HarperCollins, 1990.

Comer, Krista. *Landscapes of the New West: Gender and Geography in Contemporary Women's Writing*. Chapel Hill: U of North Carolina P, 1999.

Corbett, William. "Fairfield Porter and Jane Freilicher: 'Intimate Interiors.'" *Modern Painters*, Summer 1999, 95–96.

Cormin, Bruce. Conversation with the author, August 1999.

Costello, Bonnie. *Shifting Ground: Reinventing Landscape in Modern American Poetry*. Cambridge, MA: Harvard UP, 2003.

Cruz, Victor Hernandez. *Maraca: New and Selected Poems 1965–2000*. Minneapolis: Coffee House Press, 2001.

Cummings, Milton C., Jr. "Government and the Arts: An Overview." *Public Money and the Muse: Essays on Government Funding for the Arts*. Ed. Stephen Benedict. New York: Norton, 1991. 31–79.

Cunneen, Sally. *In Search of Mary: The Woman and the Symbol*. New York: Ballantine, 1996.

D'Agata. John. Rev. of *Girls on the Run*. *Boston Review*, February/March 2000. http://bostonreview.net.

Damon, Maria. "Victors of Catastrophe: Beat Occlusions." *Beat Culture and the New America 1950–1965*. Ed. Lisa Phillips. New York: Whitney Museum/Flammarion, 1995. 141–49.

Davidson, Michael. *The San Francisco Renaissance: Poetics and Community at Midcentury*. New York: Cambridge UP, 1989.

De Certeau, Michel. *The Practice of Everyday Life*. Trans. Steven Rendell. Berkeley: U of California P, 1984.

Delano, Sharon. "The Torch Singer." *New Yorker*, 11 March 2002, 48–63.

Deleuze, Gilles, and Felix Guattari. *A Thousand Plateaus: Capitalism and Schizophrenia*. Trans. Brian Massumi. Minneapolis: U of Minnesota P, 1987.

Deloria, Philip J. *Playing Indian*. New Haven: Yale UP, 1998.

De Man, Paul. "The Rhetoric of Temporality." *Blindness and Insight*. Rev. ed. Minneapolis: U of Minnesota P, 1983.

Diggory, Terence. "Allen Ginsberg's Urban Pastoral." *College Literature* 27, no. 1 (Winter 2000): 103–18.

———. "Barbara Guest and the Mother of Beauty." *Women's Studies* 30, no. 1 (March 2001): 75–94.

———. "Community 'Intimate' or 'Inoperative': New York School Poets and Politics from Paul Goodman to Jean-Luc Nancy." Diggory and Miller, eds. 13–32.

———. "'Picturesque' Urban Pastoral in Post-War New York City." *The Built Surface*. Ed. Christy Anderson and Karen Koehler. Aldershot, UK: Ashgate, 2000.

Diggory, Terence, and Stephen Paul Miller. "Introduction." Diggory and Miller, eds. 3–9.

———, eds. *The Scene of My Selves: New Work on New York School Poets*. Orono, ME: National Poetry Foundation, 2001.

Dillard, Annie. *Pilgrim at Tinker Creek*. 1974. New York: Harper Perennial, 1985.

Di Prima, Diane. Conversation with the author, January and June 2000.

———. "Decline of the West." *Los Angeles Times Book Review*. 24 March 1996.

———. "Diane di Prima" (biographical statement and five poems). *Beneath a Single Moon: Buddhism in Contemporary American Poetry*. Ed. Kent Johnson and Craig Paulenich. Boston: Shambhala, 1991. 56–61.

———. *Dinners and Nightmares*. 1961. San Francisco: Last Gasp, 1998.

———. "For Frank O'Hara, an Elegy." Berkson and LeSueur, eds. 156–57.

———. *Freddie Poems*. San Francisco: Eidolon Editions, 1974.

———. *Kerhonkson Journal 1966*. Berkeley, CA: Oyez, 1971.

———. "Light/And Keats." *Talking Poetics from Naropa Institute: Annals of the Jack Kerouac School of Disembodied Poetics*. Ed. Anne Waldman. Boulder, CO: Shambhala, 1978. 12–37.

———. *Loba*. New York: Penguin, 1998.

———. *Memoirs of a Beatnik*. 1969. San Francisco: Last Gasp, 1988.

———. *The Mysteries of Vision: Some Notes on H. D.* Santa Barbara, CA: am here books, 1988.

———. *Pieces of a Song: Selected Poems*. San Francisco: City Lights, 1990.

———. *Recollections of My Life as a Woman: The New York Years*. New York: Viking, 2001.

———. *Selected Poems 1956–1975*. Plainfield, VT: North Atlantic Books, 1975.

———. "The Tapestry of Possibility" (Interview). *Whole Earth*, Fall 1999, 20–22.

———. *Wyoming Series*. San Francisco: Eidolon Editions, 1988.

Di Prima, Diane, and LeRoi Jones, eds. *The Floating Bear: A Newsletter 1961–1969*. La Jolla, CA: Laurence McGilvery, 1973.

Dobrzynski, Judith H. "Extracting Metaphors from Life's Detritus." *New York Times*, 2 February 2000, E1.

Doty, Robert, "Interview with the Artist (Jane Freilicher), February 6, 1986." Doty, ed. 46–53.

———, ed. *Jane Freilicher: Paintings*. New York: Currier Gallery/Taplinger, 1986.

Duncan, Robert. "Often I Am Permitted to Return to a Meadow." *Postmodern American Poetry: A Norton Anthology*. Ed. Paul Hoover. New York: Norton, 1994. 36–37.

Du Plessis, Rachel Blau. "The Flavor of Eyes: *Selected Poems* by Barbara Guest." *Women's Review of Books* 13 (October 1995): 23–24.

———. "The Gendered Marvelous: Barbara Guest, Surrealism and the Feminist Reception." Diggory and Miller, eds. 189–213.

Edelman, Lee. "The Pose of Imposture: Ashbery's 'Self-Portrait in a Convex Mirror.'" *Twentieth Century Literature* 32, no. 1 (Spring 1986): 95–114.

Egan, Timothy. *Lasso the Wind: Away to the New West*. 1998. New York: Vintage, 1999.

Einzig, Barbara. "The Surface as Object: Barbara Guest's *Selected Poems*." *American Poetry Review*, January/February 1996, 7–10.

Elie, Paul. *The Life You Save May Be Your Own: An American Pilgrimage*. New York: Farrar, Straus, Giroux, 2003.

Eliot, T. S. *Selected Prose of T. S. Eliot*. Ed. Frank Kermode. New York: Harcourt/Farrar, Straus, Giroux, 1975.

Elledge, Jim, ed. *Frank O'Hara: To Be True to a City*. Ann Arbor: U of Michigan P, 1990.

Emerson, Ralph Waldo. *Selected Writings of Emerson*. Ed. Donald McQuade. New York: Modern Library, 1981.

Empson, William. *Some Versions of Pastoral*. 1935. Norfolk, CT: New Directions, 1960.

The Endless Summer. Dir. Bruce Brown. Black Diamond Films, 1964.

Epstein, Andrew. *Beautiful Enemies: Friendship and Postwar American Poetry*. New York: Oxford UP, 2006.

Ettin, Andrew V. *Literature and the Pastoral*. New Haven: Yale UP, 1984.

Evans-Wentz, W. Y. *Tibet's Great Yogi, Milarepa: A Biography from the Tibetan*. 1951. 2nd ed. New York: Oxford UP, 1971.

Everhart, Michael J. *Oceans of Kansas: A Natural History of the Western Interior Sea*. Bloomington: Indiana UP, 2005.

Feldman, Morton. "Lost Times and Future Hopes." Berkson and LeSueur, eds. 12–14.

Felstiner, John. "A Selection from *So Much Depends: Poetry and Environmental Urgency*." *American Poetry Review*, January/February 2007, 11–15.

Ferguson, Russell. *In Memory of My Feelings: Frank O'Hara and American Art*. Los Angeles: Museum of Contemporary Art, 1999.

Fletcher, Angus. *A New Theory for American Poetry: Democracy, the Environment, and the Future of Imagination*. Cambridge, MA: Harvard UP, 2004.

Flippo, Chet. "Star Is Borning." *New York*, 26 January 1981, 32–35.

Ford, Mark. *John Ashbery in Conversation with Mark Ford*. London: Between the Lines, 2003.

Foucault, Michel. "Of Other Spaces." *Diacritics* 16, no. 1 (1986): 22–27.

Fowler, Alastair. *Kinds of Literature: An Introduction to the Theory of Genres and Modes*. Cambridge, MA: Harvard UP, 1984.

Fowlie, Wallace. *Rimbaud and Jim Morrison: The Rebel as Poet*. Durham, NC: Duke UP, 1994.

Fraser, Kathleen. *Translating the Unspeakable: Poetry and the Innovative Necessity*. Tuscaloosa: U of Alabama P, 2000.

Freilicher, Jane. Conversation with the author, July 1999.

———. "It really is a sketch." Berkson and LeSueur, eds. 23.

———. *Jane Freilicher*. New York: Fischbach Gallery, 1995.

Frey, Hans-Jost. "Rimbaud's Poem 'L'Éternité.'" *Arthur Rimbaud: Modern Critical Views*. Ed. Harold Bloom. New York: Chelsea House, 1988. 35–55.

Frost, Elisabeth, and Cynthia Hogue. "Barbara Guest and Kathleen Fraser in Conversation." *Jacket* 25 (February 2004). http://jacketmagazine.com.

Fryer, Judith. "Desert, Rock, Shelter, Legend: Willa Cather's Novels of the Southwest." Norwood and Monk, eds. 27–46.

Gaines, Donna. "The Ascension of Led Zeppelin." *Rolling Stone: The Seventies*. Ed. Ashley Kahn et al. Boston: Little, Brown, 1998. 14–17.

———. *A Misfit's Manifesto: The Spiritual Journey of a Rock and Roll Heart*. New York: Villard, 2003.

Gaines, Steven. *Philistines at the Hedgerow*. Boston: Little, Brown, 1998.

Gangel, Sue. "John Ashbery." *American Poetry Observed*. Ed. Joe David Bellamy. Urbana: U of Illinois P, 1984. 9–20.

Gang of Souls. Dir. Maria Beatty. Downtown Community Television Center, 1990.

Garber, Frederick. "Pastoral Spaces." *Texas Studies in Literature and Language* 30, no. 3 (Fall 1988): 431–60.

Gilbert, Roger. *Walks in the World: Representation and Experience in Modern American Poetry*. Princeton, NJ: Princeton UP, 1991.

Ginsberg, Allen. *Collected Poems*. New York: Harper and Row, 1984.

Gioia, Dana. *Can Poetry Matter? Essays on Poetry and American Culture*. St. Paul, MN: Graywolf Press, 1992.

Gladysz, Thomas. "Verbal Entries: An Interview with Jim Carroll." *Booksmith Reader* (1999). http://booksmith.com/reader.

Glaser, Bruce. "Jackson Pollock: An Interview with Lee Krasner." Karmel, ed. 25–30.

Gooch, Brad. *City Poet: The Life and Times of Frank O'Hara*. 1993. New York: Harper Perennial, 1994.

Graustark, Barbara. "Mean Streets." *Newsweek*, 8 September 1980, 80–81.

Greenberg, Arielle. "A Sublime Sort of Exercise: Levity and the Poetry of Barbara Guest." *Women's Studies* 30, no. 1 (March 2001): 111–21.

Gruen, John. *The Party's Over Now: Reminiscences of the Fifties*. New York: Viking, 1972.

Guest, Barbara. *The Collected Poems of Barbara Guest.* Ed. Hadley Guest. Middletown, CT: Wesleyan UP, 2008.

——. *Forces of Imagination: Writing on Writing.* Berkeley, CA: Kelsey St. Press, 2003.

——. "Helen Frankenthaler: The Moment and the Distance." *Arts Magazine* 49 (April 1975): 58–59.

——. *Herself Defined: H. D. and Her World.* 1984. Tucson, AZ: Schaffner Press, 2003.

——. *Poems: The Location of Things, Archaics, the Open Skies.* Garden City, NY: Doubleday, 1962.

——. *Seeking Air.* 1978. Los Angeles: Sun and Moon Press, 1997.

——. *Selected Poems.* Los Angles: Sun and Moon Press, 1995.

——. "White Cloud Poem." Berkson and LeSueur, eds. 192.

Guest, Hadley. Correspondence with the author, April 2005.

H. D. *Collected Poems 1912–1944.* Ed. Louis L. Martz. 1983. New York: New Directions, 1986.

Hecht, Ben. "Interview with Jack Kerouac." *The Beat Generation.* Rhino Records, 1992.

Henderson, David. "Some Impressions." Lopate, ed. 76–80.

Henry, Gerrit. "Not Just Painting: New Views by Darragh Park." *Arts Magazine* 61 (April 1987): 76–77.

Herd, David. *John Ashbery and American Poetry.* New York: Palgrave, 2000.

——. "John Ashbery in Conversation." *PN Review* 21, no. 1 (September/October 1994): 32–37.

Herndon, James. *The Way It Spozed to Be.* New York: Simon and Schuster, 1968.

Hillman, Brenda. "The Artful Dare: Barbara Guest's *Selected Poems.*" *Talisman* 16, no. 1 (Fall 1996): 207–20.

Hillringhouse, Mark. "Barbara Guest: An Interview." *American Poetry Review,* July/August 1992, 23–30.

Hitchens, Christopher. "The Importance of Being Andy." MacCabe et al., eds. 1–10.

Hollander, John. "A Poetry of Restitution." *Yale Review* 70, no. 2 (Summer 1981): 161–86.

Imbriglio, Catherine. "'Our Days Put on Such Reticence': The Rhetoric of the Closet in John Ashbery's *Some Trees.*" *Contemporary Literature* 36, no. 2 (Summer 1995): 249–88.

Jackson, Richard. *The Dismantling of Time in Contemporary Poetry.* Tuscaloosa: U of Alabama P, 1988.

Jacobs, Allan, and Donald Appleyard. "Toward an Urban Design Manifesto." *The City Reader.* Ed. Richard T. LeGates and Frederic Stout. London: Routledge, 1996. 164–75.

Jacobs, Jane. *The Death and Life of Great American Cities.* 1961. New York: Vintage, 1992.

Jamison, Andrew, and Ron Eyerman. *Seeds of the Sixties*. Berkeley: U of California P, 1994.

Johns, Jasper. *Writings, Sketchbook Notes, Interviews*. Ed. Kirk Varnedoe. New York: Museum of Modern Art/Abrams, 1996.

Johnson, Joyce. *Minor Characters*. Boston: Houghton Mifflin, 1983.

Johnson, Paul E. *A Shopkeeper's Millennium: Society and Revivals in Rochester, New York, 1815–1837*. 1978. New York: Hill and Wang, 2004.

Kane, Daniel. *All Poets Welcome: The Lower East Side Poetry Scene in the 1960s*. Berkeley: U of California P, 2003.

———. *What Is Poetry: Conversations with the American Avant-Garde*. New York: Teachers and Writers, 2003.

Kaplan, Caren. *Questions of Travel: Postmodern Discourses of Displacement*. Durham, NC: Duke UP, 1996.

Karmel, Pepe, ed. *Jackson Pollock: Interviews, Articles, and Reviews*. New York: Museum of Modern Art, 1999.

Katz, Alex. "Memoir." Berkson and LeSueur, eds. 99.

Kaufman, Bob. *Cranial Guitar: Selected Poems of Bob Kaufman*. Minneapolis: Coffee House Press, 1996.

Keller, Lynn. "Becoming 'a Compleat Travel Agency': Barbara Guest's Negotiations with the Fifties Feminine Mystique." Diggory and Miller, eds. 215–27.

———. *Forms of Expansion: Recent Long Poems by Women*. Chicago: U of Chicago P, 1997.

———. *Re-Making It New: Contemporary American Poetry and the Modernist Tradition*. Cambridge: Cambridge UP, 1987.

"Kenneth Koch Tribute." Videotape recording. New York: Teachers and Writers Collaborative, November 2002.

Keren Ann. *Nolita*. Metroblue/Blue Note Records, 2005.

Kerouac, Jack. *On the Road*. 1957. New York: Penguin, 1976.

———. *The Portable Jack Kerouac*. Ed. Ann Charters. 1995. New York: Penguin, 1996.

———. *Selected Letters, 1940–1956*. Ed. Ann Charters. New York: Viking, 1995.

Kertess, Klaus. "The Art of Jane Freilicher." Kertess, ed. 21–66.

———, ed. *Jane Freilicher*. New York: Abrams, 2004.

Kinnahan, Linda. "Reading Barbara Guest: A View from the Nineties." Diggory and Miller, eds. 229–43.

Kinzie, Mary. "Irreference: The Poetic Diction of John Ashbery, Part 1." *Modern Philology* 84, no. 3 (February 1987): 267–81.

Kirschenbaum, Blossom S. "Diane di Prima: Extending La Famiglia." *MELUS* 14, nos. 3–4 (Fall/Winter 1987): 53–67.

Klensch, Elsa. "Interview with Jane Freilicher, 1 August 1998." *CNN Style*. Cable News Network Television.

Klinkenborg, Verlyn. "Elegy to a Dumpscape" (with a photograph by Stephen Wilkes). *New York Times Magazine*, 10 October 1999, 74–75.

Knight, Brenda. *Women of the Beat Generation: The Writers, Artists and Muses at the Heart of a Revolution.* Berkeley, CA: Conari Press, 1996.

Koch, Karen. Conversation with the author, April 2007.

Koch, Kenneth. *The Art of Poetry: Poems, Parodies, Interviews, Essays and Other Work.* Ann Arbor: U of Michigan P, 1996.

———. *The Collected Poems of Kenneth Koch.* New York: Knopf, 2005.

———. "James Schuyler (Very Briefly)." *Denver Quarterly* 24, no. 4 (Spring 1990): 21.

———. *Rose, Where Did You Get That Red? Teaching Great Poetry to Children.* New York: Random House, 1973.

———. *Seasons on Earth.* New York: Viking, 1987.

———. *Wishes, Lies, and Dreams: Teaching Children to Write Poetry.* 1970. New York: Harper Perennial, 1999.

Koch, Kenneth, and Kate Farrell. *Sleeping on the Wing: An Anthology of Modern Poetry with Essays on Reading and Writing.* 1981. New York: Vintage, 1982.

Koch, Stephen. *Stargazer: Andy Warhol's World and His Films.* New York: Praeger, 1973.

Koethe, John. "An Interview with John Ashbery." *Sub/Stance* 37/38 (1983): 178–86.

Kolodny, Annette. *The Lay of the Land: Metaphor as Experience and History in American Life and Letters.* Chapel Hill: U of North Carolina P, 1975.

Kostelanetz, Richard. "How to Be a Difficult Poet." *New York Times Magazine,* 23 May 1976, 18–33.

Kroll, Jack. "Saint Andrew." *Newsweek,* 7 December 1964, 100–103.

Kundera, Milan. *The Unbearable Lightness of Being.* Trans. Michael Henry Heim. 1984. New York: Perennial Classics, 1999.

Kureishi, Hanif. *London Kills Me: Three Screenplays and Four Essays.* New York: Penguin, 1992.

Kyger, Joanne. *The Japan and India Journals, 1960–1964.* Bolinas, CA: Tombouctou, 1981.

Lauterbach, Ann. "Fifth Season." *Denver Quarterly* 24, no. 4 (Spring 1990): 69–76.

———. *The Night Sky: Writings on the Poetics of Experience.* New York: Viking, 2005.

Laycock, Deborah. *An Eighteenth-Century Sense of Place: The Urban Pastoral.* Ann Arbor, MI: University Microfilms, 1987.

Led Zeppelin. *Led Zeppelin IV.* Atlantic Records, 1971.

Lehman, David. *The Last Avant-Garde: The Making of the New York School of Poets.* New York: Doubleday, 1998.

Leibowitz, Herbert A. "A Pan Piping on City Streets: *The Collected Poems of Frank O'Hara.*" Elledge, ed. 24–28.

Leider, Philip. "Saint Andy: Some Notes on an Artist Who, for a Large Section of the Younger Generation, Can Do No Wrong." *Artforum* 3, no. 5 (February 1965): 26–28.

LeSueur, Joe. *Digressions on Some Poems by Frank O'Hara.* 2003. New York: Farrar, Straus, Giroux, 2004.

Libby, Anthony. "Diane di Prima: 'Nothing Is Lost; It Shines in Our Eyes.'" *Girls Who Wore Black: Women Writing the Beat Generation.* Ed. Ronna C. Johnson and Nancy M. Grace. New Brunswick, NJ: Rutgers UP, 2002. 45–68.

Logan, William. "Urban Poet." *New York Times Book Review,* 29 June 2008, 1.

Lopate, Phillip. "Attitude toward Teachers and the Schools." Lopate, ed. 190–98.

———. *Being with Children.* Garden City, NY: Doubleday, 1975.

———. "Conclusion: Overview—and a Look Ahead." Lopate, ed. 327–42.

———. "Interview with Herbert Kohl." Lopate, ed. 21–43.

———. "Interview with Kenneth Koch." Lopate, ed. 269–81.

———. "Issues of Language." Lopate, ed. 100–118.

———, ed. *Journal of a Living Experiment: A Documentary History of the First Ten Years of Teachers and Writers Collaborative.* New York: Teachers and Writers Collaborative, 1979.

Lundquist, Sara. "Another Poet among Painters: Barbara Guest with Grace Hartigan and Mary Abbott." Diggory and Miller, eds. 245–64.

———. "Barbara Guest." *Dictionary of Literary Biography.* Vol. 193, 6th ser., American Poets Since World War II. Detroit: Gale Research, 1998. 159–70.

———. "The Fifth Point of a Star: Barbara Guest and the New York 'School' of Poets." *Women's Studies* 30, no. 1 (March 2001): 11–41.

———. "The Midwestern New York Poet: Barbara Guest's *The Countess from Minneapolis.*" *Jacket* 10 (October 1999). http://jacketmagazine.com.

———. "Reverence and Resistance: Barbara Guest, Ekphrasis, and the Female Gaze." *Contemporary Literature* 38, no. 2 (Summer 1997): 260–86.

MacArthur, Marit J. *The American Landscape in the Poetry of Frost, Bishop, and Ashbery.* New York: Palgrave, 2008.

MacCabe, Colin, et al., eds. *Who Is Andy Warhol?* London: British Film Institute/ Andy Warhol Museum, 1997.

MacDonald, Scott. "Ten + (Alternative) Films about American Cities." *The ISLE Reader: Ecocriticism, 1993–2003.* Ed. Michael P. Branch and Scott Slovic. Athens: U of Georgia P, 2003. 217–39.

Machor, James L. *Pastoral Cities.* Madison: U of Wisconsin P, 1987.

Mack, Theresa. "So Far Away." Lopate, ed. 214–23.

Mackey, Nathaniel. *Paracritical Hinge: Essays, Talks, Notes, Interviews.* Madison: U of Wisconsin P, 2005.

Mahler, Jonathan. *Ladies and Gentlemen, the Bronx Is Burning: 1977, Baseball, Politics and the Battle for the Soul of a City.* 2005. New York: Picador, 2006.

Malanga, Gerard. *Resistance to Memory.* Santa Fe: Arena Editions, 1998.

Marx, Leo. *The Machine in the Garden: Technology and the Pastoral Ideal in America.* New York: Oxford UP, 1964.

McCorkle, James. "*Nimbus of Sensations*: Eros and Reverie in the Poetry of John Ashbery and Ann Lauterbach." Schultz, ed. 101–25.

McDarrah, Fred W. "10 Photographs." Berkson and LeSueur, eds. 69–74.

McDonagh, Donald. "The Incandescent Innocent." *Film Culture* 45 (1968): 56.

McDowell, Robert. "How Good Is John Ashbery?" *American Scholar* 56, no. 2 (Spring 1987): 275–80.

McMullen, Kate, and Jim McMullen. *I Stink!* New York: Joanna Cotler/HarperCollins, 2002.

McMurtry, Larry. "Now Voyager." *New York Review of Books*, 20 January 2000, 41–42.

McNeil, Legs, and Gillian McCain. *Please Kill Me: The Uncensored Oral History of Punk.* 1996. New York: Penguin, 1997.

Mendelson, Edward. *Later Auden.* New York: Farrar, Straus, Giroux, 1999.

Merrin, Jeredith. "The Poetry Man." *Southern Review* 35, no. 2 (Spring 1999). http:// galenet.galegroup.com.

Metheny, Pat, and Lyle Mays. *As Falls Wichita, So Falls Wichita Falls.* ECM Records, 1981.

Miles, Barry. *Ginsberg: A Biography.* 1989. New York: Harper Perennial, 1990.

Miller, Henry. *The Time of the Assassins: A Study of Rimbaud.* 1946. New York: New Directions, 1962.

Miller, Stephen Paul. *The Seventies Now: Culture as Surveillance.* Durham, NC: Duke UP, 1999.

Mitchell, J. J. "The Death of Frank O'Hara." Berkson and LeSueur, eds. 144–46.

"The Modern Gone By: Inspiration for a New Way of Art." *New York Times*, 18 November 2004, E3.

Mohanty, S. P., and Jonathan Monroe. "John Ashbery and the Articulation of the Social." *Diacritics* 17, no. 2 (Summer 1987): 37–63.

Moon, Michael. *Disseminating Whitman: Revision and Corporeality in "Leaves of Grass."* Cambridge, MA: Harvard UP, 1991.

Morley, Jeff. "Wishes, Lies, and Dreams Revisited." *Educating the Imagination: Essays and Ideas for Teachers and Writers, Volume One.* Ed. Christopher Edgar and Ron Padgett. New York: Teachers and Writers Collaborative, 1994. 267–80.

Morrow, Robert W. *"Sesame Street" and the Reform of Children's Television.* Baltimore: Johns Hopkins UP, 2006.

Motherwell, Robert. *The Collected Writings of Robert Motherwell.* Ed. Stephanie Terenzio. New York: Oxford UP, 1992.

Munn, Paul. "An Interview with John Ashbery." *New Orleans Review* 17, no. 2 (Summer 1990): 59–63.

Murphy, John. "John Ashbery" (interview). *Poetry Review* 72, no. 2 (1985): 20–25.

Myers, John Bernard. "Frank O'Hara: A Memoir." Berkson and LeSueur, eds. 34–38.

———, ed. *Poets of the New York School.* Philadelphia: University of Pennsylvania Graduate School of Fine Arts, 1969.

Myles, Eileen. *Chelsea Girls.* Santa Rosa, CA: Black Sparrow, 1994.

Neel, Alice. "I Met Frank." Berkson and LeSueur, eds. 96.

Nelson, Maggie. *Women, the New York School, and Other True Abstractions.* Iowa City: U of Iowa P, 2007.

Norris, Kathleen. *Acedia and Me: A Marriage, Monks, and a Writer's Life.* New York: Riverhead, 2008.

———. *Amazing Grace: A Vocabulary of Faith*. New York: Riverhead, 1998.

———. *The Cloister Walk*. New York: Riverhead, 1996.

———. *Dakota: A Spiritual Geography*. 1993. Boston: Mariner/Houghton Mifflin, 2001.

———. *Falling Off*. Chicago: Big Table, 1971.

———. *Journey: New and Selected Poems 1969–1999*. Pittsburgh, PA: U of Pittsburgh P, 2001.

———. *The Virgin of Bennington*. 2001. New York: Riverhead, 2002.

———, ed. *Leaving New York: Writers Look Back*. St. Paul, MN: Hungry Mind Press, 1995.

North, Charles. *No Other Way: Selected Prose*. Brooklyn, NY: Hanging Loose Press, 1998.

Norwood, Vera, and Janice Monk, eds. *The Desert Is No Lady: Southwestern Landscapes in Women's Writing and Art*. New Haven, CT: Yale UP, 1987.

O'Hara, Frank. *Art Chronicles 1954–1966*. New York: Braziller, 1975.

———. *The Collected Poems of Frank O'Hara*. Ed. Donald Allen. 1971. Berkeley: U of California P, 1995.

———. *Early Writing*. Ed. Donald Allen. Bolinas, CA: Grey Fox, 1977.

———. *Poems Retrieved*. Ed. Donald Allen. Bolinas, CA: Grey Fox, 1977.

———. *Selected Poems*. Ed. Mark Ford. New York: Knopf, 2008.

———. *Standing Still and Walking in New York*. Ed. Donald Allen. Bolinas, CA: Grey Fox, 1975.

Ortiz, Miguel. "Latin Nostalgia." Lopate, ed. 289–301.

Padgett, Ron. Conversation with the author, May 2007.

———. "Nine Years under the Masthead of Teachers and Writers Collaborative." Lopate, ed. 282–88.

———. "To a Schuyler." *That Various Field for James Schuyler*. Ed. William Corbett and Geoffrey Young. Great Barrington, MA: The Figures, 1991. 9–11.

Padgett, Ron, and David Shapiro, eds. *An Anthology of New York Poets*. New York: Random House, 1970.

Page, Max. "Uses of the Axe: Towards a Treeless New York." *American Studies* 40, no. 1 (Spring 1999): 41–64.

Pelton, Theodore. "Kenneth Koch's Poetics of Pleasure." Diggory and Miller, eds. 327–44.

Perl, Jed. *New Art City: Manhattan at Mid-Century*. New York: Knopf, 2005.

Perloff, Marjorie. *Frank O'Hara: Poet among Painters*. Braziller, 1977.

———. "Normalizing John Ashbery." *Jacket* 2 (January 1998). http://jacketmagazine.com.

———. *Poetic License: Essays on Modernist and Postmodernist Lyric*. Evanston, IL: Northwestern UP, 1990.

———. "Watchman, Spy, and Dead Man: Jasper Johns, Frank O'Hara, John Cage and the Aesthetic of Indifference." *Modernism/Modernity* 8, no. 2 (2001): 197–223.

Peterson, Iver. "The Hamptons: Sun, Sand, and Lawsuits." *New York Times*, 25 April 1999, 36.

Pinchbeck, Daniel. "Children of the Beats." *The Rolling Stone Book of the Beats*. Ed. Holly George-Warren. New York: Hyperion, 1999. 380–91.

Pollock, Jackson. "Jackson Pollock: A Questionnaire" (1944). Karmel, ed. 15–16.

———. "My Painting" (1947). *Theories of Modern Art: A Source Book by Artists and Critics*. Ed. Herschel B. Chipp. Berkeley: U of California P, 1968. 546–48.

Porter, Fairfield. *Art in Its Own Terms: Selected Criticism 1935–1975*. Ed. Rackstraw Downes. New York: Taplinger, 1979.

———. "Jane Freilicher Paints a Picture." *Art News* 55 (September 1956): 46.

———. *Material Witness: The Selected Letters of Fairfield Porter*. Ed Ted Leigh. Ann Arbor: U of Michigan P, 2005.

Poulin, A. "The Experience of Experience: A Conversation with John Ashbery." *Michigan Quarterly Review* 20, no. 3 (Summer 1981): 242–55.

Pratt, Mary Louise. *Imperial Eyes: Travel Writing and Transculturation*. London: Routledge, 1992.

Proulx, Annie. *Close Range: Wyoming Stories*. 1999. New York: Scribner, 2000.

Rabinowitz, Anna. "Barbara Guest: Notes toward Painterly Osmosis." *Women's Studies* 30, no. 1 (March 2001): 95–109.

Rasula, Jed. *This Compost: Ecological Imperatives in American Poetry*. Athens: U of Georgia P, 2002.

Ravitch, Diane. *Left Back: A Century of Failed School Reforms*. New York: Simon and Schuster, 2000.

———. *The Troubled Crusade: American Education 1945–1980*. New York: Basic Books, 1983.

Rayns, Tony. "Andy's Hand Jobs." MacCabe et al., eds. 83–87.

Reed, Lou. *Coney Island Baby*. RCA Records, 1976.

Rehak, Melanie. "A Child in Time: Questions for John Ashbery." *New York Times Magazine*, 4 April 1995, 15.

Requiem for a Dream. Dir. Darren Aronofsky. Artisan Films, 2000.

Richman, Robert. "Our 'Most Important' Living Poet." *Commentary* 74, no. 1 (July 1982): 62–68.

Rimbaud, Arthur. *Complete Works*. Trans. Paul Schmidt. New York: Harper Perennial, 1976.

Rivers, Larry. "Speech Read at Springs." Berkson and LeSueur, eds. 138.

———. *What Did I Do? The Unauthorized Autobiography*. New York: Asher/HarperCollins, 1992.

Robinson, Marilynne. *Housekeeping*. 1980. New York: Farrar, Straus, Giroux, 1997.

Rose, Barbara. "In Andy Warhol's Aluminum Foil, We Have All Been Reflected." *New York*, 31 May 1971, 54.

Rosen, Susan A. C., ed. *Shorewords: A Collection of American Women's Coastal Writings*. Charlottesville: UP of Virginia, 2003.

Rosenbaum, Susan B. *Professing Sincerity: Modern Lyric Poetry, Commercial Culture, and the Crisis in Reading*. Charlottesville: UP of Virginia, 2007.

Ross, Andrew. "Taking the Tennis Court Oath." Schultz, ed. 193–210.

Rothenberg, David, and Marta Ulvaeus, eds. *Writing on Water*. Cambridge, MA: MIT Press, 2001.

Rudnik, Lois. "Renaming the Land: Anglo Expatriate Women in the Southwest." Norwood and Monk, eds. 10–26.

Rugoff, Ralph. "Albino Humor." MacCabe et al., eds. 97–105.

Sandler, Irving. "Avant-Garde Artists of Greenwich Village." *Greenwich Village: Culture and Counterculture*. Ed. Rick Beard and Leslie Cohen Berlowitz. New Brunswick, NJ: Rutgers UP, 1993.

Savage, Jon. "Interview with James Schuyler." *James Schuyler: Interview and Reading*. Audiocassette. Prod. Mitch Cooper. New York: Thin Air Spoken Word, 1995.

Schjeldahl, Peter. "Frank O'Hara: 'He Made Things and People Sacred.'" Berkson and LeSueur, eds. 139–43.

———. "Urban Pastorals." *Art News* 69 (February 1971): 32.

Schultz, Susan M., ed. *The Tribe of John: Ashbery and Contemporary Poetry*. Tuscaloosa: U of Alabama P, 1995.

Schuyler, James. *Alfred and Guinevere*. New York: Harcourt Brace, 1958.

———. *Collected Poems*. New York: Noonday, 1993.

———. *The Diary of James Schuyler*. Ed. Nathan Kernan. Santa Rosa, CA: Black Sparrow, 1997.

———. *Hymn to Life*. New York: Random House, 1974.

———. *Just the Thing: Selected Letters of James Schuyler 1951–1991*. Ed. William Corbett. New York: Turtle Point Press, 2004.

———. "Poet among Painters." Berkson and LeSueur, eds. 82–83.

———. "Poet and Painter Overture." Allen, ed. 418–19.

———. *Selected Art Writings*. Ed. Simon Pettet. Santa Rosa, CA: Black Sparrow, 1998.

Schuyler, James, and Darragh Park. *Two Journals*. New York: Tibor de Nagy Editions, 1995.

Seiberling, Dorothy. "Jackson Pollock: Is He the Greatest Living Painter in the United States?" *Life*, 8 August 1949, 42–45.

Sennett, Richard. *The Fall of Public Man: On the Social Psychology of Capitalism*. New York: Vintage, 1978.

"Shadows." Reading Is Fundamental television commercial (1973). http://rif.org.

Shapiro, David. *John Ashbery: An Introduction to the Poetry*. New York: Columbia UP, 1979.

Shaviro, Steven. "Warhol before the Mirror." MacCabe et al., eds. 89–95.

Shaw, Lytle. *Frank O'Hara: The Poetics of Coterie*. Iowa City: U of Iowa P, 2006.

Shklovsky, Victor. "Art as Technique." *Russian Formalist Criticism: Four Essays*. Trans. Lee T. Lemon and Marion J. Reis. Lincoln: U of Nebraska P, 1965. 3–24.

Shoptaw, John. *On the Outside Looking Out: John Ashbery's Poetry*. Cambridge, MA: Harvard UP, 1994.

Sidney, Sir Philip. *The Old Arcadia*. Ed. Katherine Duncan-Jones. Oxford: Oxford UP, 1994.

Siebert, Charles. *Wickerby: An Urban Pastoral*. New York: Crown, 1998.

Siegel, Barbara. "Teaching Art: Examining the Creative Process." Lopate, ed. 244–47.

Simic, Charles. *Dime Store Alchemy: The Art of Joseph Cornell.* 1992. New York: New York Review Books, 2006.

Simon and Garfunkel. "The Only Living Boy in New York." *Bridge over Troubled Water.* Columbia Records, 1970.

Sinagra, Laura. "The Listings: Pop." *New York Times*, 28 November 2005, E26.

Smith, Hazel. *Hyperscapes in the Poetry of Frank O'Hara: Difference/Homosexuality/Topography.* Liverpool: Liverpool UP, 2000.

Smith, Patricia Clark, and Paula Gunn Allen. "Earthy Relations, Carnal Knowledge: Southwestern American Indian Women Writers and Landscape." Norwood and Monk, eds. 174–96.

Snyder, Gary. *Myths and Texts.* 1960. New York: New Directions, 1978.

———. "North Beach." *The Old Ways: Six Essays.* San Francisco: City Lights, 1977. 45–48.

———. *Turtle Island.* New York: New Directions, 1974.

Sobule, Jill. *California Years.* Pinko Records, 2009.

Soja, Edward. *Postmodern Geographies.* London: Verso, 1989.

Solomon, Deborah. *Utopia Parkway: The Life and Work of Joseph Cornell.* New York: Farrar, Straus, Giroux, 1997.

Sontag, Susan. "Notes on Camp." *A Susan Sontag Reader.* 1982. New York: Vintage, 1983. 105–20.

Southgate, Patsy. "My Night with Frank O'Hara." Berkson and LeSueur, eds. 119–21.

Spike, John T. *Fairfield Porter: An American Classic.* New York: Abrams, 1992.

Spring, Justin. *Fairfield Porter: A Life in Art.* New Haven, CT: Yale UP, 2000.

Springsteen, Bruce. *Greetings from Asbury Park, N.J.* Columbia Records, 1973.

Spurr, David. "An Interview with Kenneth Koch." *Contemporary Poetry* 3–4 (1978): 1–12.

———. "Kenneth Koch's Serious Moment." Diggory and Miller, eds. 345–56.

Stafford, William. *The Way It Is: New and Selected Poems.* St. Paul, MN: Graywolf Press, 1999.

Stitt, Peter. "The Art of Poetry XXXIII: John Ashbery." *Paris Review* 90 (1983): 30–59.

———. *Uncertainty and Plenitude: Five Contemporary Poets.* Iowa City: U of Iowa P, 1997.

Suzuki, Shunryu. *Zen Mind, Beginner's Mind.* New York: Weatherhill, 1970.

Swift, Jonathan. "A Description of a City Shower." *The Norton Anthology of Poetry.* 5th ed. Ed. Margaret Ferguson et al. New York: Norton, 2005. 569–70.

Tapscott, Stephen. *American Beauty: William Carlos Williams and the Modernist Tradition.* New York: Columbia UP, 1984.

Taylor, Richard P. "Order in Pollock's Chaos." *Scientific American*, December 2002, 116–21.

Tonkinson, Carole. *Big Sky Mind: Buddhism and the Beat Generation.* New York: Tricycle/Riverhead, 1995.

Varnedoe, Kirk. "Comet: Jackson Pollock's Life and Work." *Jackson Pollock*. Ed. Kirk Varnedoe and Pepe Karmel. New York: Museum of Modern Art, 1998. 15–85.

Velvet Underground. *1969: The Velvet Underground Live*. Mercury Records, 1974.

———. *The Velvet Underground*. MGM Records, 1969.

———. *VU*. Verve Records, 1985.

Vendler, Helen. "Frank O'Hara: The Virtue of the Alterable." Elledge, ed. 234–52.

———. *The Music of What Happens: Poems, Poets, Critics*. Cambridge, MA: Harvard UP, 1988.

———. *Soul Says: On Recent Poetry*. Cambridge, MA: Harvard UP, 1995.

Vickery, Ann. "'A Mobile Fiction': Barbara Guest and Modern Pastoral." *TriQuarterly* 116 (2003): 246–61.

Vincent, John. *John Ashbery and You: His Later Books*. Athens: U of Georgia P, 2007.

Virgil (Publius Vergilius Maro). *The Pastoral Poems: The Text of the Eclogues*. Trans. E. V. Rieu. Baltimore: Penguin, 1967.

Waldman, Anne. "Interview with Diane di Prima" (1978). *Rocky Ledge* 7 (February/March 1981): 35–49.

———. "Paraphrase of Edwin Denby Speaking on 'The New York School.'" Berkson and LeSueur, eds. 32–33.

Waldman, Anne, and Lewis Warsh, eds. *The Angel Hair Anthology*. New York: Granary Books, 2001.

Ward, Geoff. *Statutes of Liberty: The New York School of Poets*. 2nd ed. New York: Palgrave, 2001.

Warhol, Andy, and Pat Hackett. *The Philosophy of Andy Warhol: From A to B and Back Again*. New York: Harcourt, Brace, Jovanovich, 1975.

Warner, Marina. *Alone of All Her Sex: The Myth and the Cult of the Virgin Mary*. 1976. New York: Vintage, 1983.

Warsh, Lewis. "Introduction." Waldman and Warsh, eds. xix–xxvii.

Wasley, Aidan. "The 'Gay Apprentice': Ashbery, Auden, and the Portrait of the Artist as a Young Critic." *Contemporary Literature* 43, no. 4 (Winter 2002): 667–708.

Watkin, William. *In the Process of Poetry: The New York School and the Avant-Garde*. Lewisburg, PA: Bucknell UP, 2001.

Watson, Steven. *The Birth of the Beat Generation: Visionaries, Rebels, and Hipsters, 1944–1960*. New York: Pantheon, 1995.

———. *Factory Made: Warhol and the Sixties*. New York: Pantheon, 2003.

Welish, Marjorie. "The Lyric Lately." *Jacket* 10 (October 1999). http://jacketmagazine.com.

Whitehead. Colson. *The Colossus of New York*. 2003. New York: Anchor, 2004.

Whitman, Walt. *Leaves of Grass*. Ed. Sculley Bradley and Harold W. Blodgett. New York: Norton Critical Editions, 1973.

Williams, Alex. "Lord Jim." *New York*, 24 April 1995, 64–66.

Williams, Raymond. *The Country and the City*. New York: Oxford UP, 1973.

Williams, Terry Tempest. *Refuge: An Unnatural History of Family and Place*. 1991. New York: Vintage, 2001.

Williams, William Carlos. *Selected Poems*. Ed. Charles Tomlinson. New York: New Directions, 1985.

Wishes, Lies and Dreams: Kenneth Koch Teaching Children to Write Poetry. Dir. Eric Breitbart and Alan Jacobs. National Endowment for the Arts, 1970.

Wolf, Reva. *Andy Warhol, Poetry, and Gossip in the 1960s*. Chicago: U of Chicago P, 1997.

Wordsworth, William. *The Prelude, 1799, 1805, 1850*. Ed. Jonathan Wordsworth et al. New York: Norton Critical Editions, 1979.

Yau, John. "The Pleasures of Doubting." Doty, ed. 38–45.

Yingling, Thomas E. *Hart Crane and the Homosexual Text: New Thresholds, New Anatomies*. Chicago: U of Chicago P, 1990.

Neel, Alice, 206n, 222n
Neill, A. S., 130
Nelson, Maggie, 23, 206n, 207n
New American Poetry: as Donald Allen
 anthology, 3, 70, 74, 100, 108, 126; as
 movement, 3, 32, 129
New School for Social Research, 16, 79,
 125, 131–32, 140
New York School of Painters, 1, 16, 100,
 110, 119
New York School of Poets, 1–3, 7, 10, 16,
 20, 30, 32–34, 40–43, 53, 74, 87, 96, 98,
 100–03, 105, 111, 115, 119, 123–26, 156,
 187; and gender politics, 70–72; as
 "placeless" community, 27–28, 44, 57,
 60, 67, 69, 145; and second-generation
 writers, 6, 8, 125–26, 152–53, 174–76,
 192–93
Niedecker, Lorine, 90
Norris, Kathleen, 6, 9, 11, 131–32, 168,
 176–79, 186, 193–204; *Acedia & Me*,
 193; *Amazing Grace*, 193, 225n; "At a
 Window, New York City," 195; "Bean
 Song," 195–96; childhood of, 186, 193;
 The Cloister Walk, 193; "The Consuming Angel," 197–98; *Dakota*, 193,
 196, 203; "Evaporation Poems," 225n;
 "Excerpts from the Angel Handbook,"
 198–99, 201; "Falling Off," 195; "Fragment from a Death Festival," 225n;
 "Her Application to Elysium," 198;
 "Kansas Anymore," 195; *Leaving New
 York*, 194; "The Middle of the World,"
 197; "The Most Secret Angel," 197–98;
 "Tomorrow," 198; *The Virgin of Ben-
 nington*, 194, 200; "Why the Image of
 a Starry Womb Is Not Poetic Claptrap
 but Good Science," 196
North, Charles, 71–73
Notley, Alice, 28, 207n

O'Hara, Frank, 1–2, 5, 8, 10–11, 14–41,
 44–45, 65, 70–72, 79, 88–89, 100–05,
 111, 114–16, 125–27, 152, 159, 183, 186–
 88, 203; "1951," 24; "Autobiographia
 Literaria," 19; "Chez Jane," 111; child-

hood of, 19, 43, 48, 54; "Commercial
 Variations," 19; "Corresponding
 Foreignly," 24; "The Day Lady Died,"
 21, 29, 34; "Dear Jap," 39; death of, 2,
 8–9, 35, 37–41, 156, 163, 175; "Digression on *Number 1, 1948*," 224n; "For a
 Dolphin," 207n; "For Bob Rauschenberg," 19; "For James Dean," 33; "Four
 Little Elegies," 36–37; "Grand Central,"
 30–31; "Having a Coke with You,"
 22–23; "In Memory of My Feelings,"
 30, 35–37, 207n; "Interior (with Jane),"
 29, 111; "Joe's Jacket," 23; "Les Luths,"
 207n; "Meditations in an Emergency,"
 25, 30; "Nocturne," 30–32; "Ode to
 Michael Goldberg ('s Birth and Other
 Births)," 19; "On Rachmaninoff's
 Birthday (I am so glad)," 30; "A Pastoral Dialogue," 25; "Personal Poem,"
 21–23; "Personism," 23, 29, 146; "Second Avenue," 30, 207n; "Sleeping on
 the Wing," 32–33, 116, 145–46; "Song
 (I'm Going to New York!)," 206n;
 "Southampton Variations," 32–33; "A
 Step Away from Them," 21, 34; "Steps,"
 24, 210–11n; *Stones* (with Larry Riv-
 ers), 207n; "Thinking of James Dean,"
 37–38; "To the Harbormaster," 23, 186;
 "To the Mountains of New York," 25;
 "A True Account of Talking to the
 Sun at Fire Island," 38–39; "Two Shep-
 herds, a Novel," 25
O'Keeffe, Georgia, 158
Oliver, Mary, 3, 98
Olson, Charles, 3, 169
Onassis, Jackie, 123
Ondine (pseudonym), 178, 223n4,
 224n14
Ortiz, Miguel, 133

Padgett, Ron, 25, 70, 125, 137, 216n, 218n
Park, Darragh, 117, 216–17n
Parmigianino, Francesco, 48
pastoral mode: 3–5, 13, 43, 62, 81–82, 100,
 104–05, 177, 190; and Catholicism,
 177–78, 180, 185–86; and *locus amoe-*

Contemporary North American Poetry Series

Industrial Poetics: Demo Tracks for a Mobile Culture
BY JOE AMATO

On Mount Vision: Forms of the Sacred in Contemporary American Poetry
BY NORMAN FINKELSTEIN

Jorie Graham: Essays on the Poetry
EDITED BY THOMAS GARDNER
University of Wisconsin Press, 2005

Gary Snyder and the Pacific Rim: Creating Countercultural Community
BY TIMOTHY GRAY

Urban Pastoral: Natural Currents in the New York School
BY TIMOTHY GRAY

We Saw the Light: Conversations between the New American Cinema and Poetry
BY DANIEL KANE

History, Memory, and the Literary Left: Modern American Poetry, 1935–1968
BY JOHN LOWNEY

Paracritical Hinge: Essays, Talks, Notes, Interviews
BY NATHANIEL MACKEY
University of Wisconsin Press, 2004

Frank O'Hara: The Poetics of Coterie
BY LYTLE SHAW

Radical Vernacular: Lorine Niedecker and the Poetics of Place
EDITED BY ELIZABETH WILLIS